Critical acclaim for *The Emerging Democratic Majority*

"Eye-opening. . . . Republicans have work to do, beginning with a book to read."

—George Will, *Newsweek*

"One of the freshest looks in years at the changing dynamics of American elections. . . . Thinkers in both parties will have to grapple with their insights."

—Ronald Brownstein, *The American Prospect*

"So crisply clear in its exposition and so skillfully supported by statistical evidence and analysis that it may finally turn conventional wisdom on its head."

—*The Economist*

"*The Emerging Democratic Majority* does much to explain how power is shifting in this country. It is this season's most important and insightful political book and could have impact for years to come."

—*Chicago Sun-Times*

"A marvelous volume by two excellent writers. . . . Judis and Teixeira, with their research, deserve to be taken seriously."

—*The Boston Globe*

"Certain to galvanize and energize their fellow Democrats. . . . *The Emerging Democratic Majority* is actually two things in one: a substantive analysis and a call to arms."

—*The Washington Times*

"One of the most impressive overviews of American politics in recent years."

—*Foreign Affairs*

"The most penetrating and prescient look at American politics you're likely to read for some time."

—Joshua Micah Marshall, *Talking Points Memo*

"The most interesting political book of the year."

—Fareed Zakaria, author of *The Future of Freedom*

"Judis and Teixeira are among the shrewdest students of American politics, and they've written an important book that puts recent events in a new context. It's filled with insight, intelligence, and previously unnoticed data. Democrats will take heart from its message. Republicans need to know the dangers they face."

—E. J. Dionne, author of *Why Americans Hate Politics*

"John Judis and Ruy Teixeira are two of the most intelligent, and most honest, political observers in America today. Whether you are Democrat or Republican, this book will sharpen your thinking about the future of our country."

—David Brooks, author of *Bobos in Paradise*

"This is the most cogent, prophetic, and hopeful book on the future of American politics."

—Sidney Blumenthal

"A very convincing account of the Democratic future. With the same daring as Kevin Phillips more than thirty years ago, Judis and Teixeira expose the trends that will govern the party politics of the coming era."

—Stanley Greenberg, pollster to President Clinton and Vice President Gore

"A brilliant analysis of contemporary American politics."

—Thomas Edsall, *The Washington Post*

"At a time when many Americans are anxious about our changing demographic profile, Judis and Teixeira show how the optimism and energy of our nation's diverse population can be constructively channeled into a new political majority."

—Henry Cisneros, secretary,
Department of Housing and Urban Development, 1993–97

"Every Democrat . . . should read this book."

—Elaine Kamarck, senior policy adviser to Vice President Al Gore

"A vivid and accurate picture of the rapidly changing twenty-first-century electorate."

—Al From, founder and CEO, Democratic Leadership Council

"A fine compass for navigating the confusing political currents that are swirling around us."

—Randall Kennedy, professor of law, Harvard University

Also by John B. Judis

William F. Buckley, Jr.:
Patron Saint of the Conservatives

Grand Illusion:
Critics and Champions of the American Century

The Paradox of American Democracy:
Elites, Special Interests and the Betrayal of Public Trust

Also by Ruy Teixeira

Why Americans Don't Vote:
Turnout Decline in the United States, 1960–1984

The Disappearing American Voter

America's Forgotten Majority:
Why the White Working Class Still Matters *(with Joel Rogers)*

THE EMERGING DEMOCRATIC MAJORITY

John B. Judis
and Ruy Teixeira

A Lisa Drew Book

SCRIBNER
New York London Toronto Sydney

A LISA DREW BOOK/SCRIBNER
1230 Avenue of the Americas
New York, NY 10020

First Lisa Drew/Scribner trade paperback edition 2004

For information about special discounts for bulk purchases,
please contact Simon & Schuster Special Sales:
1-800-456-6798 or business@simonandschuster.com.

DESIGNED BY ERICH HOBBING

Text set in Adobe Garamond

Manufactured in the United States of America

1 3 5 7 9 10 8 6 4 2

The Library of Congress has cataloged the Scribner edition as follows:
The emerging democratic majority/John B. Judis and Ruy Teixeira.
p. cm.
"A Lisa Drew book."
Includes bibliographical references and index.
1. Democratic Party (U.S.) 2. Republican Party (U.S.: 1854–)
3. United States—Politics and government—2001–
I. Teixeira, Ruy A. II. Title.

JK2316.J83 2002
324'.0973—dc21
2002066882

ISBN 0-7432-2691-7
0-7432-5478-3 (Pbk)

For James Weinstein and Eli Zaretsky

—JBJ

For Charles Falkenberg, Leslie Whittington, Zoe Falkenberg, and Dana Falkenberg, all of whom died on Flight 77 out of Dulles Airport on September 11, 2001

—RT

THE EMERGING DEMOCRATIC MAJORITY

CONTENTS

The Politics of Postindustrial America

Exactly a week after the September 11 terrorist attack against the World Trade Center and the Pentagon, Virginia attorney general Mark Earley, who was the Republican candidate for governor, began airing commercials declaring that he would make "the safety and security of our families and our schools his top priority." During the last week of the campaign, Earley and New Jersey Republican gubernatorial candidate Bret D. Schundler both ran endorsement ads from New York mayor Rudolph Giuliani, who had been nationally acclaimed for his response to the terrorist attack, and Earley also touted an endorsement from President George W. Bush. The subliminal message that both Earley and Schundler meant to convey was that, by electing them, voters would be endorsing Giuliani's and Bush's responses to the terrorist attack. But the public didn't make this association. Earley was decisively defeated by Democrat Mark Warner and Schundler was routed by Democrat Jim McGreevey, ceding to the Democrats offices that Republicans had occupied since 1993.

The Democrats also scored other impressive victories in November 2001. In Dayton, Ohio; Syracuse, New York; Los Angeles; and Raleigh and Durham, North Carolina, Democrats replaced Republican incumbents. The victory in Dayton, coming on the heels of a Democratic win in Columbus in 1999, meant that all of Ohio's major cities were under Democratic control. North Carolina's Research Triangle, one of the fastest-growing areas of the state, is now entirely in Democratic hands. In the longtime Republican stronghold of Nassau County, Long Island, a Democrat won the county executive race, and Democrats also captured the county legislature. Democrats had not held the legislature and the executive in Nassau County since 1917. The one outstanding Republican victory occurred in New York City. But the Republican mayoral candidate, Michael Bloomberg, was a liberal Democrat who had rented the Republican label because he stood a better chance of winning the Republican than the Democratic primary.

When parties win elections like this, it doesn't always portend significant long-term changes. In 1946, Republicans captured the Congress from the Democrats, but the Democrats won it back in 1948. The 1946 elections reflected voters' lack of support for the new Truman administration and their weariness with fourteen years of Democratic rule. But what was remarkable about the November 2001 elections was that they took place amidst widespread support for the Bush administration's conduct of the war. After the September 11 attacks, many Republican and Democratic strategists assumed that public support for Bush would carry over to Republican candidates. That it did not is evidence that these elections were, indeed, part of a longer trend, one that is leading American politics from the conservative Republican majority of the 1980s to a new Democratic majority. Democrats aren't there yet, but barring the unforeseen, they should arrive by the decade's end.

American politics has gone in cycles where one party and its politicians have predominated for a decade or more—winning most of the important elections, and setting the agenda for public policy and debate. From 1932 to 1968, New Deal Democrats were in command of American politics, even when a Republican was president; from 1980 to 1992, conservative Republicans prevailed, even when the House of Representatives was in Democratic hands. During these periods of ascendancy, the dominant party hasn't necessarily gotten everything it has wanted, but it has set the terms on which compromises have occurred. Since the 1992 elections, we have been in the midst of a political transition, similar to the period of 1968 to 1980, in which neither party has been able to establish a clear majority. And while the transition of 1968 to 1980 led from a Democratic to a Republican majority, this one is leading in the opposite direction.

The transition is from one coalition to another. American political majorities are composed of coalitions of different interests, classes, regions, religious persuasions, and ethnic and racial groups. The conservative Republican majority of the 1980s brought together Republican managers, executives, and business and farm owners with white middle-class and working-class Democrats, many of them Protestant evangelicals, who were alienated by their party's support for civil rights and for the sixties counterculture. They also blamed the Democrats for the stagflation—combined inflation and unemployment with slow economic growth—of the late 1970s and the decline of American power overseas. This new Republican majority was based in the Sunbelt, which stretched from Virginia down to Florida, across to Texas and over to California, but also included traditionally Republican farm states. There was considerable disagreement among groups within the coalition—over abortion, free trade, and deficit spending, for instance—but the leadership was distinguished by its laissez-faire economic views (government is the problem, not the solution), its opposition to the original civil rights acts and the ongoing program of the civil rights movement, and its opposition to modern feminism. And the coalition supported the new religious right and the rollback, not merely the containment, of Soviet communism.

Much of the conservative Republicans' success—and their ability to hold together their coalition—came from widespread popular disgust with the extremes to which liberal Democrats and New Left movements had gone in the late sixties and the seventies. The civil rights movement had become identified with ghetto riots and busing; feminism with bra burners and lesbians; the antiwar movement with appeasement of third world radicals and the Soviet Union; and liberal Democrats with grandiose schemes that were supposed to stimulate the economy but that would increase taxes for the white middle class and only benefit the poor and minorities. As long as these partly justifiable stereotypes endured, Republicans were able to win elections easily. But in the early nineties, as the Cold War ended, a recession began, and the Democrats moderated their economic and social message, the conservative Republican majority finally began to erode.

The Republicans suffered significant defections in the early nineties from white working-class voters in the North and the West who became disillusioned with the party's free-market economics and from upscale suburban voters who rejected the Republicans' support for the religious right. Some of these voters supported H. Ross Perot in 1992, but enough of them backed Democrat Bill Clinton for him to defeat George Bush for the presidency. The Democrats lost these voters in the November 1994 congressional elections, but Clinton won many of them back after the Republicans, who took control of Congress, tried to revive the program of Reagan Republicanism. The new Democratic majority that began to emerge in the 1996 election included some white working-class Reagan and Bush Democrats, but it also featured three important groups of voters that were becoming a larger and more powerful part of the electorate. Professionals, who included teachers, engineers, and nurses, had earlier been one of the most Republican groups, but started moving toward the Democrats in 1972 and, by 1988, had become solidly Democratic. Women voters had once been disproportionately Republican, but, starting in 1964 and accelerating after 1980, they became disproportionately Democratic. And minority voters, including blacks, Hispanics, and Asians, who had been variously committed to the Democratic Party, became overwhelmingly Democratic in the 1990s, while expanding from about a tenth of the voting electorate in 1972 to almost a fifth in 2000.

In the three presidential elections from 1992 to 2000, the Democrats won twenty states and the District of Columbia all three times. These represented a total of 267 electoral votes, just three short of a majority. They provide the Democrats with a base on which to construct a new majority. In the 2000 election, Democratic candidate Al Gore, hobbled by Clinton-era scandals and by his own ineptitude as a campaigner, nonetheless got more votes than Republican George Bush, and together with left-wing third-party candidate Ralph Nader, won 51.1 percent of the popular vote. This emerging Democratic majority was strongest in the Northeast, the upper Midwest, and the Far West, including California, but it commanded a following in many of the new metropolitan areas. These areas join city and suburbs and include high numbers of professionals. The Virginia suburbs of Washington, D.C., helped elect Governor Mark Warner; North Carolina's Research Triangle has become solidly Democratic, as have most of Florida's high-tech and tourist centers.

The outlook of this new Democratic majority is by no means uniform, but as represented by Clinton, Gore, and other leading politicians, it is different from both conservative Republicans and from the liberal Democrats and New Left movements of the 1970s that the conservative Republicans supplanted. As columnist E. J. Dionne first noted, the new Democrats closely resemble the progressive Republicans who dominated American politics at the beginning of the twentieth century.[1] Like them, they envisage government as an instrument of public good that can be used to reduce the inequities of the private market; and they see modern science, nurtured by government, as a tool of progress rather than as a threat to biblical religion. Like the Republican Progressives, who were surrounded by socialists on one side and laissez-faire conservatives on the other, the Democrats see themselves as being neither "left-wing" nor "right-wing," but as a centrist alternative to the New Left and to conservative Republicanism. They could best be described as "progressive centrists."

The Democrats' progressive outlook is most apparent in their view of government. Unlike Republican conservatives, they do not subscribe to the gospel of deregulation and privatization. They want to supplement the market's invisible hand with the visible hand of government to ensure that the public interest is served. They favor government regulation of business to protect the environment, ensure the safety and quality of consumer goods, prevent investor and stock market fraud, and protect workers from dangers to their health and safety. They want to strengthen social insurance programs, including medicare and social security, and to widen the availability of health insurance. They uphold the freedom of companies to expand or contract as the market requires, but they also want to shield workers from the insecurities created by global trade and economic downturns. They want a larger and stronger social safety net and generous spending on education and worker training.

The new Democrats also reflect the outlook of the social movements that first arose during the sixties. They support equality for women in the workplace and their right to have an abortion. They oppose government interference in people's private lives—from censorship to antisodomy laws. They reject government imposition of sectarian religious standards on both personal behavior and on scientific research. They envision America as a multiethnic and multiracial democracy, and they support targeted programs to help minorities that trail the rest of the population in education and income.

But they also see themselves as centrists. They favor government intervention, but not, except in very special circumstances, the government's supplanting and replacing the operation of the market. They want government, in David Osborne's phrase, "to steer, not to row."[2]

They want government to equip Americans with the tools to be effective workers in a high-tech society, but they don't want government to guarantee everyone a job through public spending. They worry about budget deficits and are wary of large tax cuts. They want incremental, careful reforms that will substantially increase health-care coverage and perhaps eventually universalize it, but not a large new bureaucracy that will replace the entire private health-care market. They want aid to minorities, but they oppose the large-scale imposition of quotas or the enactment of racial reparations.

Like the old progressive Republican majority, the emerging Democratic majority reflects deep-seated social and economic trends that are changing the face of the country. At the beginning of the last century, the progressive Republicans oversaw the transition from an Anglo-Saxon Protestant society of farms and small manufacturers to an urban, ethnic, industrial capitalism. Today's Democrats are the party of the transition from urban industrialism to a new postindustrial metropolitan order in which men and women play equal roles and in which white America is supplanted by multiracial, multiethnic America. This transition is occurring in the three critical realms of work, values, and geography.

Work: In agrarian and industrial America, work was devoted primarily to production of foodstuffs and manufactured goods. Beginning in the 1920s, the United States began to shift toward a postindustrial economy in which the production of ideas and services would dominate the production of goods. The transition slowed during the Great Depression, speeded up in the decades after World War II, and then accelerated again in the 1990s with the widespread introduction of the networked computer and the Internet. New service industries arose; in addition, the production of ideas came to dominate goods production. Auto manufacturers engineered annual design changes; clothing companies no longer produced clothes, but fashions. The numbers of blue-collar factory workers shrank; the number of low-wage service workers and of high-wage college-educated professionals grew proportionately. America, once a land of farms and factories, has become a land of schools, hospitals, offices, hotels, stores, restaurants, and "schedule C" home offices.

Immigrants from Latin America and Asia filled many of the positions in the new workforce. So did women, who, freed from the imperative to produce large families and from onerous household chores, such as growing food and making clothes, joined the workforce on an increasingly equal footing with men. Over half of the new professionals were women. While the low-wage service workers thought and voted like New Deal Democrats—supporting Democrats as the party of the minimum wage, social security, and collective bargaining—the new professionals saw their work as the crafts workers of the late nineteenth century had seen theirs. They sought to create or to offer a high-quality good or service; and when they became frustrated by the imposition of market imperatives, they looked to the Democrats as the party of regulated rather than laissez-faire capitalism.

Values: In agrarian and industrial America, workers and owners were supposed to practice self-denial and self-sacrifice for the economy to grow and for their souls to ascend to heaven. The prevailing Protestantism emphasized salvation in the afterlife through sacrifice in this one. It viewed the enjoyment of leisure, including sex separate from reproduction, as idleness and sin. It envisaged the family as a patriarchal unit of production and reproduction. This view of life was reinforced by the demands of work. Aesthetic contemplation and higher education were strictly the province of the upper classes. But after the Great Depression and World War II, all this changed—due partly to the changing dynamic of American capitalism.

In the wake of the Depression, American business became concerned that workers would not be willing or able to purchase the goods and services that it produced. Advertising, buttressed by American movies and television, convinced Americans to consume rather than save; on a deeper level, it directed Americans to be more concerned about the quality than the sanctity of their lives. Graced with higher incomes and a shorter workweek, American workers also began to seek out and experience the pleasures and satisfactions that had formerly been reserved for the upper classes. American companies, in search of new outlets for investment, reinforced this new preoccupation, creating service industries aimed at popular recreation, travel, education, and physical and mental health.

During the sixties, the transformation of values came to a head. Americans' concern about their quality of life overflowed from the two-car garage to clean air and water and safe automobiles; from higher wages to government-guaranteed health care in old age; and from equal legal and political rights to equal opportunities for men and women and blacks and whites. Out of these concerns came the environmental, consumer, civil rights, and feminist movements of the sixties. As Americans abandoned the older ideal of self-denial and the taboos that accompanied it, they embraced a libertarian ethic of personal life. Women asserted their sexual independence through the use of birth control pills and through exercising the right to have an abortion. Adolescents experimented with sex and courtship. Homosexuals "came out" and openly congregated in bars and neighborhoods. Initially, these new values and pursuits inspired a sharp reaction from the religious right and conservative Republicans. Republicans used Democrats' identification with postindustrial values to pillory them among an older generation raised in a different America. But over the last decades, these values have spread throughout the society and have become an important basis for a new Democratic majority.

Geography: Industrial America was originally divided between city and country, and then after World War II among city, suburb, and country. Typically, manufacturing took place within cities, farming within the countryside, and home life in the suburbs. In the seventies, the suburbs became the focus of white flight from integrated urban public schools, and suburban areas like Long Island became prime turf for the new Republican majority. But in the last two decades, inspired in part by computer technology, a new geographical formation has emerged—the postindustrial metropolitan area. It combines city and suburb in a seamless web of work and home. As manufacturing has moved to the suburbs and even the country, cities like Boston and Chicago have become headquarters for the production of ideas. Both city and suburb have become filled with the shops, stores, and institutions of postindustrial capitalism, from café-bookstores to health clubs to computer learning centers. Many are the site of major universities, which since the sixties have been the crucible of the new postindustrial work and values. Some suburban states like New Jersey are now almost entirely composed of contiguous postindustrial metropolitan areas.

These new postindustrial metropolises—from the San Francisco Bay Area to Chicago's Cook County to Columbus, Ohio, and down to North Carolina's Research Triangle—are peopled by the new professionals who live according to the ethics of postindustrial society. Their socially liberal values and concerns with the quality of life permeate the population, including the white working class. The result is widespread and growing support for the Democrats' progressive centrism. In the past, cities like Chicago, Philadelphia, and San Francisco were Democratic, while the surrounding suburbs were Republican. Now the entire metropolitan area in many of these locations has become strongly Democratic. And as more of America becomes composed of these postindustrial metropolises, the country itself becomes more Democratic.

As we write, America is still at war and coming out of a recession. By itself, the economic downturn might have been expected to accelerate the turn toward the Democrats and was already having that effect prior to September 11. But the terrorist assault on the United States—and the Bush administration's successful prosecution of the war in Afghanistan—cast Bush and the Republicans in a far more favorable light. And even if the war did not affect the local and gubernatorial elections in November 2001, a continuing public preoccupation with national security will certainly benefit the Republicans (and generally incumbents) in November 2002 and at least mitigate whatever gains the Democrats might have expected from a recession occurring during the Bush presidency. Yet when the fear of terror recedes, and when Americans begin to focus again on job, home, and the pursuit of happiness, the country will once again become fertile ground for the Democrats' progressive centrism and postindustrial values.

CHAPTER ONE

The Rise and Fall of the Conservative Republican Majority

In 1969, a year after Richard Nixon won the presidency, Kevin Phillips, an aide to Attorney General John Mitchell, published a book entitled *The Emerging Republican Majority.* The apparent confirmation of its thesis in 1972—not to mention Phillips's proximity to the administration—eventually landed it on the best-seller lists.

Like other books of its kind, however, it was cited more often than it was read, and its actual thesis has been clouded by its notoriety. Phillips did not argue that Republicans had already created a majority—in fact, when he wrote his book, Democrats still controlled both houses of Congress, plus the majority of statehouses. What he argued was that the era of "New Deal Democratic hegemony" was over. Phillips predicted that a new Republican majority would eventually emerge out of popular disillusionment with big government programs and the collapse of the Democratic coalition—a collapse the 1968 candidacy of Alabama governor George Wallace had foreshadowed. And a Republican majority finally did emerge in 1980, but only after the GOP had rebounded from the Watergate scandal.

Our view is that we are at a similar juncture—but one that will yield the opposite result. We believe that the Republican era Phillips presciently perceived in 1969 is now over. We are witnessing the "end of Republican hegemony." The first signs appeared in the early 1990s—not merely in Bill Clinton's victory in 1992, but in H. Ross Perot's third-party candidacy and the rise of new kinds of independent voters. The Republican takeover of Congress in November 1994 seemed to show that Clinton's win and Perot's strong showing were flukes. Indeed, many confidently predicted that 1994 heralded the beginning of still another conservative realignment. But the 1994 Republican wins turned out, in retrospect, to be the same kind of false dawn that the Democrats had experienced twenty years earlier because of Watergate.

Ever since 1994, Republicans have lost ground in Congress and in the country. Like the Democrats of the 1970s, they have also begun to suffer serious divisions within their ranks—from Pat Buchanan on the right to John McCain and Jim Jeffords on the left. Bush's aggressive prosecution of the war against the terrorists in the fall of 2001 lifted him in public esteem and may have delayed a Republican collapse in 2002. But once the clouds of war lift, and Americans cease to focus on threats to their national security, Republicans are likely to continue their slide, and the movement toward a Democratic majority is likely to resume.

The Republican majority that Phillips foresaw represented a "realignment" of American politics. A realignment entails a shift in the political coalitions that dominate American politics and in the worldview through which citizens interpret events and make political judgments. Realignments happened before in 1860–64, 1896, and 1932–36. These past realignments followed or took place during cataclysmic events—the conflict over slavery and the Civil War, the depression of the 1890s, and the Great Depression of the 1930s—that polarized the country along either regional or class lines. No similar cataclysm has shaken the political system since then, and as a result, realignments have occurred more gradually, with the fall of a prior majority and the rise of a new one separated by a decade-long transition period. It took from 1968 to 1980 for the New Deal majority to collapse and for a new conservative Republican majority to be born; and it is taking from 1992 until sometime in this decade for the conservative Republican majority to disintegrate and for a new Democratic majority to emerge.

I. HOW REALIGNMENTS WORK

Political scientist Walter Dean Burnham called realignments America's "surrogate for revolution."[1] It is a good way to think of them. Realignments respond to the sharp clashes between interests, classes, regions, religions, and ethnic groups brought about by tectonic shifts in the economy and society.* In other countries, these conflicts might have led to insurrection and revolution, but with the exception of our Civil War, in the United States they have resulted in changes in party control and the emergence of a new political zeitgeist. The tensions that industrialization stirred within a peasant economy contributed to the Russian revolutions of 1905 and 1917, but in the United States similar tensions produced the Populist Party, its absorption within the Democratic Party, and eventually the triumph of William McKinley and Theodore Roosevelt's new Republican coalition, which dominated American politics (with a brief interregnum) from 1896 to 1930. The economic collapse of the 1920s propelled the Fascists to power in Italy and the Nazis in Germany. In the United States, by contrast, the crash of 1929 simply ushered one governing coalition—Herbert Hoover's Republicans—out of power, so that another—Franklin Roosevelt's New Deal Democrats—could take over.

Realignments take place because a dominant political coalition fails to adapt to or to contain a growing social and political conflict. A political movement like the Southern civil rights movement can precipitate this sort of conflict. So can differing political responses to major changes in the country's economy or position in the world. The Jacksonian Democrats' rise in the 1820s was partly the result of conflict between the farmers of the new frontier states, who demanded easy credit, and Eastern bankers and merchants who wanted the stability of the Second Bank of the United States. The Republican Party was born in 1856 out of the conflict between the free-labor North and the plantation South over the extension of slavery. The McKinley Republicans put the United States squarely on the side of its industrial future rather than its agrarian past. And the New Deal Democrats expanded the scope and responsibilities of the federal government to overcome the inability of modern capitalism, acting on its own, to prevent poverty, unemployment, and incendiary class conflict.

*The theory of realignment, which was devised by political scientists V. O. Key and Walter Dean Burnham, is not a scientific theory like Newton's theory of motion. It can't be used to predict the exact time and circumstance of party changes, and the exact dates and degree of realignment have always been subject to debate. Did the New Deal realignment start in 1930, 1932, or 1936, for instance, and how profound was the realignment of 1896 that replaced one Republican majority with another? But it remains a valuable tool—a metaphor—for understanding a process of periodic change that has occurred in American politics.

Year	Realigning Party
1828	Jacksonian Democrats
1860–64	Lincoln Republicans
1896	McKinley Republicans
1932–36	New Deal Democrats
1968	Transition: Disintegration of New Deal Majority
1980	Conservative Republican Majority
1992	Transition: Disintegration of the Republican Majority
2004–8	New Democratic Majority

In each realignment, the emerging majority party creates a new coalition by winning over voters from its rival party and by increasing its sway over its own voters, whose ranks have typically increased through birth, immigration, and economic change. In 1896, the Republicans won over Northern workingmen who had voted Democratic in the past, but who blamed the Democrats for the depression and were turned off by presidential candidate William Jennings Bryan's agrarian appeal for free silver. The addition of these voters gave the Republicans a solid majority in the North and the Far West. And that majority held until 1932, when anger over the Great Depression drove a number of groups—industrial workers, small farmers, blacks, Catholics, and Jews—back into the Democratic Party. Together with the party's existing base in the South, this coalition gave the Democrats an enduring majority, reducing Republicans to their loyal business supporters in the Northeast and Midwest, farmers in the Western plains states, and rural Protestants in the Midwest and Northeast.

Majority coalitions are not necessarily homogeneous. They are like old cities that are periodically rebuilt. They may be recognizable by their newest buildings and streets, but they also contain older structures and streets. Similarly, a new majority coalition is distinguished by a set of leading constituencies, but also includes other groups that have traditionally supported that party and still find more reasons to support it than the opposition. At the heart of the New Deal were Franklin Roosevelt, New York senator Robert Wagner (the author of the National Labor Relations and Social Security Acts), and trade unionists like the Clothing Workers president Sidney Hillman, but it also included white Southern conservatives who had voted Democratic since before the Civil War and were typified by Roosevelt's first vice president, Texan John Nance Garner.

Realignments have been accompanied by the creation of a new dominant political worldview or zeitgeist. Like the coalition itself, a worldview is made up of heterogeneous elements, but it also has a leading set of ideas. The leading New Deal Democrats—Franklin Roosevelt rather than Garner or brain truster Rexford Tugwell rather than brain-truster-turned-critic Raymond Moley—held a far wider view of government's economic responsibility—and of what government could do—than did the Coolidge-Hoover Republicans. A Republican of the 1920s could not have conceived of, let alone condoned, the federal government paying the unemployed to go to school or to paint a mural. The New Deal Democrats also took a far more favorable view of labor unions and a far more skeptical view of business than did contemporary Republicans. But of course not all Democrats who voted for Roosevelt subscribed to these ideas about unions and government, just as, later, not all Republicans who voted for Reagan would support his ideas about banning abortion or reinstituting school prayer.

There is, finally, a kind of metaworldview that has distinguished the two parties. From Andrew Jackson through Franklin Roosevelt and Bill Clinton, Democrats have defined themselves as the party of the average American and Republicans as the party of the wealthy and powerful. The Democrats have not necessarily stigmatized the rich and powerful, but they have insisted that their priorities lie elsewhere. The Whigs and their successor, the Republicans, have been more consistently sympathetic to business and the wealthy. They have not defined themselves solely as the party of business, but they have defined America's interests as identical to those of its business class. Even when they have appeared to cast their lot rhetorically with the average American, as Reagan or former congressman Jack Kemp did, they have done so in a way that identifies the worker with the executive and the member of the middle class with the member of the upper class. They have shunned any evocation of class conflict or class resentment.*

One indication that a realignment is imminent has been the rise of third parties that defy the existing political consensus. The Liberty and Free Soil parties of the 1840s arose because both the Democrats and the Whigs were unwilling to oppose slavery. The Progressive Party of 1924, which ran Robert La Follette for president and received a respectable 16.6 percent of the vote, pointed to rising disillusionment by farmers and industrial workers with the two major parties' support for laissez-faire economics. And in 1968, Wallace's third party arose because neither the Democratic nor the Republican leadership were willing to oppose the civil rights movement. Sometimes, the revolt against the prevailing worldview occurs within the opposition party itself. In 1928, Al Smith, a "wet," a Catholic, and an advocate of liberal reform, challenged the prevailing consensus; Barry Goldwater did so in 1964; and George McGovern in 1972. The opposition gets clobbered, but it does surprisingly well among constituencies that would become the heart of a new majority. Smith was routed by Hoover nationally, but he ran unusually strongly among urban Catholic voters, who had deserted the Democrats in 1896, but would return in the 1930s.[2] Goldwater was also routed, but he created a new Republican base in the Deep South. And McGovern, as we shall soon see, tapped into the source of a future Democratic majority—one just coming into view now.

Realignments used to occur every thirty-two to forty years. By this count, a realignment should have occurred between 1968 and 1976. But the realignment cycle coincided with the business cycle. Both the realignments of 1896 and 1932 were precipitated by depressions. After World War II, Keynesian fiscal policy didn't eliminate, but did reduce, the downward trajectory of the business cycle. And by eliminating massive depressions, it made it less likely that political realignments would occur

*Democrats and Republicans most often put their overall rhetorical differences into practice when they formulate tax policy, with Democrats favoring progressive taxation and the Republicans some version of a flat tax that they (disingenuously) claim will benefit all classes equally. In the 1980 campaign, Reagan championed the Kemp-Roth tax plan that would cut tax rates by 30 percent for every taxpayer. In a campaign commercial Reagan declared, "If there's one thing we've seen enough of, it's the idea that for one American to gain, another American has to suffer. . . . If we put incentives back into society, everyone will gain. We have to move ahead. But we can't leave anyone behind."

exactly on time and as dramatically as before. That didn't lead to the end of realignments, but to a transitional period between the end of one majority and the beginning of another. This transition period created illusions of party dealignment and permanent equilibrium, but finally culminated in a new majority. The realignment of 1980 was prefaced by a twelve-year transition in which the old Democratic majority splintered, and the coming realignment is being preceded by a period of transition that began in 1992 in which the Republican majority has disintegrated.

II. THE COLLAPSE OF NEW DEAL LIBERALISM

In the sixties, two clear signs that a conservative Republican realignment might be imminent were Goldwater's nomination in 1964 and Wallace's independent campaign in 1968. In 1964, Goldwater directly challenged the New Deal and Cold War worldview that had united Republicans like Nixon and New York governor Nelson Rockefeller with Democrats like John Kennedy and Lyndon Johnson. The Arizonan and his conservative supporters opposed the New Deal welfare state, including social security and the minimum wage; they favored the rollback rather than containment of Soviet communism; and they rejected a commitment to racial equality, even opposing the Civil Rights Act of 1964 that guaranteed blacks equal access to public facilities. In the election, Goldwater was routed in the North and the West, but carried five Deep South states that had not backed the Republicans since Reconstruction (see chart). County by county, the pro-Republican shifts were phenomenal. For example, the average county in Mississippi moved Republican by an amazing 67 percentage points in 1964, while the average Louisiana county increased its Republican support by 34 points over 1960. These Deep South states would become bulwarks of the new conservative Republican majority.

In the 1964 Democratic presidential primaries and running as an independent candidate in 1968, Wallace challenged the consensus of both parties even more brazenly by advocating racial segregation. He waged an openly racist campaign that appealed to white Democrats who had been alienated by the civil rights movement and by the ghetto riots, which had begun in 1964. Wallace linked race to a cluster of concerns about the welfare state, taxes, spending, crime, local political power (blacks had already

Presidential Voting in Key Southern States, 1960 and 1964 Elections

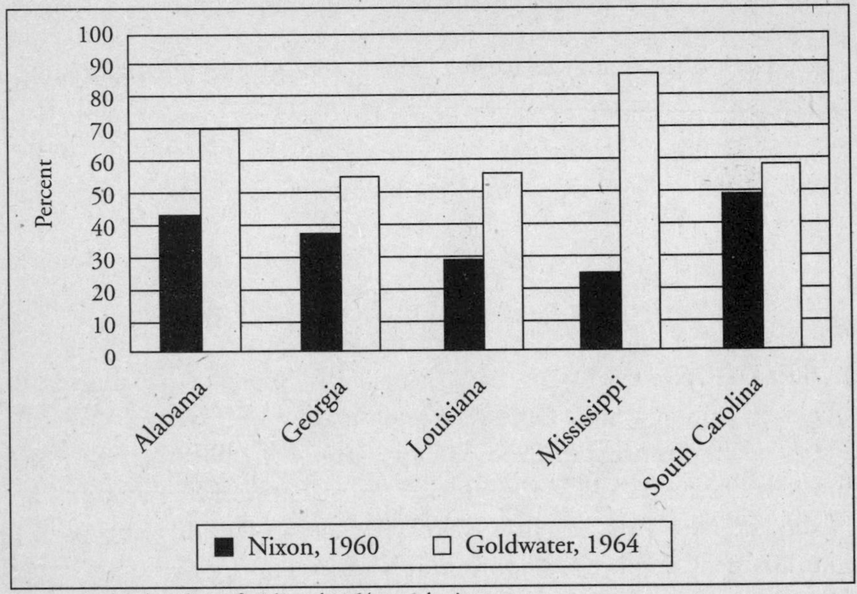

Source: Authors' analysis of 1960 and 1964 state election returns.

run for mayor in Cleveland and Gary), and the power of the federal government. This explosive cluster of issues, which had opposition to civil rights at its core, split the New Deal Democratic coalition. Phillips described this process in *The Emerging Republican Majority*:

> The principal force which broke up the Democratic (New Deal) coalition is the Negro socioeconomic revolution and liberal Democratic ideological inability to cope with it. Democratic "Great Society" programs aligned that party with many Negro demands, but the party was unable to defuse the racial tension sundering the nation. The South, the West, and the Catholic sidewalks of New York were the focus points of conservative opposition to the welfare liberalism of the federal government; however, the general opposition . . . came in large part from prospering Democrats who objected to Washington dissipating their tax dollars on programs which did them no good. The Democratic Party fell victim to

> the ideological impetus of a liberalism which had carried it beyond programs taxing the few for the benefit of the many . . . to programs taxing the many on behalf of the few.[3]

In the 1968 election, Wallace got 13.5 percent of the vote nationally, and forty-six electoral votes from five states in the Deep South. In twenty-four additional states, he got more votes than the difference between Nixon and Democratic candidate Hubert Humphrey. In 1972, Wallace's campaign for president as a Democrat was cut short by an assassin's bullet. When the Democrats nominated McGovern, who endorsed the civil rights movement agenda on welfare and crime, as well as on school integration, Nixon inherited Wallace's vote.

In forty-five of fifty states, Nixon's vote in 1972 closely matched the sum of his and Wallace's vote in 1968. (The exceptions were Maine, Hawaii, Massachusetts, Rhode Island, and West Virginia.) In some states, including seven in the South, it looked as if Wallace's votes had simply been transferred to Nixon (see chart below).[4]

Presidential Voting in Selected States, 1968 and 1972

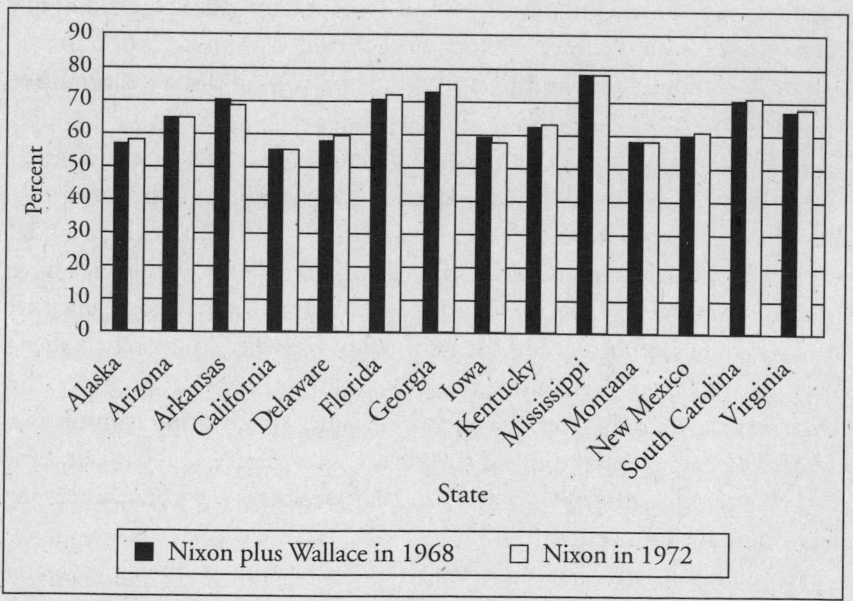

Source: Authors' analysis of 1968 and 1972 state election returns.

On the presidential level, Nixon's victory in 1972 was equivalent to Roosevelt's landslide in 1932 and seemed to augur a new conservative Republican majority. But there was one important difference: in 1932, Democrats won the White House and the Congress, while in 1972, Nixon and the Republicans were not able to win the Congress. Democrats retained a 57–43 edge in the Senate—even picking up two seats from 1970—and a 244–191 advantage in the House of Representatives.[5] Republicans failed to take the Congress partly because opposition to civil rights was not sufficiently strong in the North and Far West to overcome the voters' commitment to Democratic economics. Liberal Democrats defeated Republicans in Colorado, Delaware, Iowa, and Maine.

Republicans failed to win support in the South below the presidential level. If political position alone had mattered, the South would probably have gone solidly Republican in Congress in 1968 or 1972. Many of the Democrats it elected, such as Mississippi senator James Eastland or Arkansas Senator John McClellan, espoused exactly the same positions as the most conservative Republicans. But Southern voters, still mindful of the Republican role in the Civil War and Reconstruction, were not willing to support the creation of local Republican organizations. While the Republican Party had established a strong presence in North Carolina, South Carolina, and Tennessee, it could not recruit viable candidates in most of the South. In 1972, Democrats controlled 68 percent of both the Senate and House seats in the South, and virtually all the state legislative positions.[6]

To make matters worse for the Republicans, Nixon became embroiled in the Watergate scandal, which led to his resignation and cast a pall over Republican candidates in the 1974 and 1976 elections. The scandal was, of course, the result of Nixon's malfeasance, but it would not have become so public or led to his resignation and to Republican defeats if congressional Democrats and the national press (whom Nixon had alienated) had not been determined to do Nixon in; or, for that matter, if the Democrats had not had control of congressional investigating committees. The Watergate scandal did not simply weaken the Republicans; it happened in part because of the party's relative weakness—because a realignment had not yet occurred.

Yet while a Republican realignment had not occurred, the Democratic majority was already unraveling. Even in the shadow of Watergate,

Democrat Jimmy Carter barely eked out a victory over Gerald Ford in 1976. And while the Democrats held sixty-two seats in the Senate at the end of that year, fourteen of those senators were conservative Southern Democrats. When Carter tried to get Congress to enact the Democratic agenda of progressive tax reform, energy conservation, and consumer protection, these Southern Democrats joined their Republican counterparts to block his initiatives and to pass measures such as a reduction in capital gains taxes that would ordinarily have reflected a Republican majority.

III. THE TRIUMPH OF REAGAN REPUBLICANISM

In 1980, the Republican majority finally came to pass. Reagan won a landslide in the electoral college. He won the entire West, the South except for Carter's Georgia, and the Midwest except for Vice President Walter Mondale's Minnesota. The Republicans won a majority in the Senate and established parity in the South. The Democrats narrowly retained a majority in the House, but only because congressional results were lagging the general Republican trend in the South. Seventy of the seventy-eight Southern Democrats in the House were conservatives who would support Reagan's program and allow the Republicans to pass their legislative agenda of regressive tax cuts and reductions in social spending during Reagan's first term. In 1984, Reagan would do even better, winning 59 percent of the popular vote and every state but Minnesota and the District of Columbia against Mondale.

Two main factors propelled the Republicans into a majority. White opposition to civil rights continued to be a major factor in Democratic defections to the Republican Party. The cluster of issues that Wallace had evoked had, if anything, expanded, for now they included busing and affirmative action. As politicians were quick to understand, evoking any part of this cluster called up the whole and created a ready-made constituency among angry downscale whites who would otherwise have been expected to vote Democratic. By the time Ronald Reagan ran for president in 1980, it wasn't necessary any longer for politicians to make explicit racial appeals. He could use traditional code words such as *state's rights,* as Reagan did in his opening September campaign speech in Philadelphia, Mississippi, or could champion one of the issues at the margins of the racial cluster such as "law and order," "welfare cheating," or even capital punishment.[7]

The power of these issues was reinforced and supplemented by the stagflation of the late 1970s. Though stagflation first appeared during the 1973–75 recession, it had persisted during the Carter administration and was peaking on the eve of the 1980 election. As the economy slid once more into recession, the inflation rate in that year was 12.5 percent. Combined with an unemployment rate of 7.1 percent, it produced a "misery index" of nearly 20 percent. The stagflation fed resentments about race—about high taxes for welfare (which was assumed to go primarily to minorities) and about affirmative action. But it also sowed doubts about Democrats' ability to manage the economy and made Republican and business explanations of stagflation—blaming it on government regulation, high taxes, and spending—more plausible. In 1978, the white backlash and doubts about Democratic economic policies had helped to fuel a nationwide tax revolt. In 1980, these factors led to a massive exodus of white working-class voters from the Democratic ticket. These voters had once been the heart of the New Deal coalition, but in the 1980 and 1984 elections, Reagan averaged 61 percent support among them.[8]

In some working-class areas, race seemed like the predominant consideration. In these areas, the old Wallace vote transferred to Reagan. For instance, white working-class Lorain County, to the west of Cleveland, had once been solidly Democratic. But Nixon got 40 percent of the vote in 1968, with Wallace taking another 10. In 1980, Reagan won the county with 50 percent—exactly the sum of Nixon and Wallace's vote. White working-class Jefferson County, just south of St. Louis, had been staunchly Democratic before 1968. But in that year, Nixon had got 38 percent and Wallace 20 percent. In 1980, Reagan won the county with 52 percent.

Blue-collar Macomb County, just north of Detroit, had been the most Democratic suburban county in the country in 1960, going 63 percent for Kennedy in that year; in 1968, it had given 30 percent of its votes to Nixon and 14 percent to Wallace; in 1980, it gave 52 percent to Reagan. Then in 1984, it rewarded Reagan with a whopping 66 percent. In trying to discover why Macomb's disaffected Democrats had voted for Reagan, pollster Stanley Greenberg uncovered a cluster of issues at the center of which was racial resentment. "Blacks constitute the explanation for their vulnerability and for almost everything that has gone wrong in their lives," Greenberg wrote afterward.[9] According to Greenberg, Macomb's disaffected Democrats saw the federal government "as a black domain where whites cannot expect reasonable treatment." This view "shapes their attitudes toward government, particularly spending and taxation and the linkage between them. . . . There was a widespread sentiment, expressed consistently in the groups, that the Democratic party supported giveaway programs, that is, programs aimed primarily at minorities."

Other voters appeared to be moved primarily by doubts about Democratic economic policy. Wallace had made little headway among these voters, but they still went for Reagan in 1980 and 1984. For instance, five counties in Pennsylvania (Carbon, Erie, Lackawanna, Luzerne, and Northampton) backed Humphrey in 1968, while giving Wallace less than 5 percent of the vote. But in 1980, all except for Lackawanna went for Reagan, including predominately rural Carbon County (52–41) and blue-collar Erie (47–45). Reagan would carry these counties by similar margins in 1984. Reagan also won support from moderate Republicans who disagreed with his social conservatism and his rejection of environmental regulation and conservation, but nonetheless believed that Carter had proven incapable of managing the economy. Bergen County in northern New Jersey, just outside of New York City, and Montgomery County in Philadelphia, housed lawyers, doctors, bankers, and stockbrokers who had voted Republican for most of the twentieth century, but they were moderates who had balked at supporting Goldwater in 1964. In 1980 and 1984, however, they were back in the GOP fold, voting overwhelmingly for Reagan.

Two other factors contributed to Reagan's and the Republicans' victories in 1980—and in the next two general elections. Just as many Americans believed Carter and the Democrats had become incapable of managing the economy, many Americans also began to doubt Carter and the Democrats' leadership in foreign policy. During Carter's years, Soviet allied regimes took power in Angola, Ethiopia, Yemen, and Nicaragua and seemed on the verge of taking power in El Salvador. In 1979, the Khomeini regime in Iran, which had overthrown the shah with Carter's tacit support, took over fifty Americans hostage, creating a daily visual reminder of America's impotence. Of course, some working-class Democrats had begun to harbor doubts in the early 1970s about the Democrats' willingness to stand up to Soviet communism and third world radicalism, but the events of the Carter years convinced voters who were worried by Reagan's missile-rattling anticommunism that it was nonetheless time for a change.

Reagan and the Republicans were also able to draw on some voters' discomfort with the counterculture of the sixties, including feminism, gay rights, abortion rights, decriminalization of drugs, and sexual freedom. As early as 1966, Reagan, running for governor of California, had successfully singled out the "filthy speech movement" (a successor to the "free speech movement") in winning blue-collar votes. In 1972, Nixon had campaigned against "acid, amnesty, and abortion," a slogan he borrowed from McGovern's Democratic critic Senator Henry Jackson. These appeals exploited the generation gap between parents and children, but also the gap between the blue-collar and middle-class taxpayers who funded universities and the long-haired upper-middle-class students who attended them.

In the 1980 election, Reagan and other conservative Republicans were able to pick up votes from antiabortion Catholics in many former Democratic strongholds. But the most important defection over values came from white Protestant evangelicals in the South. These voters made up about two-fifths of the white electorate in the South and about one-seventh of the white electorate elsewhere.[10] In 1976, Jimmy Carter, who identified himself as a "born-again Christian," won 52 percent of their vote.[11]

In the late seventies, however, many of these voters began to desert the Democratic Party. The impetus came partly from leaders like the Reverend Jerry Falwell. Angered by the Carter administration's refusal to grant tax-exempt status to segregated Christian academies and by Democratic support for abortion rights, they turned to the Republicans, who, for their part, began to court them actively. Reagan won 63 percent of their support against Carter in 1980 and then 80 percent against Mondale in 1984.[12] By the late eighties, the Protestant evangelicals had become the most important single group within the Republican Party in the South, while also contributing to Republican support in the Midwest and the plains states.

Reagan's Republican coalition drew together all these voters—from the

Midwestern blue-collar Democrats that Scammon and Wattenberg had written about (who were now dubbed Reagan Democrats) to the traditional farm-state Republicans to Northeastern moderates. But Reagan's primary political base was in the Sunbelt states stretching from Virginia down to Florida, and across to Texas and to southern California. Many of these states had been the center of resistance to racial integration; they contained the bulk of the nation's Protestant evangelicals; and they were home to many of the country's military bases and defense installations and factories. While some moderate Republicans in the Northeast were put off by the conservatives' call to roll back communism and to hike military spending, these positions were extremely popular in defense-heavy states such as Virginia, North and South Carolina, Georgia, Mississippi, and Texas and in southern California. While the Republican Party still lagged in the South for historical reasons, Reagan's appeal was unmistakable. Reagan won 61 percent of white Southern voters in 1980 against a Southern candidate and 71 percent in 1984 against Mondale.[13]

Reagan Republicans incorporated the views of the Goldwater Republicans—they wanted to roll back communism, dramatically increase military spending, eliminate government intervention in the market, and end support for racial equality. Like Goldwater, Reagan adopted Andrew Jackson's antistatist populism to justify an attack on government environmental, consumer, and labor regulations. But the Reagan Republicans abandoned Goldwater's opposition to the basic New Deal programs of the minimum wage and social security and focused instead on the social welfare programs like Johnson's Great Society that had been adopted after the 1930s or that had been greatly expanded in the sixties and seventies—programs that they insinuated were aimed primarily at minorities. (Reagan would rail against the "welfare queen" in Chicago who had "eighty names, thirty addresses, twelve social security cards" and whose "tax-free income alone is over one hundred and fifty thousand dollars."[14]) In that way, Reagan, unlike Goldwater, could appeal to white working-class Democrats outside the Deep South.

Reagan also adopted the social agenda and rhetoric of the newly formed religious right. He supported a constitutional amendment banning abortion (though he had signed the nation's most permissive abortion law as governor of California); he called for restoring school prayer to the public schools; and he counseled abstinence ("just say no") to restless teenagers. Reagan and the Republicans put forth an older ideal of the churchgoing American family in which the husband was the sole breadwinner, in which women knew their place, and in which children went bowling and to church socials. This ideal was, of course, irrelevant to a growing number of Americans, but it also had wide appeal among what was then a growing constituency of politically active evangelicals.

Not all Republicans embraced all the tenets of this worldview, but then, majority coalitions are never homogeneous. The New Deal Democrats included Northern blacks and Southern whites, Wall Street investment bankers and Detroit autoworkers, Protestant small farmers from the Midwest and Catholic machine politicians from the Northeast. Despite their disagreements with each other and with some Roosevelt administration policies, these groups each saw reasons to remain within the coalition. Similarly, the conservative Republican coalition that Reagan forged contained disparate parts. Wealthy suburbanites from New Jersey's Bergen County might find little in common with the white parishioners at a small Baptist church in rural Southside Virginia; an unemployed Chrysler worker in Macomb County might also find little to share with Walter Wriston, the chairman of Citicorp. But in the early eighties, they all found sufficient reason to support Reagan.

This coalition was strong—strong enough, in fact, to carry a much weaker candidate, George Bush, to victory in 1988. Bush, who could not conceal his Eastern prep school pedigree, lacked credibility among the downscale Democrats who had backed Reagan. But, trailing by 17 percent in the polls on the eve of the Republican convention, Bush defeated Dukakis by calling forth the cluster of issues around race and the counterculture, as well as by criticizing him on foreign affairs (in which Dukakis had no experience). The Bush campaign repeatedly attacked Dukakis for having furloughed a black convict, Willie Horton, who subsequently attempted murder, and for vetoing a state bill requiring Massachusetts schoolteachers to lead their students in reciting the Pledge of Allegiance.[15]

Like Reagan, Bush got the support of white working-class voters, beating Dukakis 60–40 among that group. In the South, Bush won 67 percent of white voters. And he did even better among evangelical voters than Reagan, winning 81 percent of white Protestant evangelicals.[16] But this election was to be the last clear triumph for the conservative Republican coalition that Goldwater had first assembled in 1964 and that Reagan had finally consolidated in 1980.

IV. THE DISINTEGRATION OF THE CONSERVATIVE REPUBLICAN MAJORITY

What doomed the Republican majority was the uneven growth of the Reagan economy. The Midwest—hit by the loss of manufacturing jobs—never fully recovered from the 1982 recession. The trade deficit climbed in the mideighties, creating a widespread impression that the United States was losing ground to its economic rivals. Then in 1990, the country fell into recession. In technical terms, the recession lasted barely a year, but unemployment remained stubbornly high for another five years. This economic slowdown, along with the specter of international decline, removed an important prop from under the Republican majority. Specifically, it discredited the argument that Republicans would manage the economy better than Democrats—which was, after all, the reason many moderate Republicans had voted for Reagan in spite of their distaste for his agenda on social issues and the environment. Along with the business scandals of the late eighties, it also rekindled suspicions among white working-class Democrats that Republicans favored the wealthy.

In 1986, Republicans lost control of the Senate, and in 1988, Dukakis, perhaps the dullest Democratic candidate since John W. Davis in 1924, scored surprisingly well in the industrial Midwest, winning Minnesota, Wisconsin, and Iowa while barely losing Illinois, Pennsylvania, and Missouri. Dukakis also did impressively well in some upscale moderate Republican counties. California's San Mateo County and Santa Clara County (the site of Silicon Valley) had voted for Reagan in 1980 and 1984, but Dukakis won them both easily in 1988. Then, in 1989, the Supreme Court ruled in *Webster v. Reproductive Health Services* that states could limit access to abortion, sowing fear among many women voters that a Republican would eventually overturn *Roe v. Wade.* That year, Democratic candidates for governor in New Jersey and Virginia both won strong support in upscale suburbs—and were elected—by attacking their opponent for his opposition to abortion.

But the coup de grâce to the Republican majority was delivered in 1992 by Bill Clinton and H. Ross Perot. Perot's challenge to Bush was a lot like Wallace's challenge to Humphrey. Perot claimed to be nonpartisan, but almost all of his closest aides and a large majority of his backers were former Republican voters. According to the National Election Study, over 70 percent of Perot voters had voted for Bush in 1988. And in one post-election poll, 62 percent of Perot backers said they had not only voted for Bush in 1988 but also for Reagan in either 1980 or 1984.[17] Just as Wallace had represented a dissident faction within the Democratic Party, Perot represented a dissident outlook among Republicans and among renegade Democrats who had previously voted for Reagan and Bush.

Perot's outlook was a direct repudiation of the conservative Republican worldview. He rejected the triumphalism of their outlook—"it's morning in America," Reagan had proclaimed in 1984—warning instead that America was in economic decline. He blamed the Reagan and Bush tax cuts for creating record budget deficits. He rejected Bush's continuing preoccupation with resolving the Cold War, putting forth instead a more narrowly focused economic nationalism. He rejected the religious right's intolerance and its crusade to ban abortions and restore prayer in public schools. Perot got 18.9 percent of the vote to 43 percent for Clinton and 37.4 percent for Bush. Perot didn't win any electoral votes, but he got more than the difference between Bush and Clinton in forty-seven states.

Clinton's campaign drew on several distinct political strands to weave together what would later become a new Democratic worldview of progressive centrism. With the economy faltering, Clinton tapped the Democrats' New Deal legacy to promise new jobs and greater economic security; he invoked Democratic populism, promising to "put people first" and flaying Bush and the Republicans for favoring the rich; and he sounded sixties-era commitments to protect the environment (reinforced by his choice of Al Gore as running mate) and to defend women's rights and civil rights. He was, in these respects, similar to other liberal and New Left Democrats of the seventies and eighties. But Clinton's campaign also reflected a decade-old effort to create a new post–New Deal, post-sixties Democratic politics.

In the early eighties, several Democratic politicians, including Massachusetts senator Paul Tsongas and Colorado senator Gary Hart, argued for a "neoliberal" focus on encouraging economic growth rather than redistributing existing wealth. In 1985, after Mondale's landslide defeat, two Democratic congressional staffers, Al From and Will Marshall, founded the Democratic Leadership Council (DLC), aimed at creating a new politics that could appeal to middle-class suburbanites and Southerners. The DLC preserved the Democratic commitment to civil rights, but it advocated "inoculating" Democrats against the cluster of issues with which Republicans had made covert racial appeals. The DLC proposed welfare reform; it urged Democrats to be tough on crime and to support the death penalty.

In 1992, Clinton, who had been chairman of the DLC two years before, sought to mute the older liberal and New Left message with the centrist lessons of the neoliberals and the DLC. After Clinton and Gore got the nomination in July 1992, the campaign unveiled a commercial declaring, "They are a new generation of Democrats, Bill Clinton and Al Gore. And they don't think the way the old Democratic Party did. They've called for an end to welfare as we know it, so welfare can be a second chance, not a way of life. They've sent a strong signal to criminals by supporting the death penalty. And they've rejected the old tax-and-spend politics."[18]

This eclectic worldview resonated among voters and drew together the rudiments of a new coalition. White working-class voters, who had embraced the Republicans in hopes that they could restore prosperity or put blacks in their place, gave a slight plurality of their votes to Clinton in 1992. Nationwide, over 90 percent of formerly Democratic counties like Carbon and Erie—where Wallace had never been an attraction, but which had embraced Reagan in the 1980s—went for Clinton.[19] Missouri's Jefferson County, a Wallace stronghold that Reagan and Bush had carried in the eighties, also went for Clinton. So did Monroe County in Michigan, a heavily white, working-class suburb south of Detroit, which had gone solidly Reagan. Los Angeles County, where the aerospace industry was suffering, had gone for Reagan in 1980 and 1984, but went for Clinton by 53–27 percent, contributing to Clinton's 14 percent margin over Bush in California. Moderate Republicans who had overlooked Reagan's and Bush's commitments to the religious right in the hope that they could restore prosperity now abandoned the Republicans over their social conservatism. Clinton, for instance, won Pennsylvania's Montgomery County, and California's historically Republican Santa Barbara and San Luis Obispo counties.

The 1992 election demonstrated that the old conservative era was over: without California, and without moderate Northeasterners and Reagan Democrats, the Republicans simply could not command a consistent political majority in the country. And yet 1992 didn't demonstrate a new Democratic majority, either. In fact, Clinton didn't get significantly more votes than Democrat Michael Dukakis had received in 1988. He won because many erstwhile Republicans and Reagan Democrats voted for Perot rather than for Bush. For them, Perot represented either a protest against Bush's brand of Republicanism or a way station between their apostasy and their return to the Democratic fold.

Clinton, alas, didn't grasp how tenuous his victory was. Convinced that he was the second coming of Franklin Roosevelt, and that his first year should be comparable to Roosevelt's "First Hundred Days,"[20] he proposed a comprehensive national health-insurance plan. (He even called it a campaign for "health security," consciously evoking the language of FDR's signature achievement.) Republicans and business opponents of the plan were able to discredit it by stoking popular anxiety about Democratic "tax and spend" policies. Clinton further antagonized his white working-class supporters by championing causes like the admission of gays into the military. And to make things worse, he hadn't yet delivered on his promise to bolster the economy, which did not really begin to grow strongly until the spring of 1996.

In November 1994, Democrats paid a dear price for Clinton's miscalculation, as Republicans won the House and Senate for the first time since 1952. Yet the Republicans failed to understand the basis of their victory. Even though the Republicans had campaigned on an apolitical antigovernment platform designed to appeal to Perot voters, they portrayed the 1994 election as the dawn of a new conservative era. Lobbyist Grover Norquist wrote, "Winning control of the House of Representatives is as historic a change as the emergence of the Republican Party with the election of Lincoln or the creation of the Democratic Party majority in the 1930–1934 period with the Depression and Franklin Roosevelt."[21] Former Bush administration official William Kristol said, "The nation's long, slow electoral and ideological realignment with the Republican Party is reaching a watershed."

But the Republicans' victory in 1994 turned out to be similar to the Democratic congressional victory in 1974 and presidential victory in 1976. It represented the Indian summer of an older realignment rather than the spring of a new one. For one thing, some of the GOP's gains reflected completion of the old Republican majority—not the formation of a new one. In the House, twenty-one of the fifty-eight new Republican seats were from the South, including Kentucky and Oklahoma. In the Senate, half of the net gain of eight seats were from the South.[22] These new Southern seats were simply the final step in the South's partisan realignment dating back to Goldwater's run in 1964, rather than a new Republican breakthrough.

And it soon became clear that the new Republican Congress had no greater mandate than Clinton had had two years earlier. Once in power, Newt Gingrich and the Republicans, after briefly adopting some of the good-government reforms in the Contract With America, began trying to complete the "Reagan revolution" that they had promised their business and religious-right backers. They introduced measures that would virtually have eliminated government regulation of the environment and workplace health and safety and would have threatened medicare and medicaid. They passed a huge cut in capital gains taxes. And they tried to do away with the Department of Education, a Christian-right bugaboo, and to ban abortion and reinstitute school prayer. The result was a massive backlash among voters in the North and West, who wanted no part of such aggressive conservatism, and a renewed mobilization effort by Democratic interest groups, particularly the AFL-CIO. Indeed, for the AFL-CIO, the Democratic losses in 1994 were instrumental in provoking a revolt against its president, Lane Kirkland, and his replacement by a new leadership explicitly committed to using labor's clout to defeat Republicans and elect Democrats.[23] In the 1996 elections, Bill Clinton routed Bob Dole by hitting the Republicans on medicare, education, and the environment, and Democrats in the House and the Senate began to recoup the losses they had suffered outside the South.

More important than the actual wins, though, was the way Democrats had won. In 1996, Democrats continued to win among moderate, well-to-do voters who had supported Reagan and Bush. For example, Bush had won New Jersey's Bergen County in 1988 by 58–41 percent; in 1992, he edged Clinton there by 2 percent. But in 1996, after the Republican takeover of Congress, Bergen County threw its support to Clinton by a substantial margin—53–39 percent. Four years later, it would back Gore by 55–42 percent. Reagan Democrats also continued to desert the Republicans. Bush narrowly won Michigan's Macomb County in 1992, by 42–37 percent, but Clinton would win it by 49–39 percent in 1996, and Gore would take it by 50–48 percent in 2000. (Nader would get 2 percent in Macomb, bringing the potential Democrat total to 52 percent.) Clinton won California, the linchpin of the conservative Republican majority of the 1980s, by 13 percent in 1996, and Gore would win it by 12 percent in 2000, despite never having campaigned there. The old conservative Republican majority was finally, and very clearly, dead.

V. AN EMERGING DEMOCRATIC MAJORITY?

But what will take its place? Among those for whom the present is always the future, it's become popular to predict that the current rough parity between the parties, with third parties and political independents tipping the balance one way or the other, will continue indefinitely. But the rise of third-party candidates like Perot and Ralph Nader have usually foreshadowed a partisan realignment; after one election, most of their supporters settle back into one of the two parties. (That Nader tipped the election to Bush will, after all, quite likely discourage future third-party bids from the left.[24]) As for the increased importance of independents, that's a bit murky, too. Yes, there are more of them: according to the University of Michigan's National Election Studies, voters who are willing to identify themselves as "independent" have increased from 23 percent in 1952 to 40.4 percent in 2000.[25] But while independents are making a political statement of a sort, they do so not with a single voice and not in a way that finally affects the two-party system itself.

In the South after 1960, many former "yellow dog" Democrats who couldn't reconcile themselves to registering Republican described themselves as independent. But, as far as election arithmetic is concerned, they have been reliably Republican voters. In the Northeast, upper Midwest, and Far West, many voters now identify themselves as independents as a protest against the venality and corruption they see in Washington and in party politics. But although they occasionally vote for an independent candidate—as Minnesotans did for Jesse Ventura in 1998—they usually support candidates from one of the major parties. Indeed, when the new independent vote is broken down, it reveals a trend toward the Democrats in the 1990s and a clear and substantial Democratic partisan advantage. The National Election Studies show that about 70 percent of independents will say which party they are closer to, and, once these "independents" are assigned to the party they are closer to, Democrats enjoy a 13 percent advantage over the Republicans, which is close to the advantage Democrats enjoyed among the electorate in the late 1950s and early 1960s.[26]

The Democratic leanings of the new independents are even clearer if one looks at the states that boast the highest percentage of independents. Ten of the top fifteen—Connecticut, Illinois, Iowa, Maine, Massachusetts, Minnesota, New Jersey, Rhode Island, Vermont, and Washington—are solidly Democratic, two—Arkansas and New Hampshire—are swing states, and only three—Alaska, Montana, and North Dakota—are dependably Republican in national elections.[27] Thus, a close look at today's independent voters suggests that the most likely successor to the dying Republican majority is another major-party majority—a new Democratic majority.

There is also a striking analogy between the period from 1968 to 1976, which preceded the birth of the last realignment, and the period from 1992 to the present. The Wallace defection of 1968 had a similar effect on the Democratic Party that the Perot defection of 1992 had on the Republican Party. Nixon and Clinton were both transitional presidents who maneuvered amidst shifting coalitions. Nixon had to face a Democratic Congress, and Clinton after 1994 a Republican Congress. Both were capable of sharp turns in their political outlook that bedeviled their supporters—Nixon on China and wage-price controls, Clinton on government itself ("the era of big government is over") and on the provisions of welfare reform. Both understood that they were on the verge of assembling new political majorities, but both were prevented from doing so by scandals. These scandals were partly the result of their own misdeeds or misbehavior but also of a fierce political opposition that was determined to undermine them.

Both men unwittingly inspired a political revival among their opponents—the Democratic congressional victories of 1974 and 1976 and the Republican congressional victory of 1994. By leaving a trail of scandal behind them, they also made it difficult for the men who tried to succeed them. Both Ford and Gore had to overcome problems of political trust that they were not principally responsible for creating. If not for Watergate, Ford—indeed, almost any Republican candidate—would have been elected president in 1976. And if not for the shadow of the Clinton scandals, Al Gore would almost certainly have defeated George W. Bush. According to Gore pollster Stanley Greenberg's extensive postelection poll, lack of trust in Gore was the single most important factor dogging his candidacy and seriously hurt him among voters that had begun moving Democratic in Clinton's successful 1996 campaign.

There are even remarkable similarities between Carter, who won in 1976, and George W. Bush, who won in 2000. Bush, like Carter, is a relatively inexperienced governor who was elected president on a platform that stressed character rather than program, and who took office amidst growing divisions within his own party and an opposition determined to foil him. And Bush, like Carter, will have to face a sputtering economy that could easily be the final catalyst for a new realignment.

There is also an analogy between the South's role in the conservative Republican realignment and the North's role in this new realignment. Just as the Democrats' continued hold on Congress depended on the partisan loyalty of Southern Democrats, the Republicans' narrow 221–213 margin in the House depends on the partisan loyalty of about thirty moderate Republicans—ranging from Maryland's Connie Morella to New York's Peter King—who often vote with the Democrats.[28] These House members generally represent districts that strongly backed Clinton in 1996 and Gore in 2000, but they continue to be reelected based on their personal popularity. In the absence of strong provocation—a conflict with their leadership, the recapture of the House by the Democrats—they are unlikely to switch parties, but once they retire, they are likely to be replaced by Democrats. In the Senate, one Republican, Vermont's Jim Jeffords, did leave the party in May 2001, turning the Senate itself over to the Democrats.

But the most important arguments for a new Democratic majority do not rely on analogies. A look at the voting patterns for president and Congress during the 1990s clearly indicates that while the conservative Republican majority was crumbling, a new Democratic majority was germinating. It would include white working- and middle-class Democrats, such as those from Lorain or Jefferson counties, who have returned to the Democrats in the nineties because they (or their progeny) believe the Democrats are more responsive to their economic situations. They are responding primarily to the Democratic Party's Jacksonian and New Deal past—its commitment to economic security for the average American.

But it would also include three groups of voters who clearly appeared in George McGovern's loss to Richard Nixon: minority voters, including blacks, Hispanics, and Asian-Americans; women voters, especially single, working, and highly educated women; and professionals. While the ranks of white working-class voters will not grow over the next decade, the numbers of professionals, working, single, and highly educated women, and minorities will swell. They are products of a new postindustrial capitalism, rooted in diversity and social equality, and emphasizing the production of ideas and services rather than goods. And while some of these voters are drawn to the Democratic Party by its New Deal past, many others resonate strongly to the new causes that the Democrats adopted during the sixties. These new causes help ensure that these groups of voters will continue to support Democrats rather than Republicans, paving the way for a new majority.

George McGovern's Revenge: Who's in the Emerging Democratic Majority

Nothing has inspired such scorn as George McGovern's 1972 campaign. Immediately afterward, Jeane Kirkpatrick, who was then a Democrat, described McGovern's constituency as "intellectuals enamored with righteousness and possibility; college students, for whom perfectionism is an occupational hazard; portions of the upper classes freed from concern with economic self-interest; clergy contemptuous of materialism; bureaucrats with expanding plans to eliminate evil; romantics derisive of Babbitt and *Main Street.*"[1] Even today, liberals still regard the campaign as having been quixotic and destructive. Margaret Weir and Marshall Ganz compare it unfavorably to Goldwater's campaign in 1964: "Although the 1964 Goldwater campaign laid a foundation for subsequent grassroots organization on the right, the equally unsuccessful 1972 McGovern campaign seemed to have just the opposite effect on the left."[2]

Perhaps it is time to reappraise the McGovern campaign—not as a model of how to win presidential elections, but as an election that foreshadowed a new Democratic majority in the twenty-first century. Although McGovern lost to Richard Nixon 60.7–37.5 percent, the third-largest margin ever, several groups that would become important components of today's Democratic Party made a clear statement during that election. According to the Gallup Poll, McGovern actually did slightly better among nonwhite voters than Hubert Humphrey did in 1968—winning 87 percent of their vote. And though McGovern lost the vote among women as well as men, he showed unforeseen strength among working women. The Democrats had opened up a gender gap among employed voters starting in 1964, but this gap ballooned in

2. McGovern did 13 percentage points better among working women than among working men.[3]

McGovern also won college communities that had once been Republican. These included the University of California at Berkeley's Alameda County, the University of Wisconsin's Dane County, and Washtenaw County, where the University of Michigan is located. And he did astonishingly well among highly skilled professionals. This group, which had been solidly Republican and had given Humphrey only 36 percent of its vote, gave McGovern 42 percent.[4] He did better among these voters than he did among blue-collar workers.

At the time, of course, these results were scant consolation. What did it matter if McGovern won Alameda County and San Francisco but decisively lost Los Angeles and San Diego? Or that he did better among working women than working men, and among professionals than blue-collar workers, but still lost a majority of all these voters? Thirty years later, however, these anomalies loom larger. Women are still voting more Democratic than men, but they are also voting much more Democratic than Republican, particularly women who now work outside the home, single women, and women with college degrees. Minorities, once about 10 percent of the voting electorate, now constitute 19 percent; extrapolating from recent trends, they could make up nearly a quarter of voters by 2010. They, too, are continuing to vote Democratic. Democrats are winning even more decisively in college towns, and these towns and their schools have become linked to entire regions such as Silicon Valley and North Carolina's Research Triangle. And skilled professionals have become a much larger and a dependably Democratic voting group.

The outlook of these groups differs from that of the white working-class voters who were the heart of the New Deal Democratic majority. Professionals, working women, and minorities have been shaped by the political and economic events of the last half century: the tumultuous sixties—a period that really stretches from 1956 to 1974—which saw the rise of the civil rights movement, the revival of the women's movement, and the growth of consumer and environmental movements; and by the transition from an industrial to a postindustrial economy, which really begins in the 1920s, but erupted in the sixties, and then accelerated during the "information revolution" of the nineties. As a new Democratic majority began to emerge in the 1990s, these three groups joined forces with white working-class voters, many of whom had voted for Nixon, Reagan, and Bush, but returned to the Democratic fold in 1992 or 1996. The resulting coalition, evident in Clinton's 1996 victory, reflected the diverse outlooks of all these groups, but above all, that of professionals.

I. POSTINDUSTRIAL SOCIETY AND THE RISE OF THE PROFESSIONALS

No group used to be as dependably Republican as highly skilled professionals, a group that includes architects, engineers, scientists, computer analysts, lawyers, physicians, registered nurses, teachers, social workers, therapists, designers, interior decorators, graphic artists, and actors. This group dutifully backed Eisenhower in 1952 and 1956, Nixon in 1960, 1968, and 1972, Ford in 1976, and Reagan in 1980 and 1984. But their anti-Democratic proclivities began to soften as early as 1972, and by 1988, they were supporting Democrats for president and have continued to do so. In the fifties, their political choices didn't matter that much: they made up only about 7 percent of the workforce. But by 2000, they made up 15.4 percent.[5] Moreover, they have the highest turnout rate of any occupational group.[6] As a result, they compose about 21 percent of the voting electorate nationally and are likely near one-quarter in many Northeastern and Far Western states.[7]

The growth of professionals as a group is partly a function of the introduction of technology into the production process, which has increased the role of scientists and engineers in relation to blue-collar workers and has fueled the growth of public and private education. In 1900, there was one engineer for every 225 factory workers; in 1950, one for every 62; now, it is one for every 8.[8] But engineers make up only 11.4 percent of professionals.[9] The main reason for the growth of professionals is the transition from an industrial society, in which labor was primarily devoted to goods production, to a postindustrial society, in which the labor is primarily directed at producing ideas and services.

In the industrial society of the late-nineteenth and early-twentieth centuries, most workers were engaged in manufacturing and farming. In 1900, 38 percent worked on farms, and 36 percent were manual workers, primarily in factories—together making a total of three out of four

American workers. Twenty years later, the number of farm laborers had declined to 27 percent, but the proportion of manual workers had climbed to 40 percent. It looked as though America were going to become a giant factory, divided between a small white-collar managerial-professional class, which in 1920 made up about 12 percent of the workforce, and a huge blue-collar proletariat, much of which lived on the edge of poverty.[10] But in the 1920s, America began the transition to a postindustrial society.[11]

During the 1920s, the introduction of electricity and scientific management on the factory floor and of the gas-driven tractor and harvester in the fields made it possible for the goods-producing workforce to shrink while goods production expanded dramatically. Potentially, this promised release from unremitting toil and sacrifice, but in the near term, it created a threat of overproduction. If the wage-earning class shrank, while production grew, who would buy the growing array of new foodstuffs and cars? America failed to find a solution to this problem during the Great Depression, but over the next decades, government and business adapted to the challenge posed by the new productivity. Government's role in the economy was transformed. The federal government began to use fiscal and monetary policy to temper the business cycle. The federal government even did the unthinkable—encouraging consumer demand through running deficits. It would fund consumer housing purchases and college attendance and use public investment to build roads, bridges, schools, and hospitals, as well as aircraft carriers, and to reward farmers for not planting crops.

Private industry would also alter its practices. Businesses had begun offering installment plans in the 1920s, but after World War II, they established charge accounts and later credit cards to encourage consumer spending. Advertising also exploded after the introduction of television. Advertising budgets went from $1 billion in 1929 to $6.5 billion in 1951 to $12 billion in 1962.[12] Advertising encouraged Americans to spend rather than save, and to seek happiness on earth rather than in the afterlife—to worry about the "quality" of their life. Businesses expanded into new realms that had been previously reserved for upper-class luxuries or for production at home. They built restaurant chains, hotels, theme parks, casinos, auditoriums, and opened television and movie studios. They sold sexual pleasure and mental and physical health. They imbued the material objects they produced with the new ethic of consumerism. They marketed not merely edible food, but gourmet delights and prepackaged and frozen food. They sold fashion and not merely clothes. They didn't just sell a standard car like the Model T or Model A; they produced a new model or style annually.

These measures transformed the face of the economy, as the production of things became secondary to the production of services and ideas. By 1970, only 35 percent of the workforce was devoted to goods production; the rest was devoted to services and ideas.[13] Since then, computer automation has accelerated the transition from industrial to postindustrial society. During the 1990s, manufacturing output increased by over a third, while factory employment declined by 4.4 percent. By the decade's end, manufacturing employment accounted for only 14.3 percent of the nation's jobs. About eight in ten American workers were producing services or ideas[14]—a dramatic change from the beginning of the century, when the corresponding figure was only about three in ten.[15]

If you look at this new postindustrial workforce, it is far more diverse than the workforce of 1900 and 1920. At the top are executives, administrators, and managers. At the bottom are unskilled manufacturing and service workers, still a considerable, though shrinking, portion of the workforce. Among those groups in between are professionals, now the largest of the major occupational groups.* They are the workforce, above all, of the new postindustrial society.

In the 1990s, the ranks of professionals swelled 30 percent[16]; and the

**Professionals* is a term used by the Census Bureau to distinguish white-collar, highly skilled, credentialed workers from managers, administrators, and executives, on the one hand, and technicians and blue-collar mechanics and repairers, on the other hand. But in terms of the critical characteristic we cite—identification with the quality of the service or idea rather than with the market result—there is a blurring of the categories.The census lists airline pilots and navigators as technicians, but we would include them within professionals. We would also include school administrators, who have their own professional associations, as professionals rather than managers, even though they perform management functions. And we would probably cede certain kinds of public relations people and corporate lawyers—for instance, in-house counsels—to managers, administrators, and executives. All in all, the category of professionals, as we would use it, is slightly broader than, but roughly congruent with, the census category. To maintain consistency, and due to data limitations, all data cited here on professionals, in terms of occupational statistics and voting behavior, are based on the Census Bureau definition.

Labor Department projects that from 1998 to 2008, professionals will be the fastest-growing of any major occupational group. Among the professions expected to increase by more than 20 percent are a startling combination of jobs that either didn't exist or were of marginal significance in the industrial age: actors, directors, and producers, artists and commercial artists, designers and interior designers, camera operators, public relations specialists, counselors, registered nurses, therapists, coaches, special education teachers, preschool teachers, social workers, electrical and electronics engineers, architects and surveyors, agricultural and food scientists, conservation scientists and foresters, medical scientists, computer systems analysts, computer scientists and engineers, physicists and astronomers, and directors of religious activities.[17] Of course, some of these start from a small base, but their projected rapid growth tells us much about where the economy is headed.

The political views of professionals have been shaped by their experience in this transition to postindustrial society. From 1900 to 1960, when they were a tiny minority within the workforce, they saw themselves clearly linked to managers and executives. They disdained unions, opposed the New Deal and "big government," and adopted an ethic of individual success that made them the most Republican of the occupational groups. In the 1960 presidential election, professionals supported the Republican Nixon 61–38; managers backed Nixon by a more modest 52–48. But in the last four presidential elections, professionals have supported the Democrats by an average of 52–40 percent, while managers have averaged 49–41 support for the GOP.[18] Why did professionals turn so abruptly toward the Democrats?

One key to the change is the different relationship that managers and professionals have to the private market. While corporate and financial executives, accountants, and property managers are creatures of the private market who tend to gauge their own success in profit-and-loss terms, many professionals identify their success with the quality of the service they offer or the idea they produce. Software programmers worry about the "coolness" of their code; architects about the beauty and utility of their buildings; teachers about whether their pupils have learned; the doctor and nurse about the health of their patient. AnnaLee Saxenian wrote about Silicon Valley engineers of the 1990s that "status was defined less by economic success than by technological achievement. The elegantly designed chip, the breakthrough manufacturing process, or the ingenious application was admired as much as the trappings of wealth."[19]

One survey of different kinds of professionals conducted by Hart Research[20] confirmed the strong emphasis professionals put on "making a contribution," "the opportunity to be creative," and "excelling at my job" (see table below). The professional could draw a distinction, which neither the manager nor the alienated blue-collar worker could, between the quality of his or her product and the demands of the market.

As long as professionals felt that they had the opportunity to pursue excellence in their jobs, they identified themselves with the successful entrepreneur and CEO. They saw themselves as case studies of how capitalism could reward quality. But as the numbers of professionals have grown within postindustrial capitalism, they have become subject to higher authority within the private and the public sectors. And they don't

What Professionals Value

	Teachers	Nurses	Engineers	Information Technology Workers
Making a contribution	68%	54%	47%	37%
Creative opportunities	29	8	27	28
Excelling at my job	26	27	25	29
Professional autonomy	8	16	16	11
Salary and benefits	10	16	11	16
Voice on the job	4	10	7	8

Source: David Kusnet, *Finding Their Voices* (Washington, D.C.: Albert Shanker Institute, 2000).

like it. They have been forced to accede to what they see as alien market standards of performance that conflict with their own standards of excellence. They have had their autonomy undercut by corporate and institutional managers who have introduced work rules, overseen their output, controlled the prices they charge and the income they receive, and even divided up their work among more specialized but less highly trained technicians. As a result, they have increasingly made a distinction between their own priorities and those of business and the market. That has placed them much closer in outlook to the Democratic Party than to the unequivocally pro-market Republican Party.

Many midlevel professionals, including teachers, aerospace engineers, social workers, and software testers, have had a similar experience to late-nineteenth-century crafts workers—the smiths, machinists, and carpenters who evaluated their work by the quality of their product and jealously guarded their prerogatives. "In each craft," labor historian Harry Braverman recounts, "the worker was presumed to be the master of a body of traditional knowledge, and methods and procedures were left to his or her discretion."[21] When they saw their autonomy threatened by industrial capitalism, they helped to form and lead the American Federation of Labor in 1886. Similarly, many of today's professionals have responded in the last four decades by joining unions. In 2000, 19.3 percent of professionals belonged to unions—a higher percentage than all other white-collar workers and close to the level of operators and laborers.[22] And many of these unions, such as the American Federation of Teachers and the National Education Association, have become bulwarks of the Democratic Party.

Even the highest-level professionals have become subject to what Marxists called proletarianization. Doctors used to enjoy the privileges and security of a medieval guild and the income of the most highly paid executive, but in the last three decades, their work has increasingly become subject to direction from insurance companies through managed-care plans and health maintenance organizations. They are told what procedures to follow, what prices to charge, and how much they can make. About 40 percent of doctors are now salaried employees.[23] Marcia Simon, the director of government relations for the American College of Obstetricians and Gynecologists, says, "Doctors had always been quintessential small businesspeople, but now they're essentially employees of large corporations. It represents a real sea change in the role of doctors in the economy."[24]

Doctors who are not self-employed have begun joining unions. From 1997 to 1999, the number of unionized doctors went from twenty-five thousand to about forty thousand.[25] That year, the AMA also pledged support for unionization among doctors. Politically, doctors used to be one of the most dependable Republican constituencies. The American Medical Association and other doctor lobbies could be expected to give the bulk of their funds to Republicans. But as doctors have tried to fight the control of the insurance companies, they have found allies among Democrats rather than Republicans. In the first half of 2001, when Congress was considering a patients' bill of rights, the majority of AMA contributions—67 percent—went to Democrats rather than Republicans.[26] Says one doctor who used to raise money for Republicans, "The chicks have come home to roost on the GOP." The doctors' vote, he says, "is now up for grabs."[27]

The other key to the political outlook of professionals is the experience of the sixties, in which many future professionals, while attending college, became supporters and leaders of the civil rights, women's, antiwar, consumer, and environmental movements. These movements had their own rationales and impetus, but the women's, environmental, and consumer movements were shaped by the transition to postindustrial society. One feature of that transition—transmitted in the new variety of jobs and products and by the new appeal to the consumer crafted by advertisers—was a far more expansive definition of what Americans could expect from their lives and, by extension, their government. Americans of the last half of the twentieth century learned to value not only automatic transmissions on automobiles, but also clean air and water, physical and mental well-being, and safe and reliable products. And when they didn't get these from the invisible hand of the market, they demanded them from the visible hand of government.

This new understanding was nurtured in the universities, where the professionals were trained. The post–World War II members of the baby-boom generation would spend their late adolescence and early adulthood on college campuses. In 1900, 5 percent of eighteen-to-twenty-one-year-olds attended college. By 1970, 51.8 percent did. In college, they were insulated from parental authority and from labor market discipline. The college campus became ground zero for the development of a new postindustrial ethic and for the development of new political movements. One of the leading civil rights organizations was the Student Nonviolent Coordinating Committee, and the leading antiwar group was Students for a Democratic Society. The environmental movement was born on Earth Day at the University of Michigan, and the consumer movement grew out of the law schools.

Of all occupational groups, professionals would be the most clearly touched by these movements. To this day, they exhibit the most support for civil rights and feminist causes and for environmental and consumer regulation. Moreover, professionals would bring their own special outlook to them—an outlook that was markedly different from New Deal Democratic politics. New Deal Democratic politics were defined largely by industrial unions and blue-collar workers, who by the nature of their jobs were adversaries of business managers and executives. The New Deal Democrats envisaged American politics as a contest of interest groups, and they sought a "fair deal" (the name of Harry Truman's platform) for workers and ordinary Americans. But the growing army of professionals occupied a place between the alienated blue-collar worker and the manager and executive. They didn't see themselves primarily as winning a better deal from the rich and powerful. Instead, they believed they were acting on behalf of the public as a whole rather than on behalf of workers or management. They thought they represented the "public interest," and they envisaged the movements they founded as "public interest" groups. The model was Harvard Law School graduate Ralph Nader's Public Interest Research Group and Public Citizen and John Gardner's Common Cause.

These environmental, consumer, and political reform groups were initially nonpartisan, identified with neither the New Deal Democrats nor the pro-business Republicans, but by the mid-1970s they found themselves opposed by an alliance of business groups and conservative Republican politicians and think tanks. In 1977, for instance, the Business Roundtable teamed with Republicans to defeat a Nader plan, backed by the Carter administration, to establish a consumer protection agency. Four years later, Reagan appointed a host of officials to the Federal Trade Commission, Interior Department, and Environmental Protection Agency who were hostile to the environmental and consumer movements. As a result, the consumer and environmental movements—and the larger public interest movement of which they are a part—found themselves at odds with the Republican Party and increasingly identified with the Democratic Party. The many professionals who actively supported these groups or merely subscribed to their goals followed suit. It became another impetus for professionals to abandon the Republicans for the Democratic Party. (As we will see, professionals' support for feminist goals would have a similar effect on their party allegiance.)

If you look at the voting history of professionals in the light of these influences, it becomes more comprehensible.[28] Professionals began in the 1950s as a thoroughly Republican group. They identified with the market and opposed the "big government" initiatives of the New Deal and the Great Society. Like managers, and every other occupational group, they supported Johnson against Goldwater because of the latter's seeming readiness to plunge the United States into nuclear war, but they reverted to strong support for Nixon against Humphrey in 1968. In 1972, they backed Nixon, but much less so than managers because many of them supported the movements of the sixties. In 1976, they supported Gerald Ford and in 1980 and 1984, Reagan.

They continued to support Republicans largely because professionals still tended to share the economic outlook of small businessmen: they were suspicious of government spending on jobs and feared deficits were imperiling the economy. Like many Americans, they were skeptical of Carter and the Democrats' economic policies. And they distrusted government in general. Johnson's conduct of the war and Nixon's Watergate scandal had reinforced this attitude. By 1980, 81 percent of professionals believed government was "too powerful." Even so, many professionals balked at supporting Reagan. Instead, 15 percent of professionals voted for the fiscally conservative and socially liberal Anderson—a higher percentage than he got from any other occupational group.

The professionals' move toward the Democratic Party continued in the 1984 election. In that election, professionals increased their support for the Democratic presidential candidate by about 9 percent to 45 percent, while only 30 percent of managers backed Mondale. One of the reasons professionals moved to the Democrats and managers did not was their support for environmental regulation. In 1984, 52 percent of professionals favored spending more on the environment compared to 32 percent of

Democratic Margin among Professionals and Managers, 1952–2000

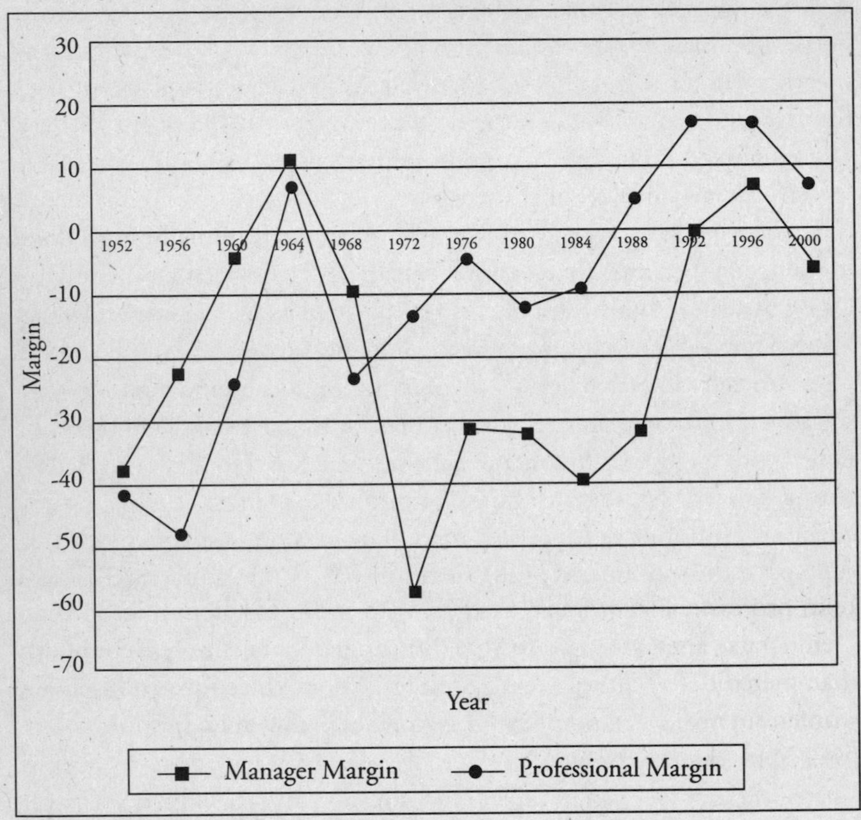

Source: Authors' analysis of National Election Study (NES) data, 1952–2000.

managers. Of all the occupational groups, professionals were also most sympathetic to civil rights and women's rights and the most supportive of campaign finance reform and other good-government issues.[29] Since 1988, professionals have strongly backed Democratic presidential candidates, while managers have remained mostly Republican (see chart).

Professionals might not have moved toward the Democratic Party, however, if the party itself had not moved toward them. If the 1972 election marked the Democrats' identification with the sixties, the 1984 election marked the end of the Democrats as the party of indiscriminate big spenders and the beginning of the party's commitment to more incremental reform. It was the first intimation of the Democrats' progressive centrism. In that election, Mondale attacked Reagan for running deficits and promised to reduce the deficit, even if that meant raising taxes. Such a stance probably hurt him among blue-collar Democrats, but it may have helped him among professionals worried by looming deficits. Dukakis, Clinton, and Gore continued in their campaigns to promise fiscal restraint. Clinton, for example, despite the more ambitious experiments of his first two years in office, would end up running on a program of moderate, fiscally prudent reform in the 1996 campaign, and Gore followed in 2000 with a similar approach that emphasized the importance of not endangering the budget surplus. This general approach has helped to reassure professionals leery of overly ambitious government programs and to make the Democratic Party the natural home of the professional voter.*

II. WOMEN AND THE FEMINIST REVOLUTION

Like professionals, women used to vote more for Republicans than Democrats. They also used to vote disproportionately more Republican than men did. In 1956, according to the National Election Study survey, women supported Eisenhower 63–37 percent while men supported him 56–43 percent. In 1960, women supported Richard Nixon 53–46 percent against Democrat John Kennedy, but men backed Kennedy 52–48 percent. In 1964, women began to vote slightly more Democratic than men, and in 1968 and 1972 the trend grew.[30] Then, after subsiding for the 1976 election (when the Republican candidate was pro-choice, pro–equal rights Gerald Ford along with his outspoken wife, Betty), in 1980 it reappeared in force. According to the CBS/*New York Times* exit poll, men in 1980 supported Reagan over Democrat Jimmy Carter 55–36 percent—while women supported him only 47–45 percent.

*In 2000, however, some professionals, concerned about the Clinton-Gore campaign-finance scandals, voted for Nader rather than Gore. In the NES 2000 survey, professionals and technicians were the most supportive of Nader's candidacy, and professionals registered the greatest concern with reforming campaign finance of any of the occupational groups. This, of course, didn't alter the Democratic trend among professionals.

In the 1980s, women not only began voting disproportionately more Democratic than men—the so-called gender gap—but what is more important they began to vote more Democratic than Republican. As a result, Democratic candidates began to win elections on the strength of the women's vote the way they had won elections on the strength of the union vote. In 1982, Mario Cuomo got 56 percent of the women's vote—but just 48 percent of the men's—in defeating Republican Lew Lehrman for the New York governorship. In 1984, Illinois Democratic Senate candidate Paul Simon defeated incumbent Republican Charles Percy by winning 55 percent of the women's vote and only 46 percent of the men's vote.

In the 2000 elections, women's support helped the Democrats win eight Senate races. In Florida, Democrat Bill Nelson won 56 percent of the women's vote, but only 45 percent of the men's vote. In Minnesota, Democrat Mark Dayton lost the men's vote to incumbent Rod Grams 44–47 percent, but he won the women's vote 54–40 percent. In the presidential race, men supported Bush 53–42 percent, but women supported Vice President Al Gore 54–43 percent.[31] In twelve of the nineteen states that Gore won, women made up a Democratic deficit among male voters and enabled Gore to win. This change in women's voting was due to the way that the parties responded to the transformation of women's role and status that occurred after the sixties—a transformation that was itself closely bound up with the transition to postindustrial society.

In industrial society, women of all classes were defined by their subordinate role within the family to men. If they were in working-class families, they had many other duties besides mother and homemaker—they might, for instance, do piecework to supplement the family income—but their primary identity and responsibility was as wife and mother under a husband's authority. Working-class single women like Theodore Dreiser's Sister Carrie got jobs, but their goal in life was to leave the workplace when they married. Few middle- and upper-class women worked outside the home, especially if they were married. As late as 1910, only 9.2 percent of married women worked outside the home.[32] "The economic position of women in the world," Charlotte Perkins Gilman wrote in 1898, is "that of domestic servant."[33] Women's personal lives were circumscribed by the dictates of nineteenth-century Protestantism and the demands of industrial society for new workers. Sex was for reproduction—

and for creating large families. Women's cares, interests, and wants were to be directed at their children and husband.

The transition to postindustrial society after World War II changed women's lives, but didn't really change their place in society. Business and the public sector increasingly took over many of the functions that women had performed within the home—from making clothes and educating children to preparing food. New technology reduced the time women had to spend on cooking, cleaning, and doing laundry. Work itself was changing—toward the kind of service and professional jobs that women had been deemed capable of filling. And more women began to attend college. Yet married women were still discouraged from working outside the home. Wrote Betty Friedan in 1963 in her groundbreaking book, *The Feminine Mystique,* "It is more than a strange paradox that as the professions are finally open to women in America, *career woman* has become a dirty word."[34]

Women's personal lives were also in flux. Freed from the social imperatives of the farm and factory, they were no longer enjoined to have large families. Through birth control, they could have sex without the threat of reproduction (and with the introduction of the pill, they could have some control over the process themselves). The new ethic of consumerism and personal fulfillment—put forth by advertisers and reflected in popular entertainment—depicted women as sexual beings. The fashion of the fifties—epitomized by Dior's "New Look"—emphasized women's curves.[35] Yet women were still constrained by Victorian ideals of feminine behavior. They were educated to have minds of their own, but were discouraged from displaying them by the official culture.

In the sixties, these looming contradictions gave rise to the modern women's movement. While the older movement had limited itself to demanding political equality for women, the new movement of the sixties demanded equality within the home, school, and workplace. NOW was founded in 1966 and Friedan became its first leader. Its membership climbed to 15,000 in 1972 and to 220,000 in 1982. In the late sixties, hundreds of local women's groups also grew up under the aegis of the New Left's women's liberation movement—which was modeled on the black liberation movement. While the women's movement's membership was largely drawn from college students, young educated women in their twenties, and professionals, its impact was universal. It changed the way women envisaged all aspects of their working and personal lives—from their responsibility as parents to their sexuality.

The women's movement challenged the barriers to women's equality—whether in the workplace or in university funding of athletics; the movement pressured states and finally the Supreme Court into eliminating most restrictions on abortion. The women's movement also spearheaded women's massive entry into the workplace, which began in the 1960s. Women's labor force participation went from 37.7 percent in 1960 to 43.3 percent in 1970 to 51.5 percent in 1980 and to 57.5 percent in 1990 (see chart). Among twenty-five-to-thirty-four-year-old women—those who would be expected to leave the workforce after marriage—participation rates went up by 20.5 percent during the 1970s.[36] As women entered the labor force, they also moved up within it. In 1970, fewer than 10 percent of medical students and 4 percent of law students were women; by the early 1990s, more than 40 percent of first-year law and medical students were women.[37] By the end of the twentieth century, 55 percent of professionals were women.[38]

Women's Labor Force Participation: 1950–2000

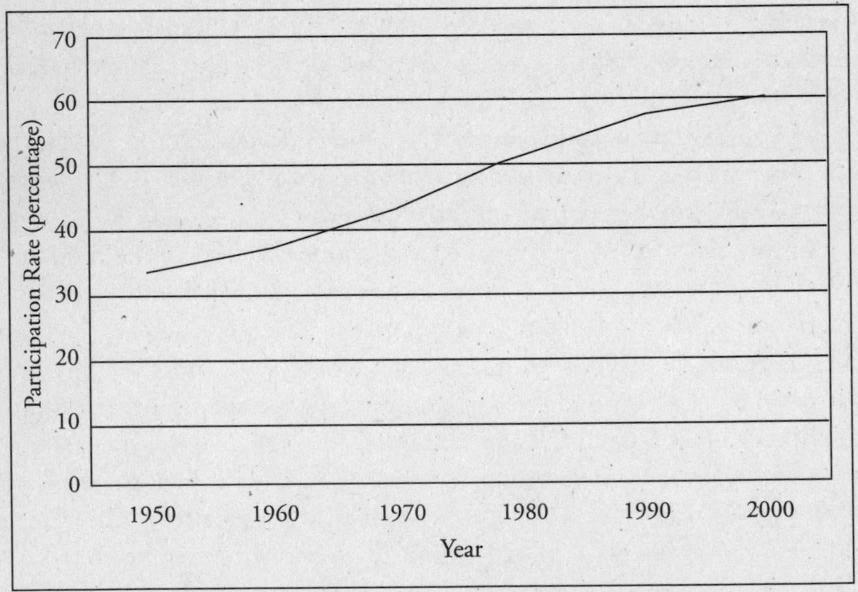

Sources: Howard N. Fullerton Jr., "Labor Force Participation," *Monthly Labor Review*, December 1999; and Bureau of Labor Statistics Web site.

The rise of the women's movement and women's accelerated entry into the labor force also changed the way women thought about politics. Women's disproportionate support for Republicans before 1964 was largely attributable to the political outlook of women who did not work outside the home. These homemakers made up almost two-thirds of female voters, and they were much more likely to support Republicans than working women or men were.[39] (Even then, working women were more Democratic than working men.) In 1952, for instance, only 38 percent of nonworking women supported the Democrat Stevenson against Eisenhower, compared to 44 percent of working men and 48 percent of working women. While demographic differences had some influence, the main reason nonworking women were disproportionately Republican was because their position in the home made them more politically conservative. They represented the vestiges of an earlier ethic, and as such, they were more likely to favor the Republicans, who still represented the small-town mores of the Protestant Midwest.

The presixties women's movement was also pro-Republican. The members of the main women's organization, the National Woman's Party, were often Republican businesswomen. In addition, Republicans were more likely before 1973 to back the Equal Rights Amendment (ERA), which the NWP championed. The first major party candidate to endorse the ERA was Republican Thomas Dewey in 1948, and Eisenhower was the first president to endorse it (in 1957). New Deal Democrats from Franklin Roosevelt through John Kennedy opposed the ERA because they feared that it would undercut state labor legislation aimed at protecting working women from overtime and heavy lifting.[40] But Friedan and many of the leaders of the new women's movement came out of the political left and were inclined to link the women's movement, if at all, with the Democratic rather than the Republican Party. In 1972, feminist political leaders, including Congresswoman Bella Abzug and *Ms* magazine founder Gloria Steinem, attended the Democratic convention. Actress Shirley MacLaine and Los Angeles official Yvonne Braithwaite Burke headed the California delegation. In 1968, 13 percent of the Democratic delegates were women; by 1972, 38 percent were. McGovern staffers talked of a "nylon revolution" in the party.[43]

But the great divide between women and the parties did not occur until after 1973. Liberal feminists and labor Democrats had come out in favor of the ERA after an amendment to the 1964 Civil Rights Act prohibited discrimination in employment on the basis of sex. That, and the fact that women were increasingly working in services and in professions that didn't need special protection, undercut the older liberal objections to the ERA. In 1972, Nixon and Republicans had backed the ERA, but in 1973, new right leader Phyllis Schlafly began a successful crusade to turn the Republicans and the country against the amendment. In January of that year, the Supreme Court ruled in *Roe v. Wade* that states could not outlaw all abortions. While Democrats endorsed abortion rights in 1976, conservative Republicans got the Republican Party to come out in favor of a constitutional ban.

In 1980, the religious right became an important constituency of the Republican Party, and the party went on record in favor of women's traditional place in the family. It even removed support for child care from the platform. Reagan spoke repeatedly for banning abortion and in opposition to affirmative action for women. In 1983, the Reagan administration attempted to gut Title IX, which required federally subsidized colleges to offer equal facilities to women.[42] The women's organizations moved closer to the Democrats, and in 1984 NOW actually endorsed Mondale for president.

Of course, women in this era were concerned about a range of issues from affirmative action to breast cancer research. Evidence is particularly strong that working women, as they experienced the vagaries of the marketplace, developed distinctly positive views of government's role in providing services and mitigating economic insecurity. These views disposed working women naturally toward the Democratic Party and account for much of the move toward the Democrats among women as a whole.[43]

But one issue that concerned female voters directly as women and clearly turned many college-educated women toward the Democratic Party was the Republican Party's opposition to abortion. It struck at the heart of women's claims to a new independence and identity outside the traditional role of mother and wife. It impinged on women's ability to work outside the home and to have sex for pleasure rather than for reproduction. Tanya Melich, a longtime Republican Party activist who finally broke with the party in the 1990s over its hostility to women's rights, wrote later of the centrality of abortion as an issue: "A woman's right to determine whether she has a child strikes at the core of her being, affecting how she lives and what she does, who she is, and what she will be."[44]

One poll taken after the 2000 election showed that abortion was still a defining issue for many women. Stanley Greenberg, who served as Gore's pollster, asked over two thousand respondents to identify three reasons (out of eighteen choices) why they voted, or considered voting, for Gore and three reasons (out of thirteen choices) why they had doubts about voting for George Bush. Among all women voters, Bush's "opposition to a woman's right to choose" was the single biggest reason for opposing him. In addition, Greenberg found that for white college-educated females and white females making over $75,000, protecting a woman's right to choose was both their most important reason for supporting Gore and for having doubts about Bush. Thirty-nine percent of white college-educated females said defending a woman's right to choose was their main reason for supporting Gore, and 33 percent said it was their main source of doubt about Bush.

Some women's support for Democrats can, of course, be attributed to factors other than their experience as women. It could be argued, for instance, that African-American women support Democrats simply because they are African-American. Yet even here there is good evidence that the feminist revolution has had its special effect. African-American women voted for Gore by 94 percent, a 9 percent gender gap over their male counterparts.

Women's support for Democrats is also not universal. It is particularly concentrated among working and single women and among college-educated women, especially those with a postgraduate education—exactly those groups that would experience most clearly the effect of feminism and of the transition to postindustrial society. Single working women, for instance, backed Dukakis in 1988 by 57 to 42 percent; Clinton in 1992 by 62 to 24 percent; and Clinton in 1996 by 72 to 21 percent. Women college graduates supported Gore by 57 percent compared to 39 percent for Bush, and 63 percent of women with advanced degrees backed Gore.[45] But these are the groups that, as a proportion of the female electorate, have been steadily growing since the end of World War II and will continue to do so.

III. MINORITIES AND THE DEMOCRATIC MAJORITY

Until recently, America's minority groups—defined in distinction to the white Indo-European majority—had widely differing political allegiances. Mexican-Americans, typical of many new immigrants, generally voted for Democrats. African-Americans were Republicans from the Civil War to 1936. Chinese and Cuban-Americans were anticommunist Republicans. But over the last few decades, these diverse minorities, with the exception of Miami's Cubans, have converged on the Democratic Party and have given it a large potential advantage in national and some state elections over Republican candidates.

Blacks

Blacks did begin voting for Democrats during the New Deal, but as late as 1960, almost a third of the black electorate voted for Republican Richard Nixon for president.[46] The big change came after 1964 when Democrats sponsored the Civil Rights Act of 1964, and when Republicans, who as a party had been supportive of civil rights legislation, nominated Goldwater for president, who had voted against it. That November, blacks voted for Johnson against Goldwater 94–6 percent.[47] As Democrats cemented their commitment to civil rights and conservatives took over the Republican Party, blacks supported Democrats overwhelmingly. Between 1968 and 2000, they never gave Democratic presidential candidates less than 83 percent of their vote and usually quite a bit more.[48] In 2000, blacks gave Gore 90 percent, Nader 1 percent, and Bush 9 percent.

At the same time as blacks were voting Democratic, the black vote increased as a proportion of the electorate. In 1960, only 29 percent of Southern blacks were registered to vote; by 1976, after passage of the Civil Rights Act of 1965 guaranteeing blacks the right to vote, 63 percent of Southern blacks were registered.[49] The black proportion of the electorate went from less than 6 percent in 1960 to 10–12 percent in the 1990s.[50]

The single most important reason why blacks supported Democrats was, of course, civil rights. They saw Democrats supporting civil rights and

Republicans doing what they could to take advantage of the white backlash to it—from Nixon's thinly veiled pledge to restore "law and order" to Reagan's stories about the "welfare queen" in Chicago. Many blacks also supported Democrats for economic reasons. African-Americans disproportionately occupied the lower rungs of the occupational ladder, and many lived in cities beset by poverty and crime. They saw government not only as providing much needed aid and benefits, but also as an important source of upwardly mobile employment. They backed the New Deal and the Great Society. They wanted the minimum wage raised, and welfare payments expanded. They favored national health insurance and a massive program of urban aid. While Democratic politicians like Clinton and Gore balked at the most ambitious of these programs, they still represented to black voters a viable alternative to Republicans, who tended to oppose or to seek to weaken even basic New Deal programs.

Hispanics

Some Mexicans had settled in the Southwest and West before American settlers had wrested these lands from Mexico. In the late nineteenth and early twentieth century, Mexican laborers were lured into the Southwest and West to help build the railroads and work on farms. They were given citizenship but were discouraged from voting and denied adequate schooling. In the 1930s, some were forcibly deported. But unlike blacks, they were never enslaved. Instead, they faced the kind of discrimination that blacks experienced in the North in the twentieth century. Like Northern blacks, many Mexican-American and Central American immigrants have also occupied the lower rungs on the occupational ladder. They worked as migrant farm laborers and, over the last three decades, have filled many of the service industry jobs created by the postindustrial economy.

Except for the Cubans who emigrated after the revolution, a majority of Hispanics have voted Democratic. John and Robert Kennedy both wooed Mexican-Americans, and in 1972, Mexican-American political leaders became active in the national party. In McGovern's California delegation to the national convention, 17 percent were Mexican-Americans.[51] In the 1960s, the Hispanic civil rights movement, which included sepa-

California Latino and White Views of Economic Issues, May 1998

Taxes and Spending	**Latinos**	**Whites**
Should spend more on social programs, even if it means increasing taxes	58%	46%
Should reduce taxes, even if it means spending less on social programs	38	46
Government Regulation		
Regulation of business is necessary to protect public interest	63	49
Regulation of business does more harm than good	33	48

Source: Mark Baldassare, *California in the New Millennium: The Changing Social and Political Landscape* (Berkeley, Cal.: University of California Press, 2000).

rate Chicano and Puerto Rican organizations, followed on the heels of the black civil rights movement; and many Hispanics supported Democrats as the party of affirmative action and opposition to discrimination. But Hispanic voters probably placed more emphasis on economic issues. Hispanics, who were concentrated in the working class, were Democrats on grounds of economics as much as on grounds of civil rights. Primarily working class, they supported the New Deal and the Great Society and wanted government to do still more (see table).

When the Democrats appeared to falter in their economic leadership in the late 1970s, some Hispanics voted for Reagan. Reagan got as high as 47 percent of the Hispanic vote in one poll taken in 1984.[52] But Hispanics returned to the Democratic Party in the 1990s—not only because of Republican support in California and in the U.S. Senate for punitive measures aimed at Mexican illegal and legal immigrants, but because they saw Democrats as the party of economic opportunity and security. Growing union membership seems to have had an important impact on

Hispanic support for Democrats, particularly in California, Illinois, New York, and New Jersey.* In the 2000 election, for example, working-class Hispanics who belonged to unions supported Gore by 37 percent (66–29); those who did not supported Gore by just 17 percent (57–40).

Hispanic support is a crucial part of a new Democratic majority. Hispanics are the minority group that is growing the most in terms of both absolute numbers and percentage of population. In 1990, they made up 9 percent of the population compared to 11.7 percent for blacks. They now make up 12.5 percent compared to 12.4 percent for blacks and are also at virtual parity in terms of the voting-age population: 11 percent compared to 11.3 percent for blacks.[53] In a quarter of the country's congressional districts, there are at least one hundred thousand Hispanic residents.[54] They are 29 percent of the potential electorate in Texas, 28 percent in California, 21 percent in Arizona, 16 percent in Florida, 15 percent in Colorado, and 14 percent in New York.[55] Their voting turnout continues to be low, albeit gradually improving, but their share of active voters has been steadily increasing thanks to their rapid increase in numbers. In 1992, they made up 3.7 percent of the presidential voting electorate. In 2000, they made up 5.4 percent of voters and possibly more.[56]

Asian-Americans

Like the term *Hispanic,* the term *Asian-American* imputes a spurious unity of belief to a diverse group of nationalities. Chinese, Japanese, Vietnamese, Korean, Indian, and Filipino immigrants have followed different political trajectories and also very different histories in America. While the Vietnamese and South Asian Indians are recent immigrants, the Chinese, for instance, began coming in the nineteenth century as "coolie" labor to build the railroads. Chinese, Japanese, and Indian immigrants have also prospered in recent decades. They are the most educated nationalities in

*In New Jersey's Fifth District, which includes Paterson, Democrat Bill Pascrell challenged incumbent congressman Bill Martini in 1996. According to Martini's polls, he was well ahead on election eve, but he lost by 51 to 48 percent to Pascrell. The reason appeared to be a Democratic surge among Hispanic voters in Paterson, inspired by organizers from the textile union UNITE.

America and have the highest proportions of professionals and managers. Nearly a quarter of Silicon Valley firms are run by Chinese or Indian immigrants.[57] On the other side, Filipinos are primarily working class and are heavily unionized. Among Asians, as among Hispanics, union members are much more likely to vote Democratic.

In the 1990s, Asian-Americans[58] had the fastest rate of increase of any minority group. Their numbers swelled 59.4 percent compared to 57.9 percent for Hispanics.[59] They have gone from 2.8 to 3.9 percent of the population[60] and are now about 2 percent of the voting electorate.[61] The largest numbers of Asians are found in California, New York, Hawaii, Texas, New Jersey, Illinois, and Washington state.[62] Since World War II, Japanese-Americans and Filipinos have been the most consistently Democratic voters. The Japanese supported the Democrats' commitment to civil rights and the Filipinos were drawn by the Democrats' New Deal economics. The Chinese who emigrated after World War II and the Vietnamese who came after the war were the most Republican, largely because they identified the Republicans with opposition to Chinese and Vietnamese communism. In addition, many of the Chinese owned small businesses and opposed Democrats as the party of labor unions and blacks.

In the nineties, however, these different groups came together in the Democratic Party. The Chinese, who are by far the single largest group of Asian-Americans, were impressed by Clinton's "new Democratic" politics and his appointments of Chinese-Americans. Says David Lee, the executive director of the Chinese American Voter Education Committee, "Clinton was a different kind of Democrat, he was a founder of the DLC, and they had distanced themselves from the party's labor and African-American roots." At the same time, Chinese-Americans were offended by a succession of Republican actions in Washington. In 1996, Wyoming senator Alan Simpson introduced a bill restricting immigration, and Republicans adopted a welfare reform measure that denied benefits to legal residents. After the 1996 election, Republicans tried to tar Asian-American contributors to the Clinton campaign, and in December 1997 Senate Republicans refused to confirm a prominent Chinese-American, Bill Lann Lee, as assistant attorney general for civil rights. By 1998, Chinese-Americans were voting Democratic. An extensive national postelection poll found Chinese-Americans backing Al Gore over George W. Bush 64–21 percent.[63]

Vietnamese also shifted their political allegiance in the 1990s. As memories of the war faded, many working-class Vietnamese began supporting the Democrats on economic grounds. A *Los Angeles Times* survey of Vietnamese voters in Orange County's "Little Saigon" concluded that these voters were becoming Democratic because they were "becoming more concerned about issues such as medicare, social security, and programs for the poor."[64] According to the national survey just cited, Vietnamese voters supported Gore over Bush 54–35 percent.[65] All in all, the survey suggested that Asian-American voters favored Gore 55–26 percent (with 18 percent refusing to state or not sure).[66]

Writing in *The Emerging Republican Majority,* Kevin Phillips mused that it was possible for Republicans to cede the minority vote and still win elections. Reagan's victory in the 1966 California gubernatorial contest tended "to disprove," Phillips wrote, that "minority group support is a mandatory ingredient of Republican victory in a big-city state." But that was when minorities were not much more than one-tenth of the electorate. Asian, Hispanic, black, and other minority voters, swelled by the enormous wave of immigration during the 1990s, now are about 19 percent of the voting electorate, and they gave Gore at least 75 percent support in the 2000 election.[67] Over the next decade, this bloc of voters is expected to continue to increase and, extrapolating from recent trends, could make up nearly a quarter of the electorate. If these voters remain solidly Democratic, they will constitute a formidable advantage for any Democratic candidate.

Democrats could suffer from an embarrassment of political riches. As Democrats have gained majorities in cities or states, assuring a politician with united Democratic support of victory, turf battles have begun to break out among the members of the Democratic coalition. These have pitted blacks against Hispanics or both against whites. In Los Angeles's 2001 mayoral election, a Hispanic candidate lost out to a white candidate who had black support. Both were Democrats, but the tension that the election caused could weaken Democratic prospects in future city elections. In New York City that year, Mark Green, a white liberal Democrat, fought a bitter primary battle against a Puerto Rican opponent, who was backed by Al Sharpton, an African-American demagogue who has thrived on creating racial division.[68] Green won the primary, but defections from Hispanics and blacks helped elect his opponent Michael Bloomberg, a former Democrat who had become a Republican because he thought he had a better chance of winning the Republican than the Democratic primary. New York remained a Democratic city, but racial divisions had prevented the Democratic candidate from winning the mayoralty. These kind of intraparty battles could eventually disrupt a national Democratic majority the way conflicts between the religious right and moderates have undermined the conservative Republican majority, but that danger probably lies well in the future—*after* the Democratic majority has emerged.

IV. THE WHITE WORKING CLASS

From 1932 to 1964, the Democrats were the party of the white working class, and particularly of blue-collar and service workers, who in 1950 constituted about half the workforce.[69] The Democrats enjoyed the overwhelming support of these workers just as Republicans enjoyed the support of upper-income business executives and professionals. From 1932 through 1960, voting for Democrats among whites was inversely proportional to their income and the power and status of their occupation. You could put a line through a pyramid depicting the distribution of income and the status of occupational groups, and you'd have a rough estimate of Democratic and Republican support (see chart). In 1960, for instance, 57 percent of blue-collar whites identified themselves as Democrats and only 26 percent as Republicans.[70] Heavy Democratic support among these and other white working-class voters, who made up well over half of the voting electorate, was enough to win elections.[71]

The Democrats sustained this support by their populist rhetoric branding the Republicans as the party of the rich and powerful (Truman asked voters in 1948 to elect a Congress "that will work in the interests of the common people and not in the interests of the men who have all the money"[72]) and by their support for New Deal reforms, including social security, the minimum wage, unemployment insurance, and the Wagner National Labor Relations Act. They also benefited from the postbellum commitment of the Confederate South to the Democratic Party and by the support of unions, which, by the late 1940s, could claim around 60 percent or more of the Northern blue-collar workforce.[73]

Since 1964, the white working class has undergone two dramatic

Democratic Presidential Vote among Whites by Socioeconomic Status: 1948 and 1960

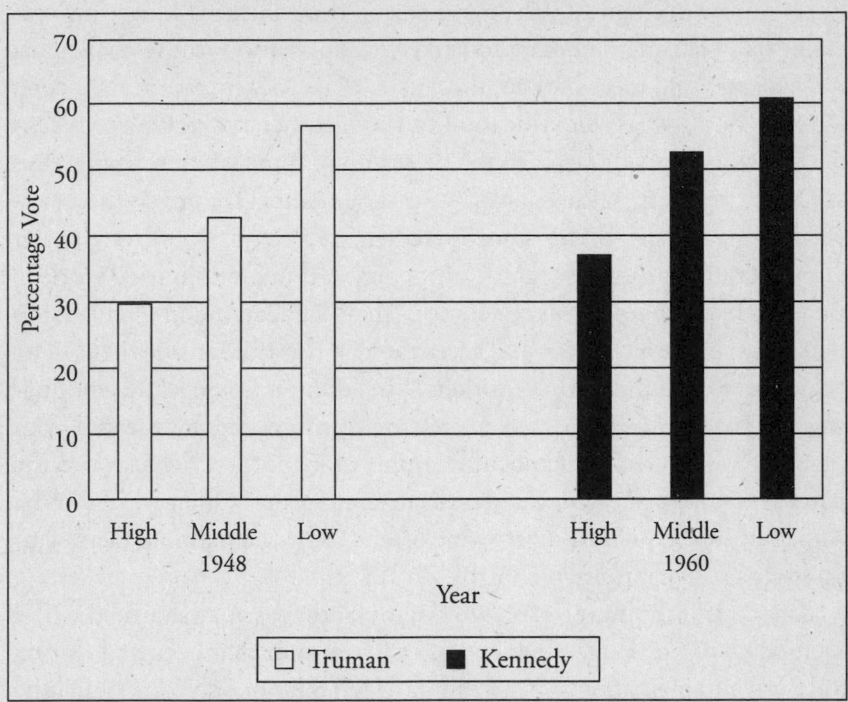

Source: Everett Carll Ladd Jr. with Charles D. Hadley, *Transformations of the American Party System: Political Coalitions from the New Deal to the 1970s* (New York: Norton, 1975).

political shifts. First, in the 1960s, it turned against Democratic candidates. In the 1968 election, 64 percent of white working-class voters supported either Nixon or Wallace against Democrat Hubert Humphrey. In 1972, 70 percent backed Nixon against McGovern. In 1980, 57 percent voted for Reagan against Carter; in 1984, 65 percent voted for Reagan against Mondale; and in 1988, 60 percent voted for Bush against Dukakis.[74] Then in the 1990s, some of these voters began to return to the Democratic Party. In the 1992 election, Clinton actually won the white working-class vote from Bush 39–38 percent (the remainder voted for Perot); and in 1996, he won it again from Dole by doing particularly well among white working-class women. Gore lost back some of these votes, but there were still significant gains for Democrats from 1988 to 2000 among these voters.

As we saw in chapter 1, the main reason that white working-class voters initially left the Democratic Party was opposition to the civil rights movement—and more broadly, the cluster of issues with race at their core. White working-class identification of the Democratic Party with blacks has remained a major factor in the defection of some white working-class voters, particularly in the South. The other principal factor was these voters' belief, after the Carter administration, that Republicans were better at maintaining prosperity than Democrats. Although unionized workers were less likely to reach this conclusion, the decline in union membership that began in the late 1950s and accelerated in the 1970s made these views more prevalent among white workers.[75] In addition, some white working-class voters in the Protestant South were influenced by the religious right. They objected to Democratic support for abortion rights and to the party's identification with the sixties counterculture. Other whites in the rural and small-town Midwest were offended by the national Democratic Party's support for gun control.

The most important reason why many of these voters returned to the Democrats in the early nineties was the recession that occurred during the Bush administration. The recession wiped out not only jobs, but white working-class confidence that Republicans could manage the economy better than Democrats. Clinton also successfully countered the image of the Democrats as the "black party" by his advocacy of welfare reform and the death penalty and by a publicized spat with the Reverend Jesse Jackson on the eve of the Democratic convention. Clinton's success in 1992 and 1996 was particularly notable among unionized white working-class voters—a group that would be most susceptible to the Democrats' economic argument. Reagan had won these voters in 1980 and 1984, and Bush had barely lost them 52–48 percent in 1988, but Clinton won them by an average of 23 percent in 1992 and in 1996.

Gore's problems with white working-class voters were due partly to his political ineptitude and to the shadow that the Clinton scandals had cast over his campaign. But they were also due, ironically, to the boom of the late 1990s; in such flush times, working-class voters thought less about the economy and more about the issues on which they preferred Republicans, such as gun control, abortion, or affirmative action. Gore did particularly poorly among white working-class voters in rural areas and in the South—the two groups most susceptible to Republican appeals on these issues. (White working-class voters in rural areas, for instance, preferred Bush over Gore by 35 percent.) But the economic slowdown that began soon after George W. Bush took office is likely to lead many of these voters to pay renewed attention to economic issues, especially as their focus shifts back from the war on terror to domestic concerns. This should benefit Democratic candidates for years to come.*

The white working class's move back to the Democrats has also been spurred by the change in the composition of the working class. In 1948, about two-thirds of the workforce was white men, and the bulk of these white men worked at blue-collar manufacturing and construction jobs or at blue-collar service jobs like janitor or warehouseman. By 2000, working-class whites still constituted about 70 percent of the working class, but they had become a much more diverse group. There were almost as many women workers as men, and only three out of ten working-class whites were engaged in goods production. Many now worked in hospitals, schools, offices, and stores. Many were government employees.

Different influences impinged on this new group. White working-class women began voting much more Democratic than white working-class men. In the states that Gore won in 2000, he got 52 percent of white working-class women, and just 40 percent of their male counterparts. Overall, white workers who lived in large metropolitan areas were more

*Some indication of how this might happen appeared in the results of the 2001 Virginia gubernatorial election. The small-town, rural districts in southern Virginia, dominated by tobacco growing and textiles, had been overwhelmingly Democratic until 1964, when, in response to the national Democrats' support for civil rights, they backed Goldwater in 1964, and Nixon and Wallace in 1968. In subsequent elections, this area, dubbed Southside, supported either Republicans or very conservative Democrats. But in 2001, as unemployment in the area rose, moderate Democratic candidate Mark Warner, promising to bring high-technology growth, won the area's voters in the November election. Warner did not fudge his commitment to civil rights, but he did promise not to strengthen the state's gun control laws and appealed to the area's voters by sponsoring a NASCAR team and recruiting country singers for campaign ads. By contrast, the Democratic candidate for attorney general, an African-American who called for tougher gun laws and a moratorium on the death penalty, lost overwhelmingly to his Republican opponent among the same voters. See John B. Judis, "Coming Attractions," *American Prospect,* December 3, 2001.

inclined to vote for the Democrats than workers who lived in small towns or rural areas. In 1988, for instance, Dukakis lost to Bush among working-class whites in large urban areas 57–44 percent. Gore won these voters in 2000, 49–46 percent. Meanwhile, Gore actually lost white working-class voters in rural areas by almost 20 points more than Dukakis did. Fortunately for the Democrats, many more white working-class voters live in metropolitan than in rural areas.

Democrats did best among those white working-class voters who had been most dramatically affected by the experience of the sixties and by the transition to postindustrial society. These included not only working women, but men and women who lived in large metropolitan areas that have been transformed over the last four decades from manufacturing centers to centers for production of services and ideas. A white working-class voter in Seattle's King County or in the Boulder-Denver area is likely to support the right to abortion and the need for environmental regulation and to place some importance on being racially tolerant. In the Denver-Boulder area, for example, working-class whites backed Gore 53–38 percent, with only a few percentage points separating men and women in the group.

The key to Democratic victories in the 1990s was combining majorities in the three McGovern constituencies—women (especially the working, single, and highly educated), professionals, and minorities—with a respectable showing among white working-class voters. This is true nationally, as well as in state-level races Democrats have won, including in those states where the national ticket has not done well. For example, if you compare Mike Easley's gubernatorial win in North Carolina to Gore's loss there, or compare Bill Nelson's five-point senatorial win in Florida to Gore's (very narrow) loss there, the key in both cases was the winning Democratic candidate's ability to attract a reasonable level of white working-class support to add to Democratic support among the McGovern constituencies.

What makes it likely that a Democratic majority will emerge over the next decade? First of all, as a result of the transition to postindustrial society, each of the McGovern constituencies will continue to grow as a percent of the electorate. And barring a sea change in Republican politics, these constituencies will continue to vote Democratic. Second of all, as postindustrial areas continue to grow, white working-class and professional voters in these areas are likely to converge on a worldview that is more compatible with Democrats than with Republicans. A continuing economic slowdown could also move white working-class voters back to the Democrats. Of course, all these constituencies overlap with one another—for instance, many working women are professionals as well as white working class—but even so, it is fair to assume that if Democrats can consistently take professionals by about 10 percent, working women by about 20 percent, keep 75 percent of the minority vote, and get close to an even split of white working-class voters, they will have achieved a new Democratic majority.

Elections in America aren't finally won, however, by collections of constituencies. Our national elections are determined by who wins states. Who controls Congress is determined by who wins state and district elections. If a new Democratic majority is to emerge, it will have to stake out a geographical as well as a numerical majority. The outlines of that geography have also become apparent during the last decade.

CHAPTER THREE

The Geography of the New Majority

After the 2000 election, political commentators began referring to the Democrats as the "blues" and the Republicans as the "reds"—terms corresponding to the blotches of states that Gore and Bush won on the electoral map. And the question of America's political future has been posed in terms of who will dominate—the blues or the reds. In American politics, that's entirely appropriate, because as the 2000 election agonizingly demonstrated, presidents don't get elected by winning national majorities, but by winning states. And longstanding majorities are not constructed out of random voters, but out of support from certain states and regions.

Until the Great Depression, the Republicans were the party of the North and Midwest and the Democrats the party of the segregated South. In the 1930s, the New Deal Democrats put the Solid South together with the growing cities of the North, Midwest, and Far West to form a new majority. The Republican "reds" were confined to New England and the farm states. In the 1980s, the Reagan Republicans turned the New Deal configuration upside down by capturing the South. They combined traditional Republican support in the prairies with a new majority in the Sunbelt—a large swatch of land stretching southward along the Virginia tidewater down to Georgia and Florida, around to Mississippi and Texas and across to southern California.

The emerging Democratic majority looks as if it will mirror the conservative Republican majority it is replacing. Its strength lies in the Northeast, the upper Midwest through Minnesota, and over to the Pacific Northwest. But like the old McKinley majority, it includes the Sunbelt prize of California. Over the last three elections, Democrats were able to win states with 267 electoral votes in these areas. That's only three short of a majority. In the 2004 election, these states will account for 260 elec-

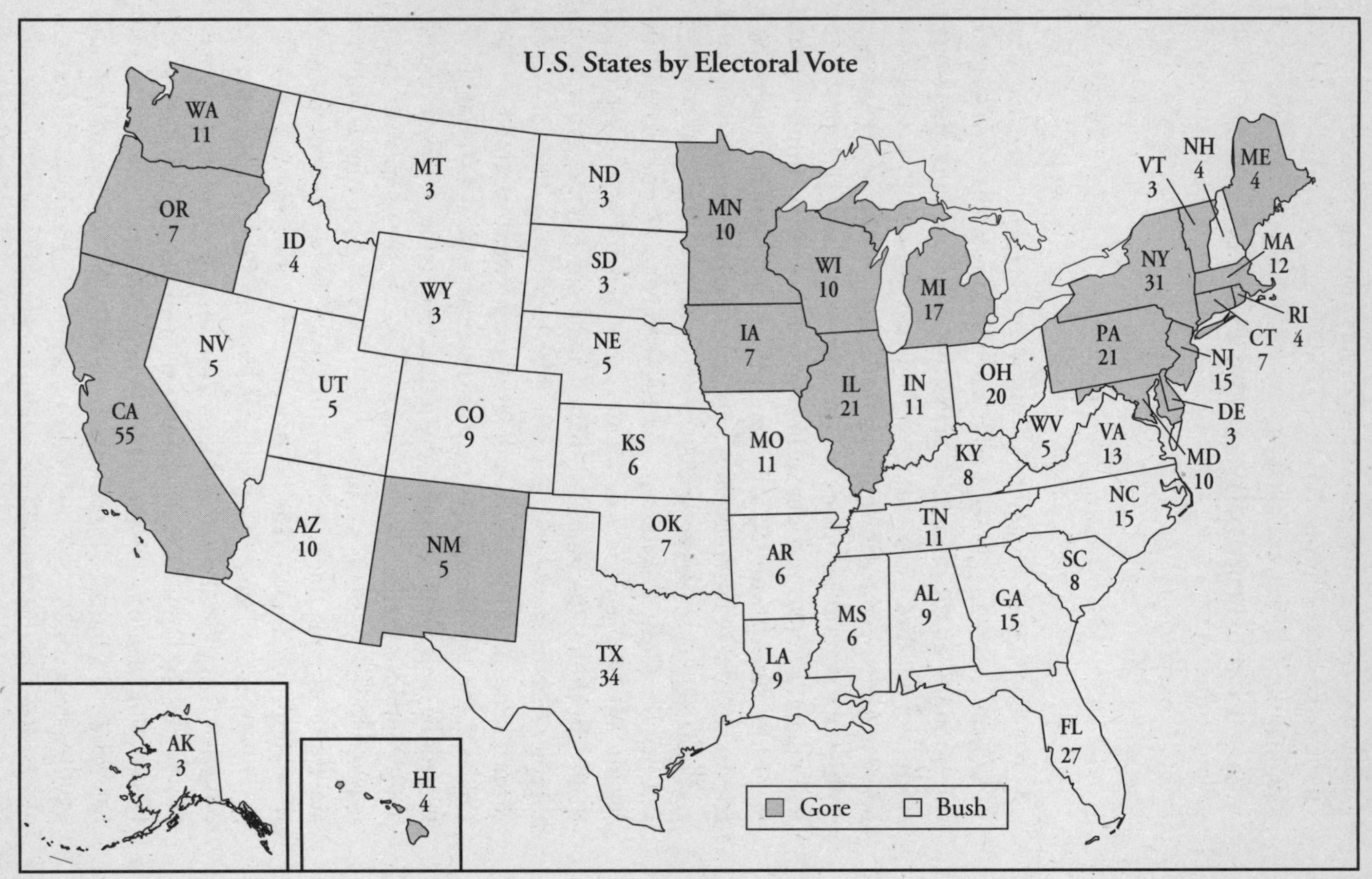
U.S. States by Electoral Vote
WA 11
OR 7
CA 55
NV 5
ID 4
MT 3
WY 3
UT 5
AZ 10
CO 9
NM 5
ND 3
SD 3
NE 5
KS 6
OK 7
TX 34
MN 10
IA 7
MO 11
AR 6
LA 9
WI 10
IL 21
MS 6
MI 17
IN 11
KY 8
TN 11
AL 9
OH 20
WV 5
VA 13
NC 15
SC 8
GA 15
FL 27
PA 21
NY 31
VT 3
NH 4
ME 4
MA 12
RI 4
CT 7
NJ 15
DE 3
MD 10
AK 3
HI 4
Gore
Bush

toral votes, ten short of a majority. This suggests that the Democrats are on the verge of establishing the same kind of "lock" on the electoral college that the Republicans enjoyed in the 1980s (see map). They won't automatically win all these electoral votes—a Republican presidential candidate from Pennsylvania, for instance, might win that state just as Mondale won Minnesota in 1984, and Republican George W. Bush, buoyed by his success in fighting terrorism, could overcome underlying trends—but, all else being equal, Democrats can be assured of beginning an election campaign at a distinct advantage over the Republicans.

The major parties also represent certain kinds of industries, which are primarily located in certain states and regions. The Jacksonian Democrats united Southern and Western farmers with urban workingmen; the McKinley Republicans spoke for the new industrial corporations and banks; and the New Deal Democrats captured the new mass-production industries in the North. The conservative Republicans were the party of the military bases, shipyards, aerospace firms, and space centers that dotted the Sunbelt. Indeed, in the 1980s, the Sunbelt had 142 military bases—more than the rest of the nation put together.[1]

The emerging Democratic majority is closely linked to the spread of the postindustrial economy. Democrats are strongest in areas where the production of ideas and services has either redefined or replaced assembly-line manufacturing, particularly in the North and West, but also including some Southern states like Florida. Republicans are strongest in states like Mississippi, Wyoming, and South Carolina (as well as in former Democratic enclaves like Kentucky) where the transition to postindustrial society has lagged. There are exceptions to this pattern, of course, but they are anomalies—states like Utah where cultural conservatism runs deep or regions like California's San Diego County where the Sunbelt military ethos is still strong. Since America is moving toward a postindustrial economy, that gives the Democrats a significant advantage in the decade to come.

This new postindustrial politics is not defined by states, however, but by metropolitan regions within states. These postindustrial metropolises, which we call ideopolises, are the breeding ground for the new Democratic majority. Insofar as they are not confined to the Northeast, Far West, and upper Midwest, but are also found in the South and Southwest, the Democrats have a chance of building a large majority and of rewriting today's political map. By our count, Democrats could enjoy by 2008 a state-by-state advantage of 332 electoral votes, well more than they need for a majority, plus a competitive position in a number of additional states that might swell that majority. The key to the development of this electoral dominance will be the spread of these ideopolises.

THE ROLE OF IDEOPOLISES

The transition to postindustrial society has transformed the economic geography of the country. After World War II, industrial society was divided into three domains: cities, which housed offices and manufacturing plants; suburbs, where many of the workers lived; and rural areas of farms, mines, and forests. Postindustrial society is organized around metropolitan areas that include both suburbs and central cities.[2] Goods production has moved out of the central city into the suburbs, or even into semirural areas in the south-central Midwest. There is a clear contrast between metropolitan and rural areas, and also a sharp difference between metropolitan areas like Silicon Valley that bear the marks of postindustrial society and other metropolitan areas like Muncie, Indiana, or Fresno, California, that are still relatively backward in telecommunications, computers, and high-tech jobs.[3]

Some of the new postindustrial metropolitan areas like Silicon Valley or Colorado's Boulder area contain significant manufacturing facilities, but it is the kind of manufacturing—whether of pharmaceuticals or semiconductors—that applies complex ideas to physical objects. The amount of labor time expended in researching and developing these ideas far outweighs that in producing the final goods. That has become true even of automobile production in eastern Michigan. While much of the actual production has moved southward, much of the research and development and engineering of automobiles (which now make extensive use of computer technology) is conducted in Michigan.[4]

Some of these metro areas specialize in producing what Joel Kotkin and Ross C. DeVol call soft technology—entertainment, media, fashion, design, and advertising—and in providing databases, legal counsel, and other business services. New York City and Los Angeles are both premier postindustrial metropolises that specialize in soft technology.[5] Most of these postindustrial metropolises also include a major university or several major universities, which funnel ideas and, more important, people into the hard or soft technology industries. Boston's Route 128 feeds off Harvard and MIT. Silicon Valley is closely linked to Stanford and the University of California at Berkeley. Dane County's biomedical research is tied to the University of Wisconsin at Madison. And all of them have a flourishing service sector, including computer learning centers, ethnic and vegetarian restaurants, multimedia shopping malls, children's museums, bookstore–coffee shops, and health clubs.

Professionals and technicians are heavily concentrated in the workforces of these postindustrial metropolises. A quarter or so of the jobs in Austin (Texas), Raleigh-Durham, Boston, or San Francisco are held by professionals and technicians.[6] Plentiful, too, are low-level service and information workers, including waiters, hospital orderlies, salesclerks, janitors, and teacher's aides. Many of these jobs have been filled by Hispanics and African-Americans, just as many of the high-level professional jobs have been filled by Asian immigrants. It's one reason that the workforces in these areas we call ideopolises tend to be ethnically diverse and more complex in their stratification (various combinations of employers, employees, contract workers, temps, consultants, and the self-employed) than the workforce of the older industrial city.

The ethos and mores of many of these new metropolitan areas tend to be libertarian and bohemian, because of the people they attract. Economists Richard Florida and Gary Gates found a close correlation between the concentration of gays and of the foreign-born and the concentration of high technology and information technology within a metropolitan area. They also found a high percentage of people who identified themselves as artists, musicians, and craftspeople.[7] Concluded Florida, "Diversity is a powerful force in the value systems and choices of the new workforce, whose members want to work for companies and live in communities that reflect their openness and tolerance. The number one factor in choosing a place to live and work, they say, is diversity. Talented people will not move to a place that ostracizes certain groups."[8]

Within metropolitan areas, ideopolises come in different stages and configurations. In the San Francisco Bay Area or the Chicago Metro area, the work and culture of the ideopolis pervades the entire metropolitan area. Many of the same people, the same businesses, and the same coffee shops or bookstores can be found in the central city or in the suburbs.

These are the most advanced and integrated ideopolises. Politically, many of these areas used to be Republican, but have become extremely Democratic in their politics. In the 2000 election, Al Gore didn't campaign in Colorado, but still carried the Denver-Boulder area 56–35 percent.[9] He won Portland's Multnomah County 64–28 percent. Princeton University's Mercer County went for Gore 61–34 percent. Seattle's King County was 60–34 percent for Gore.

The Democrats' vote in these integrated ideopolises included, of course, professionals, women, and minorities, but it also included relatively strong support from the white working class—the very group that had begun to abandon the Democrats during the sixties and that formed the backbone of the Reagan majority. In the most advanced ideopolises, the white working class seems to embrace the same values as professionals, and in some of them, white working-class men vote remarkably similarly to their female counterparts. As a result, Republican appeals to race (or resentment against immigrants), guns, and abortion have largely fallen on deaf ears, and these voters have not only rejected Republican social conservatism, but also reverted to their prior preference for Democratic economics. In Seattle's King County, white working-class voters backed Gore 50–42 percent. In Portland's Multnomah County, it was 71–24 percent.[10] By comparison, working-class whites nationwide supported Bush 57–40 percent.

Sometimes, of course, high-tech development has taken place either on the outskirts of the central city or in the suburbs—with the inner city impoverished and underdeveloped. Predictably, the politics of these areas are different, too. St. Louis, Cleveland, and Detroit, though pro-Democratic as a whole, have politics marked by familiar race and class cleavages. The most Democratic groups are minorities and college-educated women, while many, and sometimes most, white working-class and college-educated males still vote Republican. In Cleveland's Cuyahoga County, for instance, white college-educated men backed Bush 55–38 percent and white working-class voters supported him 45–42 percent, while white college-educated women backed Gore 67–28 percent.[11] Voters in St. Charles County, across the river from the black section of St. Louis, used to be Democrats, but gave Wallace 19.4 percent in 1968. Since then, these suburban voters have consistently identified Democrats with St. Louis blacks and have voted heavily for Republicans.* In 2000, St. Charles voted for Bush 56–42 percent and for extreme-right-wing Republican congressman Todd Akin.

Also, in some burgeoning metropolitan areas, a county or city has become a center of high technology or information technology, but the surrounding semirural counties have been largely unaffected by these developments. Some of the counties that surround Charlotte, North Carolina, Columbus, Ohio (where Ohio State University and the state capitol are located) and Lansing, Michigan (where Michigan State University and the state capitol are located) tend to be rural or small-town and very Republican, while the central area has become increasingly Democratic. Eventually, the culture and politics of the city will spread farther into the metropolitan area, but in the meantime, the core city or county will vote much more Democratic than the surrounding suburbs.

Finally, some postindustrial metropolitan areas are well integrated between city and suburb, but have not adopted the libertarian ethos of the ideopolis. In Salt Lake City or Colorado Springs, for instance, a conservative religious culture precludes the bohemian and libertarian spirit that normally accompanies the development of the most advanced ideopolises. But nationally these areas are the exception. In most areas where an ideopolis has arisen alongside a conservative religious culture—as in the Kansas suburbs of Kansas City—the two soon find themselves at war.

To gauge the effect of these ideopolises nationally, we looked at 263 counties that are part of metro areas with the highest concentrations of high-tech economic activity or that contain a front-rank research university.† Most of these areas used to be Republican and voted for Repub-

*When the metropolitan St. Louis area wanted to run its commuter Metrolink line out to St. Charles in the midnineties, its white inhabitants balked out of the fear that it would attract minorities to their county. Said St. Louis University political scientist Ken Warren, who did polling on the decision, "They turned it down because blacks could cross the river from St. Louis."

†For this statistical survey, we took the fifty top metropolitan areas for high-tech concentration as determined by the Milken Institute's Ross C. DeVol in his study *America's High-Tech Economy.* DeVol's study, besides having a sound methodology, is distinctive in that it rated virtually all (315) of the nation's MSAs (Metropolitan Statistical Areas) and PMSAs (Primary Metropolitan Statistical Areas), allowing us to look at metropolitan America as a whole, rather than a small subset defined by size or job growth as in other studies. To DeVol's top-fifty list, which he termed tech-poles, we added a handful of counties not included in the Milken list, but that contain one of the fifty top national universities desig-

lican presidential candidates in 1980 and 1984. In 1984, for instance, they went 55–44 percent for Reagan. But in 2000, Gore garnered 54.6 percent of the vote in these areas compared to 41.4 percent for Bush. And since Nader got 3.3 percent in these counties, the total Democratic-leaning vote in America's ideopolises can be reckoned at close to 58 percent.

By contrast, Democrats have continued to lose in rural areas in Missouri and Pennsylvania and in many low-tech metropolitan areas like Greenville, South Carolina, that have not made the postindustrial transition. In all, Gore lost the nonideopolis counties 52.9–43.6 percent. Indeed, if you compare 1980, the beginning of the Reagan era, to today, it is clear that almost all of the pro-Democratic change in the country since then has been concentrated in America's ideopolis counties (see chart).

The Democrats' victory in these postindustrial metro areas is likely to translate into a national majority over the next decade. Together, the ideopolises account for 43.7 percent of the vote nationally. They represent the most dynamic and growing areas of the country. Between 1990 and 2000, the average ideopolis county grew by 23.2 percent compared to 11.1 percent for the average U.S. county and 10 percent for the average nonideopolis county. And ideopolis counties start from a large population base—an average of 475,000 inhabitants, compared to 90,000 for all counties and just 54,000 for the typical nonideopolis county.[12] Their vote should, if anything, increase in the next decade, and if the trend toward the Democrats in these areas continues, that would give the Democratic Party a solid base for a new majority.

To see how this would translate into a presidential majority—and also a majority in Congress—we will analyze the vote in each region and

---

nated by *U.S. News & World Report.* There was considerable overlap, but this allowed us to include a number of worthy areas such as Nashville's Davidson County, Madison's Dane County, and Princeton's Mercer County that would not otherwise have made the list. We would like to have included several other counties, such as Salt Lake City's Salt Lake County, Charlotte, North Carolina's Mecklenburg County, Columbus, Ohio's Franklin County, Las Vegas's Clark County, and Lansing, Michigan's Ingham County in our statistical analysis, but we did not want to seem arbitrary in our criteria. In the text itself, however, we refer to all these counties as postindustrial areas. (Including these additional counties in our analysis would not have substantially altered the statistical results we present.)

Presidential Voting, Ideopolis vs. Nonideopolis Counties, 1980 and 2000

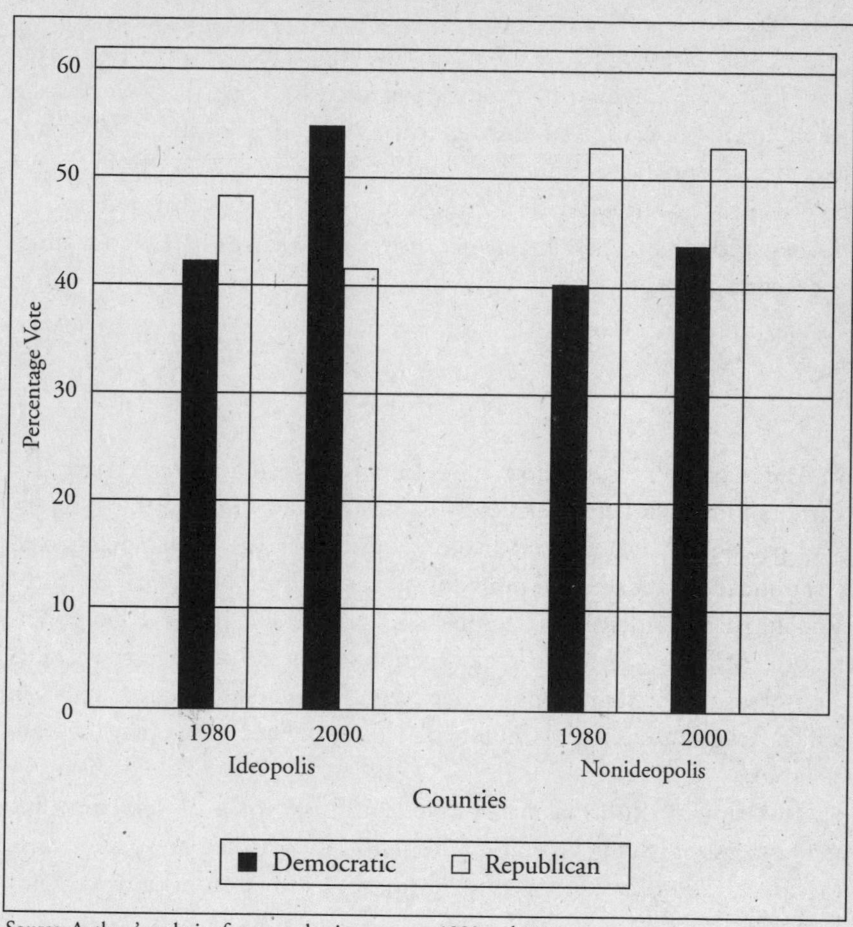

Source: Authors' analysis of county election returns, 1980 and 2000.

the key states. This survey is for readers who want to see how the new majority is actually emerging in states from California and Oregon to New Jersey and North Carolina and the major role that is being played by the development of ideopolises.

THE WEST

From 1968 through 1984, the only Western state won by a Democrat was Washington, which Humphrey captured in 1968. The West was a Republican preserve. But during the 1990s, the Pacific coast states became dependably Democratic, and Democrats have begun to make inroads in the Southwest. The most important change occurred in California, and it happened largely because of the growth of the postindustrial economy.

California

In American politics, California has long been a trendsetter. Progressive Party candidate Robert La Follette's astonishing showing in 1924—he got 33.1 percent of the presidential vote against conservative Democratic and Republican candidates—foreshadowed the coming New Deal majority. Ronald Reagan's defeat of a Republican progressive in the 1966 gubernatorial primary and of the liberal Democratic incumbent in the general election anticipated the conservative Republican realignment of 1980, in which Reagan himself and California's electoral votes would play the leading role.

This time, California may be the harbinger of a new Democratic majority. After having voted for a Republican candidate in six successive presidential elections from 1968 through 1988, Californians strongly backed Clinton in 1992 and 1996 and Gore in 2000, in each case by a margin of 12 to 13 percent. Starting in 1992, Californians elected and subsequently reelected two Democratic senators. Republicans controlled the governor's office from 1982 to 1998, but in November 1998, Democrat Gray Davis won in a landslide, and Democrats won every other state office except one. This political shift was the result of factors that also prevailed, although less dramatically, in other parts of the country: the transition to postindustrial society, which created large ideopolises in northern and southern California; the GOP's dogged and continued turn to the right; the Democrats' move to the center; and the growth of the state's minority population.

The key development was the political reconciliation of northern and southern California, which had been sundered by Reagan's candidacy in 1966. In that election, by three to one, Reagan won the support of formerly Democratic white working-class voters in the Los Angeles area. These voters, many of whom worked for the aerospace industry, took umbrage at the rise of the antiwar left on California's campuses and were disturbed by the Watts riot of 1965 and by the growing civil rights movement in the state.[13] Over the next two decades, voters in southern California, except for minority and Jewish enclaves, backed Republican conservatives, while the Bay Area in northern California remained generally Democratic, with a strong current of moderate, upscale Republicanism in San Mateo, Santa Clara, and Contra Costa counties.[14] But in the nineties, the differences between the Bay Area and Los Angeles County suddenly disappeared, and the two most populous areas in the state, making up about 45 percent of the population, both began voting strongly for Democrats.

Beginning in 1988, the Bay Area ideopolis, which includes Silicon Valley (the area with the highest concentration of high-technology and information-technology jobs in the country[15]), became even more Democratic. Voters in San Francisco and Alameda County backed Dukakis by two to one, and voters in the formerly moderate-Republican bastions in Santa Clara, San Mateo, and Contra Costa counties—wary of the Republicans' identification with the religious right—also supported Dukakis against George Bush. By 2000, the area immediately around San Francisco was supporting Gore by well over two to one, with San Francisco turning in some staggering figures—76 percent for Gore, 16 percent for Bush, and 8 percent for Nader—and even Contra Costa, the least Democratic of the Bay Area counties, going for Gore 59–37 percent. Befitting the culture of the most advanced ideopolis, there were no sharp differences between working-class and professional voters. Both college-educated and working-class white voters in the Bay Area backed Gore by roughly equal amounts—65–29 percent among the former and 70–25 percent among the latter.[16] And white female voters as a whole backed Gore 78–19 percent.[17]

As northern California went even more Democratic, the south began turning back to the Democrats. The impetus was economic. In the early 1990s, the recession and the cutbacks in military spending eliminated more than three hundred thousand manufacturing jobs in the state, many of them in the Los Angeles aerospace industry. Some of these workers, who had been essential to the conservative Republican majority, moved out of state or to neighboring Ventura, Orange, or Riverside counties. Others found employment in the new postindustrial economy that grew up in the 1990s. This economy, centered around computer services, biotechnology, and entertainment, relied on highly skilled professionals, technicians, and unskilled service workers. In 1983, there were almost twice as many aerospace workers as workers in the motion picture industry. By 2000, almost three times more workers were employed in motion pictures than in aerospace (see chart). Los Angeles County had become one of the nation's leading ideopolises.

As the economic cultures of these areas became similar, so, too, did their political cultures. According to an extensive survey conducted in 1998 by

The Transformation of Los Angeles County

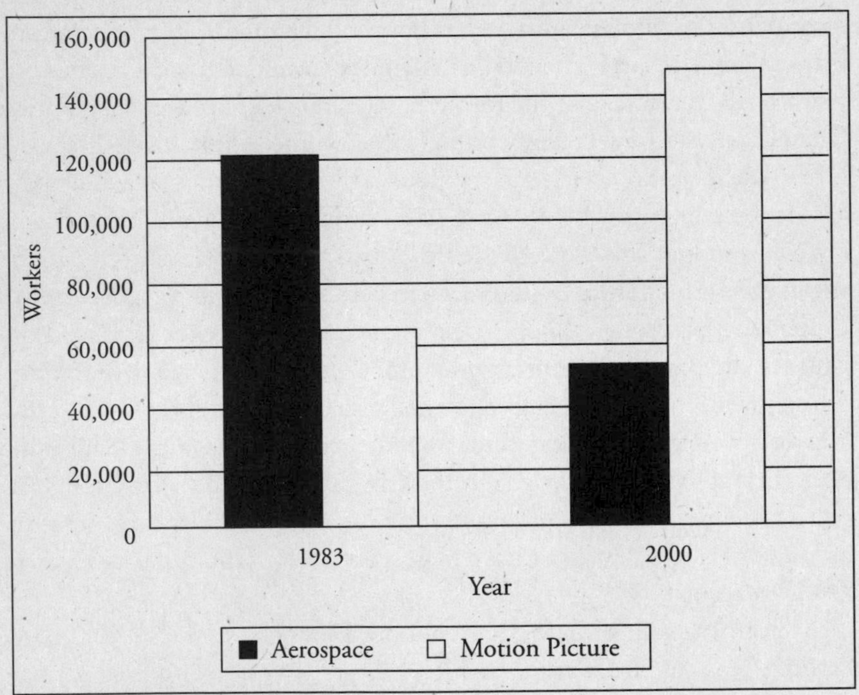

Source: California Employment Development Department Web site.

California's Public Policy Institute, Bay Area and Los Angeles residents held similar favorable views on the need for environmental regulations and the importance of government regulating business in the public interest, both thought religion should be kept out of politics, and both favored affirmative action programs.* As many as 35 percent of Los Angeles residents and 36 percent of San Francisco Bay Area residents described their views as "liberal"; all together, 69 percent of both Los Angeles and San Francisco residents described their views as either "liberal" or "middle of the road."[18]

The views in these two ideopolises are in striking contrast to those in California's primarily agricultural Central Valley, where the workforce is largely divided between manager-owners and workers, and where, except in Sacramento, there is no flourishing service sector. Even when Democratic Sacramento is included in this survey, residents of the Central Valley took a far less favorable view of government regulation of business, affirmative action, immigrants, and government assistance to the poor and were more likely to approve of politicians invoking religion. For example, residents of the Los Angeles area (61–33) and the San Francisco area (67–30) strongly endorsed the view that environmental regulation is worth the costs over the view that environmental regulation costs too many jobs. In contrast, residents of the Central Valley, again even including relatively liberal Sacramento, were split about down the middle, 48–45 percent.

As might be expected, the state's major ideopolises voted Democratic and its nonideopolis counties went Republican (see map). In 1992, Clinton defeated Bush 53–29 percent in Los Angeles and 57–25 percent in the Bay Area.[19] In 1996 and 2000, Clinton and Gore won both Los Angeles and the Bay Area by two-to-one margins.† On the other hand,

*The only anomaly in the survey was that while 74 percent in San Francisco supported a woman's right to choose, only 58 percent did in Los Angeles. The anomaly is the result of Los Angeles's Latino population, which is generally antiabortion, but which also doesn't typically evaluate candidates or parties on that basis.

†Significantly, in Los Angeles County in the 2000 election, working-class and professional voters both apparently favored the Democrats. In the city of Los Angeles, working-class whites voted 63–36 in favor of Gore, while in suburban L.A. County, where most of them live, the same group supported Gore 50–47 percent. By contrast, in the Central Valley, working-class whites backed Bush 56–34 percent. Even working-class white women voted 55–39 percent Republican. (Authors' analysis of VNS data.)

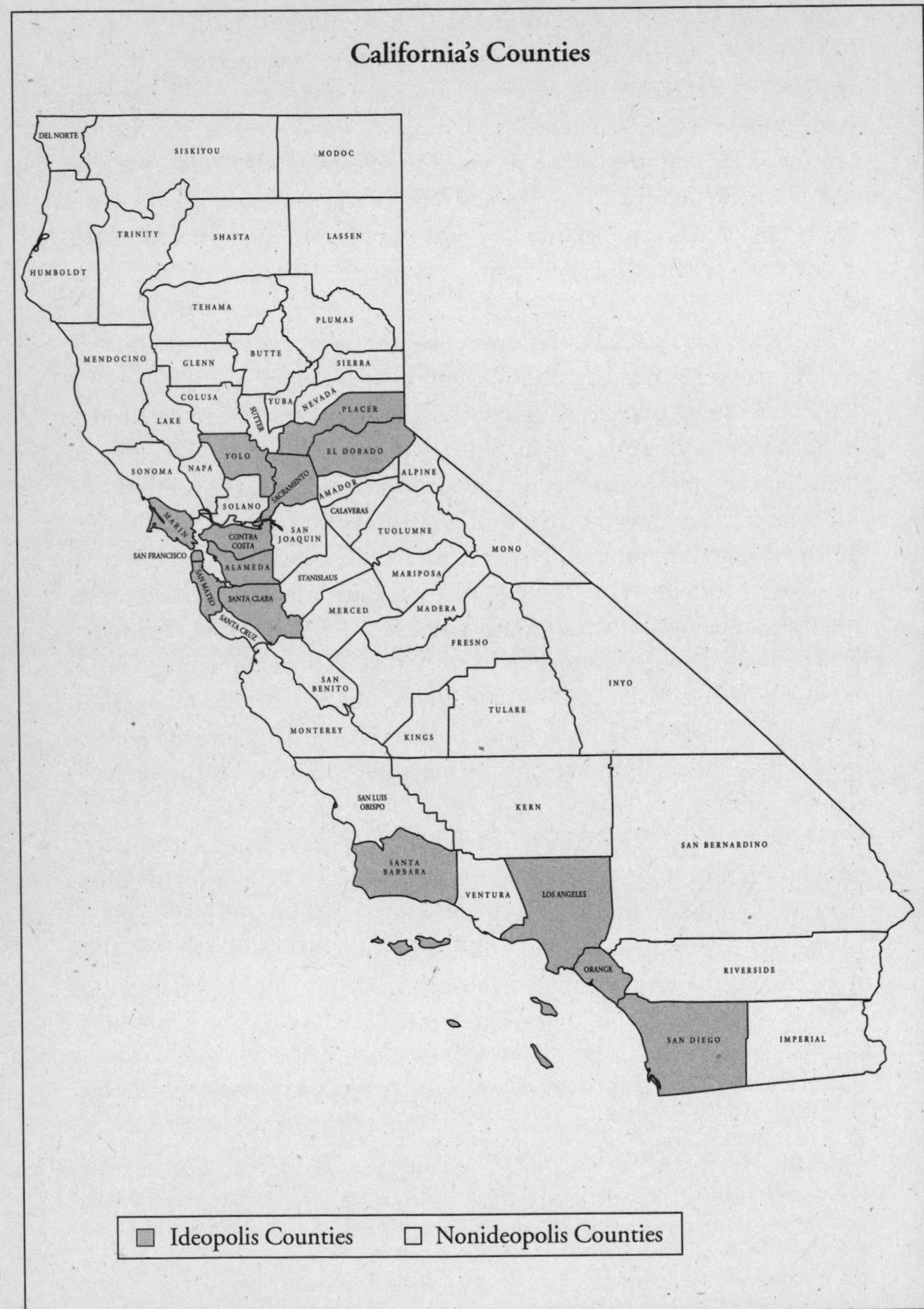
California's Counties
DEL NORTE
SISKIYOU
MODOC
TRINITY
SHASTA
LASSEN
HUMBOLDT
TEHAMA
PLUMAS
MENDOCINO
GLENN
BUTTE
SIERRA
COLUSA
SUTTER
YUBA
NEVADA
PLACER
LAKE
YOLO
EL DORADO
SONOMA
NAPA
SACRAMENTO
ALPINE
AMADOR
SOLANO
CALAVERAS
MARIN
CONTRA COSTA
SAN JOAQUIN
TUOLUMNE
MONO
SAN FRANCISCO
ALAMEDA
STANISLAUS
MARIPOSA
SAN MATEO
SANTA CLARA
MERCED
MADERA
SANTA CRUZ
FRESNO
SAN BENITO
INYO
TULARE
MONTEREY
KINGS
SAN LUIS OBISPO
KERN
SAN BERNARDINO
SANTA BARBARA
VENTURA
LOS ANGELES
ORANGE
RIVERSIDE
SAN DIEGO
IMPERIAL
Ideopolis Counties
Nonideopolis Counties

Clinton just tied 39–39 percent in the Central Valley in 1992 and lost the region by 4 percent to Dole in 1996.[20] Then, in 2000, even while winning Sacramento, Gore was handily defeated by George W. Bush 54–42 percent in the overall Central Valley.

In the state as a whole, Gore won the ideopolis counties, but lost the counties that have not yet been transformed by the postindustrial economy. California's fourteen ideopolis counties, which made up 69 percent of the overall vote, supported Gore 57–38 percent, while the forty-four nonideopolis counties supported Bush 49–46. Bush did win two areas of high-tech concentration in Orange County and San Diego County south of Los Angeles, but in these counties, the religious right has had a strong presence, and the military continues to be a leading employer. Even so, both these areas have become far less Republican over the last two decades—a result of the impact of the postindustrial economy and of the growth in the Hispanic and Asian populations. George Bush carried San Diego by 22 points in 1988, but his son carried it by only 4 points, 50–46.

The other factor that has transformed California into a Democratic bulwark is growing support from Hispanics and Asians, who by 2000 made up 44 percent of the population in California and about 20 percent of the voting electorate statewide and 57 percent of the population in Los Angeles County (see chart[21]). Latinos had been pro-Democratic throughout the twentieth century, but Reagan and other Republican candidates could hope to get as much as 40 percent of the California Latino vote. Until the 1990s, Democrats were lucky to get half of the Asian vote, which included pro-Republican Chinese-Americans and Vietnamese-Americans.

But over the next eight years, Hispanics became decidedly more Democratic than before, especially in state elections, and Asians became dependably Democratic. What moved many new Hispanics into the Democratic column was the 1994 governor's race. In that race, the Republican incumbent, Pete Wilson, faced with a stagnant economy, played a version of the race card that the party had successfully used in the sixties and seventies to win office. He tried to blame the lingering slowdown in the California economy on illegal Mexican immigrants. Wilson championed Proposition 187 to deny public services to the children of these illegal immigrants. Wilson won against an inept opponent, but he deeply alienated Hispanic voters. After Proposition 187, the Republicans' share of the Hispanic vote has consistently been low. In the 1998 guber-

California's Population by Race and Ethnic Group

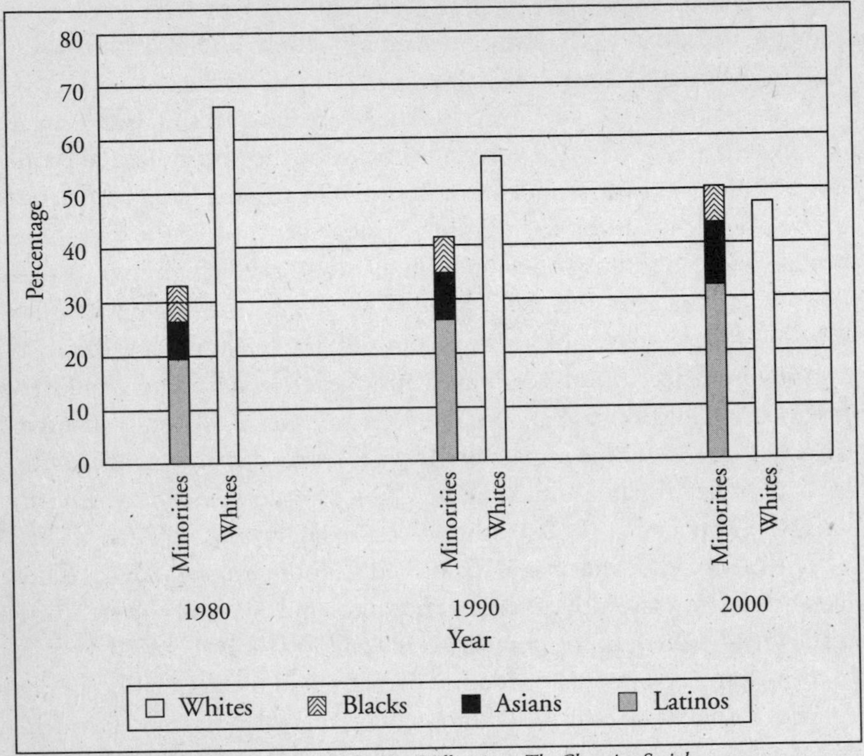

Sources: Mark Baldassare, *California in the New Millennium: The Changing Social and Political Landscape* (Berkeley, Cal.: University of California Press, 2000); and authors' analysis of 1990 and 2000 census data.

natorial race, the Republican candidate, Dan Lungren, only got about 20 percent of the Hispanic vote, which by then accounted for 14 percent of the electorate in California. In the 1996 presidential election, Clinton got about 73 percent of the Hispanic vote against Bob Dole, who championed an English-only requirement, and in 2000, Gore got 71 percent against Bush, even though Bush, speaking Spanish, vigorously campaigned among Hispanics.[22]

Asians, too, have moved Democratic. As we recounted in chapter 2, Chinese-Americans and Vietnamese-Americans, in particular, became more Democratic in the 1990s. In the 2000 election, Gore easily defeated

Bush by about 57–40 percent in California among Asian voters (one survey had the margin as high as 63–33).[23]

The growth of the Hispanic population has been particularly important in changing Orange County's politics. Hispanics make up about 31 percent of Orange County's population, but 62 percent of the forty-sixth congressional district, which includes Santa Ana, the largest city in Orange County. Until 1996, the congressional seat was held by arch-conservative Republican Robert Dornan, who won with a coalition of white and Vietnamese-American voters. But in 1996, Dornan was defeated for reelection by Mexican-American businesswoman Loretta Sanchez. And Clinton also beat Dole in the district, which had always been Republican, 49–41 percent. After the election, Dornan charged that Sanchez had stolen the election with votes from illegal immigrants. Dornan's charge further inflamed California's Hispanics and ensured that in their rematch in 1998, Sanchez would defeat Dornan easily, 56–39 percent. In 2000—a final indication of how Orange County had changed—Gore would carry this district 54–42 percent and Ralph Nader would get 2 percent of the vote.

Oregon and Washington

Both Oregon and Washington went Democratic in 1988, the same year that Democrats began to win Silicon Valley in California. Both states had residual New Deal voters, especially among unionized workers in Washington, but their dramatic shift into the Democratic column occurred because of the growth of the ideopolises around Portland's Multnomah County, which accounts for 45.7 percent of Oregon's votes, and around Seattle's King County, which accounts for 43.3 percent of Washington's vote.

Both states typify the new progressive centrist politics. The voters back regulatory capitalism, but are wary of ambitious social engineering. Perot got 24 percent in Washington in 1992, and in 1994, the state's voters, alienated by Clinton's policy failures, backed Republicans, leading to a seven-to-two Republican edge in Congress. But Clinton's increased effectiveness, especially on economics, and move to the center, combined with the Republican Party's capture by Southern conservatives, moved Washington voters back into the Democratic column. By November 2000, Democrats had six of nine congressional seats, both Senate seats (both of which were held by women), control of every major state position except commissioner of public lands, and control of both legislative houses. In both states, the Democrats' hold looks as if it will strengthen. Along with Hawaii, New Mexico (which combines a Hispanic and high-tech vote), and California, they form a solid Democratic majority in the West for years to come.

Arizona, Colorado, and Nevada

Much of Nevada votes like California's Central Valley, but the fastest-growing area in Nevada—and one of the fastest in the country—is Las Vegas's Clark County. It added about 630,000 residents in the 1990s, over a third of whom were Hispanic. Las Vegas's economy, based around entertainment, resembles that of Los Angeles, and it is voting increasingly like Los Angeles. After voting for George Bush in 1988 by 56–41 percent, it supported Clinton twice, and Gore in 2000, giving the Democratic candidate a higher percentage of the vote each time. If Clark County's population continues to grow at the rate it has been and continues trending politically as it has, Nevada could become dependably Democratic in the next decade.

In Colorado and Arizona, Democrats have begun to make inroads. Democratic hopes in Arizona, which backed Clinton in 1996, depend upon the growing Tucson-area ideopolis, which is pro-Democratic, and upon the rising Hispanic population, which went from 19 to 25 percent of the state in the 1990s. In addition, the Democrats could benefit from a continuing pro-Democratic trend in Phoenix's Maricopa County, the largest county in Arizona and the county with the largest growth in the nation. In 1988, Bush senior carried Maricopa 65–34 percent; in 2000, his son's margin was down to just 53–43, a swing of 21 points toward the Democrats.

Colorado might also go Democratic over the next decade. Granted, rural Colorado votes like Wyoming, while Colorado Springs's El Paso County is influenced by the religious right and the culture of the military. (It is home to the Air Force Academy and to conservative evangelist James

Dobson's Focus on the Family.) But the Denver and Boulder area votes like the San Francisco Bay Area. And Colorado's pro-Democratic Hispanic population grew from 13 to 17 percent of the state in the 1990s. After backing Clinton in 1992, Colorado did support Dole in 1996 and Bush in 2000, but Clinton barely lost in 1996—Nader's vote provided the difference—and Bush benefited in 2000 from an even larger Nader vote—5.25 percent—and from Gore's failure to campaign in the state. Democrats should stand a good chance of winning Colorado in the future.

The Republican West

Idaho, Wyoming, Montana, and Alaska vote like western Washington, rural Oregon, and parts of the Central Valley of California—which is to say, they view the national Democratic Party as an alien force dominated by labor, Eastern cities, and minorities. What helps Democrats in suburban California or New Jersey—support for gun control, federal land management, environmentalism, and feminism—kills them in many of these states. To win in these states—or in Nebraska, Kansas, South and North Dakota—a Democrat has to be deeply rooted in the state's culture,

Summary: Democratic Prospects in the West in the Next Decade

Solid Democratic	Leaning Democratic	Leaning GOP, but Competitive	Solid GOP
California	Nevada	Arizona	Alaska
Hawaii		Colorado	Idaho
New Mexico			Montana
Oregon			Utah
Washington			Wyoming
82 electors	5 electors	19 electors	18 electors

fight fiercely for the state's special interests, and, if necessary, distance her- or himself from the national party. A national Democratic candidate can generally only win in these states if the Republican is unpopular—as Clinton showed in Montana in 1992.

Utah contains a postindustrial area in Salt Lake City and several other smaller concentrations of high-tech research and development, but it has not adopted the bohemian culture of the ideopolis. Instead, its culture and its politics are shaped by the omnipresent Mormon religion, which opposes homosexuality, looks askance at feminism, and until 1978 prohibited blacks from being pastors. As a result, it is dependably Republican.

THE NORTHEAST

After the Civil War, the Northeast was the most Republican area in the nation for a long while. Even during Roosevelt's New Deal years, Vermont and Maine remained solidly Republican. In the 1948 presidential election, the Northeast, from Maine down to Maryland, except for Massachusetts and Rhode Island, voted for Republican Thomas Dewey. But Northeastern Republicanism bore little resemblance to the conservative Sunbelt Republicanism of Goldwater and Reagan, and after the recession of the early nineties and the capture of the Republican Party by the extreme right, the Northeast began to move strongly into the Democratic column.

The Northeast has become to the emerging Democratic majority what the South was to the conservative Republican majority of the 1980s. In the last three presidential elections, only New Hampshire and West Virginia went Republican, and only once. And while Republicans still hold some key congressional seats and governorships, it's mostly out of historical habit. Northeastern Republicans like New York congressman Jack Quinn, Maryland congresswoman Connie Morella, or Rhode Island senator Lincoln Chafee are moderates whose voting records are largely indistinguishable from moderate Democrats—and in a few cases, a little more liberal. Eventually, when these senators and House members retire, Democrats are likely to replace them. And in some cases, it may not even take that long, since there's always the possibility of defecting as did Long Island congressman Michael Forbes (who was then denied reelection when a left-wing Democrat defeated him in the primary) and as did Vermont senator James Jeffords in 2001.

New Jersey

One of the latest, and most significant, states to go Democratic has been New Jersey. Like California, it has been a bellwether state that went with the winner in the presidential election twenty-two of twenty-five times in the twentieth century. It supported the Republican nominee from 1968 through 1988, but has now backed Democrats three times in a row. Republicans controlled the governor's office and a majority of the House seats in the midnineties, but all the major state offices and a majority of House seats are now in Democratic hands.

New Jersey went Democratic for many of the same reasons that California did. In the nineties, its minority population, which votes overwhelmingly Democratic, grew from 26 to 33 percent[24]; the state's white working class, after abandoning the Democrats in the eighties, began returning to the fold with the recession of 1991; and the state's economy, once dependent upon heavy industry, has now become a leader in high-tech and information technology. New Jersey still has over four hundred thousand manufacturing jobs, about a tenth of the labor force, but many of these jobs are in the high-tech telecommunications and pharmaceutical firms that run along Highway 1 through Princeton's Mercer County and Middlesex County then eastward to Monmouth County.

New Jersey also used to be known as a collection of suburban bedroom communities, most of whose citizens actually worked in either New York or Philadelphia. But in the last two decades, firms have increasingly located in counties like Bergen and Hudson that are across the Hudson River from New York. These counties have become headquarters for securities, banking, health care, telecommunications, and publishing. The state's largest single occupational group—and the fastest growing—is professionals, who make up 23.3 percent of the workforce compared to 15.4 percent nationally.[25] And these professionals, like those in California, are now strongly Democratic.

New Jersey's shift to the Democratic Party came in an initial lurch forward, followed by a stagger backward, and then a resumption of the original movement. In the eighties, New Jersey voted for Reagan and Bush for president, and for moderate Republican Tom Kean for governor. Reagan and Bush won the biggest and third-biggest counties, Bergen in the north and Middlesex in the center, by comfortable margins. Bergen's professionals and managers were moderates who supported Republicans like Kean and Bergen County congresswoman Marge Roukema. In the eighties, Bergen's moderates backed conservative Republican presidential candidates out of opposition to Democratic economics. Blue-collar Middlesex voters, many of them pro–New Deal Irish Catholics, began voting Republican as part of the racial backlash. The same thing happened in the predominately white counties that bordered Trenton and Camden in the south. Wallace had gotten 11 percent in Middlesex in 1968 and from 12 to 15 percent in the predominately white southern counties. These votes would go to Nixon in 1972 and to Reagan and Bush in the 1980s.

But in the 1989 gubernatorial election, the Democrats reemerged as a force in state politics. Democratic representative Jim Florio, an environmentalist known as the author of Superfund legislation, ran as a moderate, pro-choice, pro-gun-control candidate against Representative Jim Courter, who was identified with the religious right's views on abortion and the National Rifle Association's position on guns. Florio won decisively, 62–38 percent, with large margins in Bergen and Middlesex counties. One key factor was women's support for Florio in the wake of the Supreme Court's *Webster* abortion decision.[26] Florio won 60–39 percent support among women under thirty.[27] Florio also gathered support in both counties for his strong environmental record and for his pledge not to raise taxes and to hold down auto insurance rates.

Although Florio's victory showed the potential for a Democrat, he squandered it by raising taxes and by championing an unpopular plan to redistribute school funds from predominately white to predominately black districts. (The school plan was mandated in some form by the state court.) Florio and his advisers believed they would mobilize the old New Deal majority on his behalf by framing the tax increase as a progressive levy. They were wrong—in a big way.[28] In 1990, the vitriolic backlash very nearly claimed the career of incumbent senator Bill Bradley simply because Bradley refused to publicly repudiate Florio. In 1992, Clinton won New Jersey, but by a smaller percentage than in neighboring states, as 19 percent of New Jerseyans backed Perot. And in 1993, Florio was defeated for reelection by moderate Republican Christine Whitman. Yet the underlying conditions for a Democratic upsurge were, if anything, stronger than before. New Jersey's recovery after the 1991 recession led to a boom in information services. Formerly blue-collar counties like Middlesex became dotted with telecommunications firms. Many of the older chemical refineries were replaced by pharmaceutical plants. The central and northeastern sections of the state became almost a continuous ideopolis.

Politically, the breakthrough came after the November 1994 election. Southern Republicans took over Congress and attempted to roll back environmental regulations—an affront to New Jerseyans, who suffer from pollution and toxic waste. The Republicans also tried to cut medicare and proposed banning abortion. At the same time, Clinton and the Democrats tailored their message so as not to scare professional and white working-class voters wary of overly ambitious social programs. As a result, New Jersey voters forgot about Florio and resumed their movement to the Democratic Party. In 1996, Clinton defeated Dole 54–36 percent, and in 2000, Gore defeated Bush by 56–40 percent, with Nader getting 3 percent. And in the 2001 gubernatorial contest, Democrat Jim McGreevey, who had been chairman of the state's DLC chapter, easily defeated a conservative Republican opponent.

In these elections, women and professionals backed the Democrats. Gore won Bergen County 55–42 percent, Mercer 61–34 percent, and Middlesex 60–36 percent. In Bergen County, Gore won 65 percent of college-educated white voters, including 77 percent of college-educated white women. In the state, he won voters with postgraduate degrees (usually a good indication of professionals) 62–34 percent. At the same time, he won 88 percent of the black vote and 58 percent of the Hispanic vote (which includes pro-Republican Cubans from Union City).[29]

The Democrats eventually picked up many of the white working-class voters who had backed Wallace in 1968 and Nixon, Reagan, and Bush from 1972 to 1988. In the face of the recession of 1991, these voters abandoned the Republicans, but many of them voted for Perot rather than Clinton. In 1996 and 2000, they went for Clinton and Gore. For instance, in white working-class Gloucester County, outside Camden and Philadelphia, where chemical plants are still located, Wallace had gotten 15 percent in 1968. The county went overwhelmingly for Reagan and

Bush in the 1980s. In 1992, Clinton got 41 percent to 36 percent for Bush and 23 percent for Perot. By 2000, however, Gore was getting 57 percent and the Republicans were still stuck under 40 percent (see chart). In New Jersey's southern counties overall in 2000, white working-class voters backed Gore 55–38 percent and white female professionals supported him 78–22 percent.[30]

In New Jersey, Democrats have created a powerful coalition of professionals, working women, minorities, and the white working class. The Republicans' principal strength is in sparsely populated rural counties such as Somerset (where billionaire Malcolm "Steve" Forbes lives), Hunterdon, and Warren. The danger that Republicans face in New Jersey is that as moderate voters abandon their party for the Democrats, they will increasingly be dominated by the most conservative voters, who will

Presidential Vote in Four Southern New Jersey Counties, 1988–2000

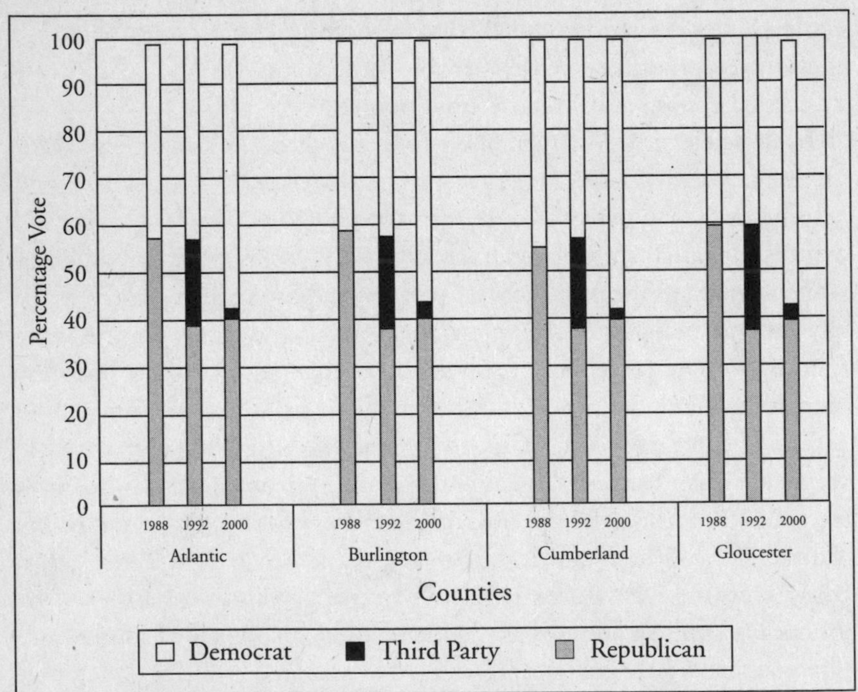

Source: Authors' analysis of county election returns, 1960–2000.

nominate candidates who can't win a general election. That clearly happened in the 2001 Republican primary for governor when New Jersey Republicans chose Bret Schundler, an antiabortion, anti-gun-control conservative, over moderate former congressman Bob Franks, dooming the party to ignominious defeat in November.

New York and Pennsylvania

New York has followed a pattern similar to New Jersey's. New York City, once a manufacturing center, has become an ideopolis, with its own "Silicon Alley." Its professionals, minorities, and white working class vote Democratic. Gore defeated Bush 80–15 percent in the city, which would have made it virtually impossible for Bush to win the state even if he had carried Long Island and upstate counties. But what has turned New York into a dependable Democratic state is the movement of the populous Long Island counties of Suffolk and Nassau into the Democratic column in presidential elections.

These Long Island counties were settled by the Italian middle and working class who called themselves Republicans primarily for the sake of ethnicity, not philosophy. (The Irish controlled the city's Democratic machines, so the Italians became Republicans.) During the tumultuous sixties, however, when New York was rocked by ghetto violence, racial tension, and rising crime, Long Island politics became consumed by the white backlash against New York liberal politics. As Jonathan Cohn has written, "Fear of, and hostility toward, New York City became the defining characteristics of Long Island politics."[31] But as New York quieted under Republican mayor Rudolph Giuliani (who, like New York's mayor during the 1930s, fellow Italian Republican Fiorello La Guardia, was closer to the national Democratic than the Republican Party), the white backlash receded. And as national Republican politics became the preserve of conservative Southerners, Long Island voters increasingly turned toward the Democrats in national elections. Like New Jersey's white working-class voters, large numbers of these voters journeyed out of the Republican Party by way of Perot, but finally ended up with the Democrats (see chart).

Pennsylvania was a dependable New Deal state. After World War II,

Presidential Vote in Two Long Island Counties, 1988–2000

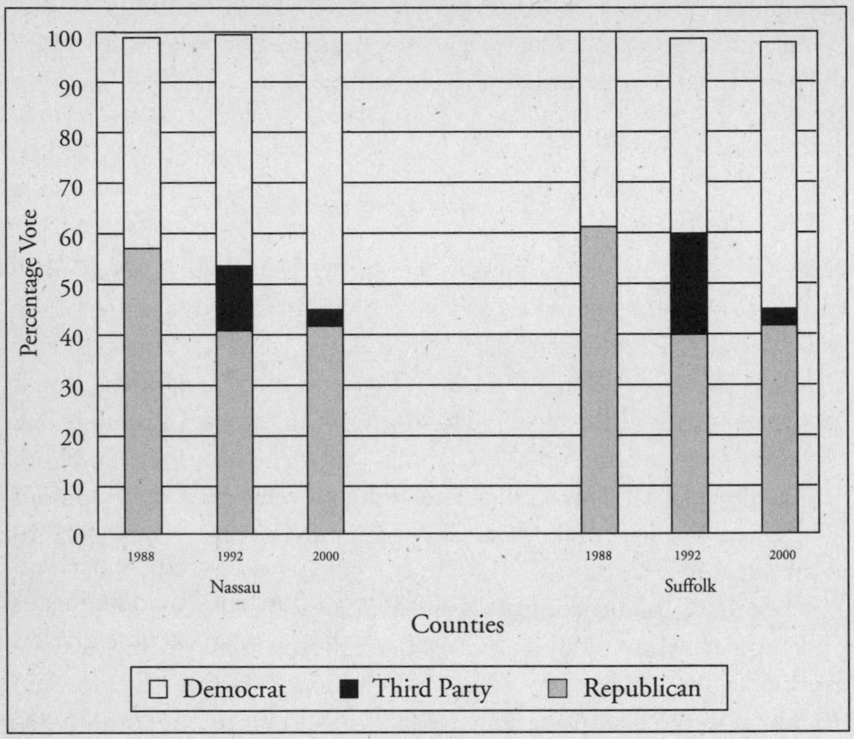

Source: Authors' analysis of county election returns, 1988–2000.

Democrats carried the state in presidential elections by overcoming the Republican vote in the primarily agricultural parts of the state and in the growing upscale Philadelphia suburbs. Democrats racked up big margins in Philadelphia and Pittsburgh and in the steel towns around Pittsburgh. In the eighties, enough blue-collar Democrats joined traditional and suburban Republicans for Reagan and Bush to carry the state, but Democrats have won it three times since then.

What changed in the nineties, though, was the way they carried it. Democrats still won the steel counties west and south of Pittsburgh, but by lower margins. Much of the disaffection is cultural, although these voters may also have blamed free-trade Democrats for the decline in the steel industry in the late nineties. (In 2000, a pro-gun, antiabortion Republican won a congressional seat in western Pennsylvania that had long been in Democratic hands.) But Democrats have made up for these losses by winning over the Philadelphia suburbs. The Philadelphia area now shows the voting traits of an ideopolis, including 58–39 percent Democratic support in 2000 among white, college-educated, suburban women and similar levels of support among white working-class voters, particularly women.[32] Overall, Gore carried Philadelphia and its Pennsylvania suburbs 61–36 percent. And the suburban counties in this area remain the fastest growing in the state—giving reason to believe that Democrats will be able to hold Pennsylvania over the next decade.

New Hampshire and West Virginia

The Democrats won every Northeastern state from 1992 to 2000 except for New Hampshire and West Virginia, which Bush narrowly won in 2000. But Republican support in both states could prove to be fleeting. What has distinguished New Hampshire in the eighties and nineties from its neighbors was that, because it did not have an income or sales tax, it became a haven for professionals and managers who worked in Massachusetts, but wanted to avoid paying its taxes. These antitax voters joined New Hampshire's rural Republicans to keep the state on the political right. But in the nineties, New Hampshire began to move left, partially out of disillusionment with Republican economics, but also because New Hampshire was developing a high-tech corridor whose voters, like professionals elsewhere, were beginning to prefer moderate Democrats. New Hampshire voted for Clinton twice and elected and reelected a Democratic governor. Gore lost New Hampshire in 2000 by 48–47 percent because he failed to anticipate Nader's 4 percent vote. Gore didn't campaign or run ads in the state and allowed Nader and Bush to brand him as a foe of the environment.[33] New Hampshire will continue to be more Republican than its neighbors, but a progressive centrist Democrat should be able to win the state in the future.

West Virginia has historically been one of the most Democratic states—it even went for Carter in 1980 and Dukakis in 1988. But the state, dependent on its declining coal industry, has been largely untouched by the high-tech boom of the 1990s. This, in turn, has fueled antipathy toward a Democratic Party identified not only with gun control but environmental regulation. In 2000, coal operators were able to rally many West Virginians against Gore and the Clinton administration, which they blamed for pushing environmental regulations that would potentially close mines throughout the state.[34] The Bush administration's political strategy is to turn West Virginia into another Republican Idaho or Wyoming. The administration has already given priority to coal in its energy plan, and the EPA chief for the West Virginia region has announced his support for letting states police their own industries—a recipe for lax enforcement of clean air standards.[35]

Summary: Democratic Prospects in the East in the Next Decade

Solid Democratic	Leaning Democratic
Connecticut	New Hampshire
Delaware	West Virginia
District of Columbia	
Maine	
Maryland	
Massachusetts	
New Jersey	
New York	
Pennsylvania	
Rhode Island	
Vermont	
113 electors	9 electors

And yet, ultimately, the state's struggling economy could push its politics back the other way. By November 2000, unemployment was also nearing 10 percent in coal counties that Democrats had carried easily in the past. Democrats can still claim the allegiance of the United Mine Workers and the support of West Virginians who look to them as the party of social security, medicare, mine-safety legislation, and the minimum wage. Plus Democrats control every major state office, both statehouses, both Senate seats, and two of three House seats. If the downturn in West Virginia's economy continues, the state is almost sure to go back to the Democrats.

THE MIDWEST

The Midwest has always been a battleground in American politics and will continue to be during the next decade. Republicans will undoubtedly retain their hold over the prairie states of Kansas, Nebraska, and North and South Dakota and over traditionally Republican Indiana. But the Democrats have established their own grip over the western Great Lakes states. The key to Democratic strength in Illinois, Minnesota, Michigan, and Wisconsin has been the revival of blue-collar support and the growth of ideopolises where older manufacturing cities used to exist. That has nowhere been more apparent than in Chicago and Illinois. It has set the pace for the emerging Democratic majority in the Midwest.

Illinois

Illinois voted for the winning presidential ticket twenty-one out of twenty-four times in the last century. It also voted for the Republican candidate from 1968 through 1988. But since then, it has gone Democratic. In 2000, Gore won the state easily, 55–43 percent, with Nader garnering 2 percent. Democrats have gained ground in the ideopolis around Champaign and in Chicago's outlying "collar" counties, but where Illinois has become irretrievably Democratic is in Chicago and its immediate Cook County suburbs.

The enormity of Chicago's shift can be gauged by looking back at the

1960 election. "In Cook County, Illinois," historian Stephen Ambrose writes, "Mayor Richard Daley . . . turned in an overwhelming Kennedy vote."[36] Nixon supporters charged that Daley had achieved this "overwhelming" vote through fraud. That may or may not have been true, but what is interesting is that Democrat John F. Kennedy's actual margin in Cook County was only 56–43 percent. It was probably closer to 65–35 percent in the city. By contrast, Al Gore defeated George Bush in Cook County in 2000 by 69–29 percent, and Gore won Chicago by an incredible 80–17 percent. With Cook County tallying about 40 percent of the votes in the state, Bush would have had to win 65 percent outside of Cook County to carry Illinois. That's an insuperable obstacle in a state that, even outside of Chicago and Cook County, is beginning to trend Democratic.

Chicago's movement to an 80 percent majority in 2000 has not been inexorable. In 1972, Nixon actually won Chicago and Cook County, and Mondale won the county by only 2.6 percent in 1984. The big shift came in the 1990s, and it coincided with important changes in Chicago's economy and politics (see chart). Like Boston, San Francisco, and Los Angeles, Chicago was once known for its manufacturing. It packed meat and made such things as household appliances, plastics, railroad equipment, televisions and radios, diesel engines, telephone equipment, candy, soap, and of course, steel.[37]

But between 1970 and 1997, Chicago lost 60 percent of its manufacturing jobs.[38] While Chicago still manufactured goods, what it made was often high-technology computer equipment such as modems or semiconductor chips. In the nineties Chicago became one of the leading areas for high technology and information technology. According to a Humphrey Institute study, the Chicago metropolitan area has the greatest number of high-technology and information-technology jobs of any metropolitan area.[39] All in all, the metro area had twice as many professionals and technicians as production workers. These included 103,910 computer and mathematical professionals; 71,000 architects, surveyors, and engineers; 49,690 community and social service professionals; 22,450 lawyers; 204,460 teachers; and 46,900 artists, designers, media professionals, athletes, and entertainers.[40]

The city itself was transformed. Once a larger version of Kansas City, it became a much larger version of San Francisco, with its theater and music, its restaurants, its funky lofts, its artists, and its visible gay popu-

Democratic Vote in Cook County

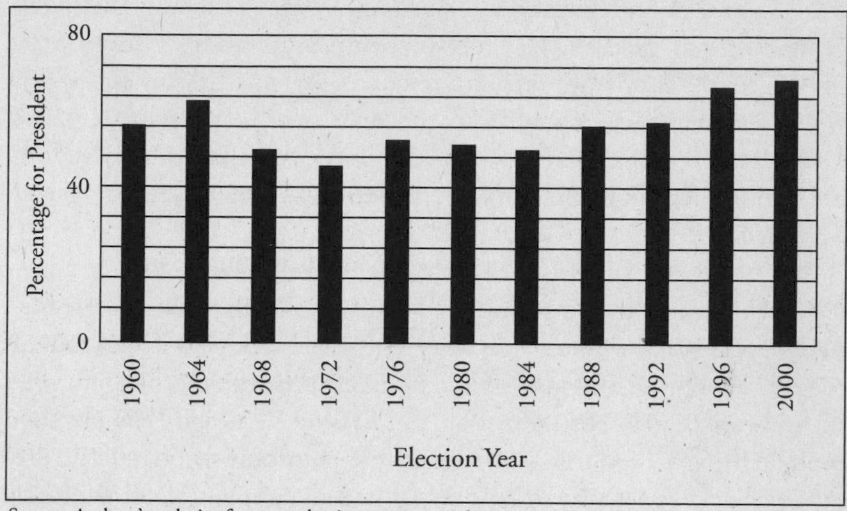

Source: Authors' analysis of county election returns, 1960–2000.

lation on the North Side. Once a city divided between white and black, Chicago became multiethnic in the nineties as its Asian and, particularly, its Hispanic populations continued to increase. The percentage of blacks in Cook County went from 25 to 26, Hispanics increased from 14 to 20, and Asians from 4 to 5. Neighborhoods, particularly on the North Side, that used to be demarcated by ethnic loyalty now became integrated.

This shift toward a postindustrial metropolis was accompanied by a dramatic change in the city's politics. Richard J. Daley governed the city from 1955 to 1976 through a New Deal coalition that combined the city's unions, ethnic groups, and blacks with its leading business interests. By the time he died, the Democratic machine was already coming apart—a victim of racial division and also of Chicago's declining industrial base. By the early eighties, Chicago looked as if it were going to become a racial Beirut. In 1983, black Democrat Harold Washington won the Democratic nomination over a divided white field. Any Democrat should have had an easy time against an unknown Republican, but Chicago's white working-class voters flocked to Bernard Epton. The low point of the campaign came on Palm Sunday when Washington and former vice president Walter Mondale were heckled by an angry crowd during a visit to a Polish-American church on the city's northwest side. "Die nigger die" was inscribed on the church door. Washington won with only 51 percent of the vote, and only 19 percent of the white vote, primarily from well-to-do lakefront wards. Washington's first term saw pitched battles between white and black Democrats and the defection of prominent white Democrats to the Republican Party. In the 1984 presidential election, many of Chicago's white ethnic voters also supported Reagan against Mondale.

But Washington died suddenly after being reelected in 1987. In a special 1989 election to succeed him, Richard M. Daley, the son of the former mayor, won the nomination over a divided black field. Daley sought to heal the political wounds, but also to redirect the city's Democratic politics toward a new postindustrial, multiethnic Chicago. His election mollified many of Chicago's white ethnic community, but Daley also made a black woman the city spokeswoman and appointed Hispanics to be the police chief and fire chief. He instituted an affirmative action policy. And he did what would have been inconceivable to his father—in June 1989, he led the Gay and Lesbian Pride Parade through Chicago's North Side. More than anything, that gesture—and Daley's subsequent overtures to gay Chicago—indicated that he knew he was dealing with an entirely different Chicago from that which his father had governed.[41] Aided by the city's boom during the nineties, Daley would not only bring Chicago together, but he would also erase the political division between Chicago and its suburbs. Chicago suburbanites, like New York City suburbanites, would no longer define themselves against Chicago, but see themselves as part of the city. That was crucial to the change in the voting pattern of the Chicago suburbs.

Chicago and its suburbs began to move Democratic in 1988, but the most dramatic change came in the 1990s. In the 1992, 1996, and 2000 elections, the Republicans would never get more than 30 percent of the vote in Cook County, and the Democratic total would rise from 58 percent in 1992 to 69 percent in 2000. In the 1992 election, Chicago's minorities and professionals voted heavily for Clinton, but some white ethnic voters hedged their bets by backing Perot, who got 13 percent in Cook County. Like voters in Long Island and southern New Jersey, these white Democrats were still leery of the national party, but in the face of a recession, they were no longer willing to vote Republican. In 1996 and 2000, these voters would return to the Democratic fold. Chicago's Polish voters, for instance, had backed Reagan both because they identified the Republicans with support for Poland in the Cold War and because they identified the Democrats with Chicago's insurgent blacks. By 1996, the Cold War was over, and Daley had largely healed the racial divisions in the city. As a result, many of these voters began to vote Democratic again. Says Chicago political consultant Don Rose, "With the Cold War's end and more of a cessation of racial hostilities, they began to vote their pocketbook and their issues."[42]

Chicago voting patterns were similar to those in other advanced ideopolises. There was not a dramatic difference between professional and working-class whites within the city. Working-class whites backed Gore 78–11 percent; and college-educated white voters (which includes many managers and business owners) backed him 69–20 percent. Overall, white men in the city supported Gore 67–32 percent and white women 78–10 percent.[43] In the past, the Cook County suburbs had been Republican in contradistinction to the city, but during the nineties, the suburbs became Democratic and backed Gore 56–41 percent in the 2000 election.*

Chicago's political shift has spilled over to the "collar counties" around Cook County that have also taken part in the transformation of Chicago's economy (see map). In the past, these counties voted like California's Orange County. Indeed, they still send Republican Phil Crane, one of the most right-wing members of the House, to Congress. But they have begun moving toward the Democrats over the last decade. Lake County backed Bush against Dukakis in 1988 by 64–36 percent; in 2000, it supported his son by just 50–48 percent, with 2 percent going to Nader. Will County backed Bush senior in 1988 by 59–40 percent. In 2000, it backed his son 50–47 percent with 2 percent to Nader. Both counties have become toss-ups and will probably become Democratic by the decade's end. The ideopolis in the Champaign-Urbana area has gone Democratic.

*In that shift, however, working-class white, minority, and women voters played the crucial role. Working-class white voters, for example, backed Gore 56–38 percent, and white college-educated women backed Gore 57–41 percent. In contrast, college-educated white men backed Bush 65–34 percent, suggesting the continued presence of managers and business owners in the suburbs who identify with Republican free-market policies. (Authors' analysis of 2000 VNS Illinois exit poll.)

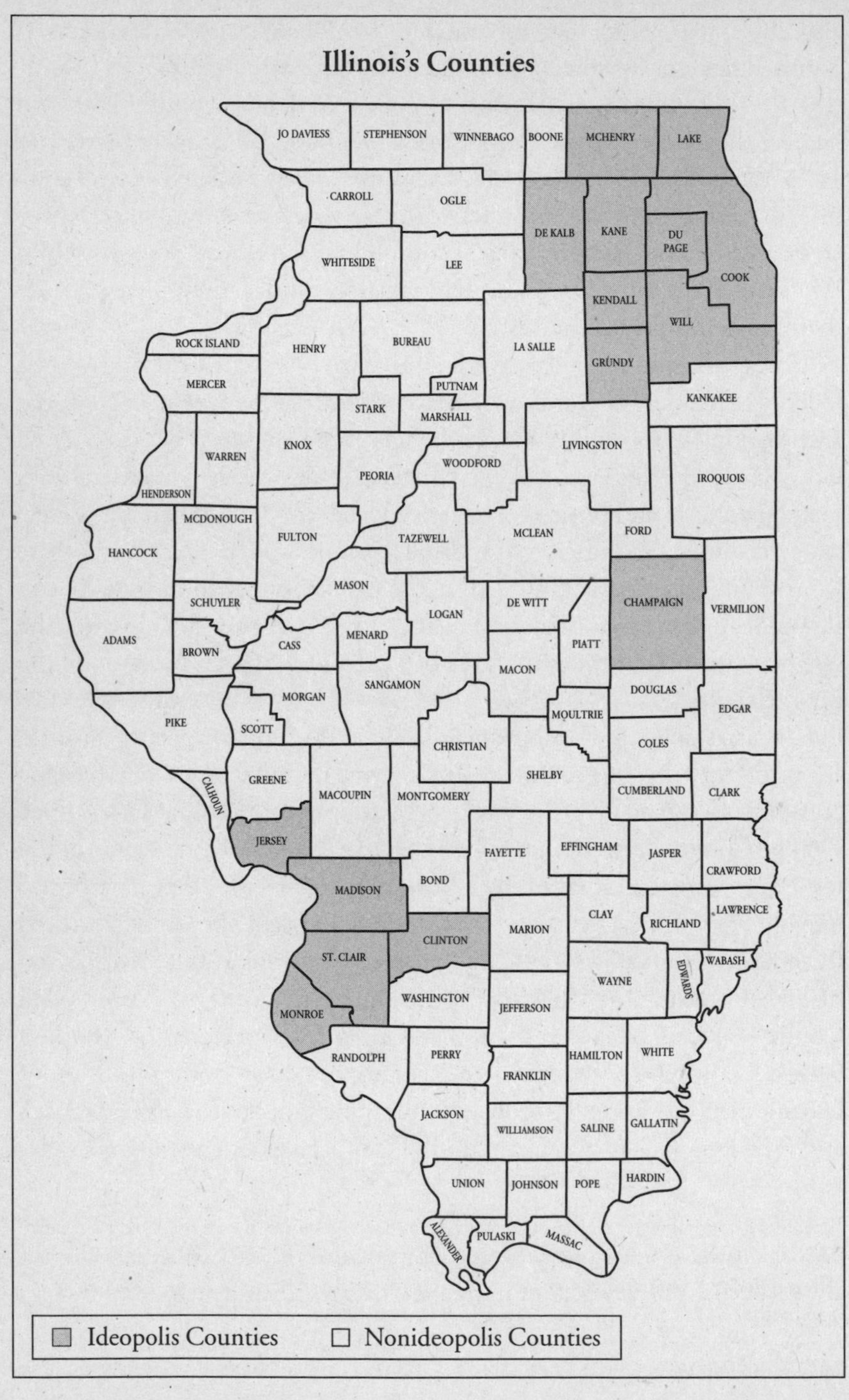
Illinois's Counties
JO DAVIESS
STEPHENSON
WINNEBAGO
BOONE
MCHENRY
LAKE
CARROLL
OGLE
DE KALB
KANE
DU PAGE
COOK
WHITESIDE
LEE
KENDALL
WILL
ROCK ISLAND
HENRY
BUREAU
LA SALLE
GRUNDY
MERCER
PUTNAM
KANKAKEE
STARK
MARSHALL
KNOX
WARREN
LIVINGSTON
WOODFORD
PEORIA
IROQUOIS
HENDERSON
MCDONOUGH
FULTON
TAZEWELL
MCLEAN
FORD
HANCOCK
MASON
CHAMPAIGN
SCHUYLER
DE WITT
VERMILION
LOGAN
ADAMS
MENARD
PIATT
BROWN
CASS
MACON
SANGAMON
DOUGLAS
MORGAN
EDGAR
MOULTRIE
PIKE
SCOTT
CHRISTIAN
COLES
SHELBY
GREENE
CALHOUN
MACOUPIN
MONTGOMERY
CUMBERLAND
CLARK
JERSEY
FAYETTE
EFFINGHAM
JASPER
CRAWFORD
MADISON
BOND
CLAY
LAWRENCE
RICHLAND
MARION
CLINTON
ST. CLAIR
EDWARDS
WABASH
WAYNE
WASHINGTON
JEFFERSON
MONROE
RANDOLPH
PERRY
HAMILTON
WHITE
FRANKLIN
JACKSON
WILLIAMSON
SALINE
GALLATIN
UNION
JOHNSON
POPE
HARDIN
ALEXANDER
PULASKI
MASSAC
Ideopolis Counties
Nonideopolis Counties

In 1988, Bush won Champaign County 52–47 percent; in 2000, Gore won it 48–47 percent, with 5 percent going to Nader.

Across the entire state, the Democrats' gains in Illinois are almost exclusively in the state's ideopolises. In 1988, these counties gave Bush and Dukakis each just under 50 percent, but in 2000, Gore won them collectively 59–39 percent. By contrast, Democrats lost the nonideopolis counties by 6.7 percent in 1988 and by 6.3 percent in 2000. Fortunately for the Democrats, the state's growth has been concentrated in the ideopolis counties. The greatest increases in population during the 1990s came (in this order) in the four ideopolis counties of Cook, Du Page, Lake, and Will. If this continues, the Democrats' hold over bellwether Illinois looks secure for the early twenty-first century.

The Upper Midwest

Minnesota and Wisconsin have voted in a similar manner to Washington and Oregon, the other states that form "greater New England." After a brief Republican interregnum in the early eighties (Minnesota supported Democrats for president, but at one point had two Republican senators and a Republican governor), both states have become dependably Democratic. The Democratic coalition has changed, however, from the New Deal days. Once dominated by blue-collar workers and small farmers, it now includes a large contingent of professionals. In Wisconsin, Democrats are strongest in Milwaukee and in Danc County, which houses the capitol and the University of Wisconsin and has become strongly Democrat in the last four decades, going 61–33 percent for Gore in 2000, with 6 percent for Nader. Dane is also the fastest-growing county in the state and together with Milwaukee accounts for about 26 percent of the voting electorate.

Minnesota is dominated by the Minneapolis–St. Paul metro area, which makes up 59 percent of the state vote. It is the home of the University of Minnesota and was the birthplace of Control Data, Honeywell, 3M, and other innovative high-tech companies. The city itself has almost always been Democratic, but in the last decades, the formerly Republican western suburbs in Hennepin County, the largest county in Minnesota, with the largest growth, have trended Democratic. In 2000, Gore won the county 54–39 percent with Nader getting over 6 percent. Along with strongly Democratic Ramsey County (57–36 for Gore, with 6 percent for Nader) this gives the Democrats overwhelming dominance of over one-third of Minnesota's vote.

Like Washington and Oregon, Minnesota and Wisconsin also have a history of supporting political reform and third-party efforts—from the farmer-labor parties of the 1920s to John Anderson, Perot, Minnesota governor Jesse Ventura, and Nader. Gore should have won easily in 2000, but barely won both states because the campaign ignored them and allowed Nader to flourish. Nader got 5 percent in Minnesota and 4 percent in Wisconsin. Many of the states' independent-minded voters supported Nader out of a commitment to political reform and good government and in opposition to the Clinton administration's scandals. In Minnesota, Gore did worse compared to Clinton in 1996 in exactly those counties that had voted for Ventura in 1998. Democratic Senate candidates—Herb Kohl in Wisconsin and Mark Dayton in Minnesota—ran far ahead of Gore. A Democrat untainted by scandal should be able to capture these states easily in the next decade.

Democrats continue to have a following among Iowa's farmers, who suffered under Republican policies in the 1980s. But more important, Democrats are strongest in the three counties that registered the largest increases in population—Des Moines's Polk County, Cedar Rapids's Linn County, and Iowa City's Johnson County. These counties, which are the sites of the state's major universities, have also moved the farthest toward a postindustrial economy. Gore failed to win decisively in Iowa, as in Minnesota and Wisconsin, because of Nader's vote and because of the shadow of Clinton's scandals. If Nader's vote is factored in, the total Democratic-leaning vote was 51 percent, more than Clinton got in 1996.

Republicans carried Michigan from 1972 to 1988 through a coalition of traditional Republicans in western and central Michigan and white working-class voters disgruntled about black Democrats and stagflation. But the Democrats revived in the late eighties and have now won the state three times in a row. One key to the Democratic revival was the return to the fold of white working-class counties like Macomb and Monroe around Detroit, Flint, and Toledo. Monroe, just north of Toledo, whose biggest single employer is a Ford auto parts factory, voted for George Bush in 1988 by 54–45 percent, grudgingly favored Clinton in 1992 by

42–34 percent (with Perot getting 23 percent), but then gave Clinton 50 percent in 1996 and Gore 51 percent in 2000. The Democrats' success in these counties signaled the diminution of race as a divisive factor and the reidentification of the Democrats as the party of prosperity.

But the other key to the Democratic revival was the growth of Michigan's postindustrial areas around Detroit–Ann Arbor, Lansing, and Kalamazoo in the 1990s. These areas have all become increasingly Democratic, going from 51–48 Republican support overall in 1988 to a 57–41 Democratic advantage in 2000, a swing of 19 percent.[44] For instance, upscale and predominately white Oakland County outside of Detroit is the home of the high-tech side of the auto industry, including Chrysler's research and development facility, Electronic Data Systems, and Fanuc Robotics. It was overwhelmingly Republican in the 1980s (Bush won it 61–38 percent in 1988), but it turned Democratic in 1996. In 2000, Gore won it 49–48 percent, with 2 percent to Nader. Oakland County also recorded the largest population growth of any Michigan county in the 1990s.

Missouri, Ohio, and Kentucky

Gore lost three Midwestern states in 2000 that Clinton had won in 1992 and 1996: Missouri, Ohio, and Kentucky. In Kentucky, Democrats still control the governor's office and one of two statehouses, but Republicans occupy both Senate seats and five of six House seats, and Gore lost decisively to Bush 57–41 percent. And while Democrats historically have had a strong working-class following in Louisville and in rural areas, many of the state's working-class voters in or around the coal and tobacco industries have abandoned the national Democrats over their environmental and public health policies. The state also lacks a postindustrial metropolis—it's thirty-ninth among states in the percentage of high-tech workers.[45]

Missouri and Ohio, by contrast, are developing politically and economically in ways that will make it very possible for a capable Democrat to win those states. Missouri, which was under Republican rule during the 1980s, began to go Democratic in the 1990s. Democrats now control one of two Senate seats and every state office except secretary of state. The shift toward the Democrats was the result of the same factors that worked in

Michigan. Many white working-class voters in the Kansas City and St. Louis areas who had backed Republicans because of race and stagflation returned to the Democrats after the recession. Jefferson County, south of St. Louis, backed Clinton in 1992 and 1996 and Gore by 50–48 percent (with Nader getting 2 percent) in 2000. And upscale voters in St. Louis's St. Louis County (which encompasses the suburbs and not the city) and in Kansas City's Clay County—both of which have become part of high-tech ideopolises—also turned Democratic in the 1990s. The Democrats had lost St. Louis County, the home of aerospace and biotechnology firms, 55–45 percent in 1988; in 2000, they won it 51–46 percent.

Gore's defeat in Missouri—at the same time Democratic candidates for Senate and governor were winning—may have been due to several special circumstances of his candidacy. He did much worse than Clinton or other Missouri Democrats among white working-class voters in rural areas and small towns. In the north and southeast parts of the state outside of the St. Louis metro area, Clinton had won white working-class voters 50–38 percent in 1996, but Gore lost them 60–38 percent, a 34-point swing. The late Mel Carnahan, running for Senate against Republican John Ashcroft, ran 11 percent better than Gore in the north and southeast parts of the state.[46]

Gore may have been hurt, ironically, by the prosperity of the Clinton years. According to St. Louis University political scientist and pollster Ken Warren, working-class voters, who had focused on jobs and the economy in the two earlier elections, focused in 2000 on "luxury" issues such as personal morality, abortion, and guns, on which they favored the Republicans. Exit polls also suggested that Missouri voters, mindful of Clinton administration scandals, were worried about whether they could trust Gore.

According to Warren, Gore suffered as well from being unable to communicate with rural voters in Missouri. While they had seen Clinton as a neighbor from Arkansas who, like them, had been born to humble circumstances, they saw Gore as a "Northeastern stuffed shirt." Says Warren, "Rural people tend to have an inferiority complex. They are intimidated by city people. Gore came across as a snob and a Northeast, Washington bureaucrat. Clinton never came across that way. And Bush came across as folksy. You have no idea how rural people hate that Northeast, Washington image."[47] The same problems seem to have affected

Gore in other Midwestern states and in Southern states such as Arkansas, Louisiana, and Tennessee, where white working-class voters are reluctant to support Democrats with whom they feel little cultural affinity.

In Ohio, Republicans control the governorship and both Senate seats. Its southern tier, including Cincinnati, is traditionally Republican, and Democrats have proven unable to field candidates with broad appeal. But Ohio's unionized industrial working class—after flirting with Republicans in the eighties—returned to the fold in 1988; and Democrats have fared increasingly well in the state's two postindustrial areas, Cleveland and Columbus's Franklin County, the site of Ohio State University and the state capitol. Democrats lost Franklin County in 1988 by 60–39 percent, but Gore won it 49–48 percent in 2000, and Nader got 3 percent. Even though the Gore campaign withdrew from Ohio almost a month before the campaign was over, Gore only lost the state 50–46 percent. With Nader's 3 percent, that amounts to a 49 percent vote for Democratic politics.

Gore suffered in Ohio from the same disabilities that sank him in Missouri: rural and small-town voters' concerns about guns, abortion, and the Clinton scandals, and Gore's difficulty in communicating with them. According to exit polls, 61 percent of Ohioans had an unfavorable view

Summary: Democratic Prospects in the Midwest in the Next Decade

Solid Democratic	Leaning Democratic	Leaning GOP, but Competitive	Solid GOP
Illinois	Missouri	Kentucky	North Dakota
Iowa	Ohio		South Dakota
Michigan			Indiana
Minnesota			Nebraska
Wisconsin			Kansas
65 electors	31 electors	8 electors	28 electors

of Clinton as a person; of those, 70 percent voted for Bush and only 26 percent for Gore. As in Missouri, a Democrat who evoked a reasonable level of trust could have won Ohio in 2000 and could win it in future elections.

THE SOUTH

The Republicans have been winning most of the South in recent elections, but the region is by no means as solid for Republicans as it was for the Democrats from 1876 to 1960. A few states, such as Mississippi, Alabama, and South Carolina, would be very unlikely to vote for a national Democrat. But one very important state, Florida, has been turning Democratic, and several other states, including North Carolina and Virginia, could go Democratic before the decade is over. These states could veer Democratic because of the growth of a postindustrial economy in their key metropolitan areas.

Florida

Of all the Southern states, the one most clearly moving toward the Democrats is Florida. Clinton won Florida in 1996, and Gore lost it only because of ballot irregularities in Palm Beach and Duval counties. In the same election, Democratic Senate candidate Bill Nelson easily defeated Republican congressman Bill McCollum. And Florida should get easier not harder for the Democrats in the future. Since 1988, Democratic strength has dramatically increased in all five counties of the state that added the most people during the last decade: Fort Lauderdale's Broward County, Miami-Dade, Palm Beach, Orlando's Orange County, and Tampa's Hillsborough County (see table).

In Palm Beach County, for instance, Bush defeated Dukakis in 1988 by 55–44 percent, but Gore won it in a landslide 62–35 percent, with 1 percent to Nader, a swing of 38 percent toward the Democrats. Similarly, Bush overwhelmingly defeated Dukakis in Orange County, 68–31 percent, but Gore won it 50–48 percent with 1 percent to Nader, a pro-Democratic swing of 39 percent. Even in Hillsborough County, where the

Democrats slid slightly backward in 2000 (although Senate Democratic candidate Nelson easily won the county against Republican McCollum), there was still a swing of 17 percent toward the Democrats over that period.

Behind this dramatic shift were the same factors that made states in the West or Northeast more Democratic. Florida has one of the most advanced economies in the South, and its largest metropolitan areas have moved toward becoming postindustrial and high-tech. In Palm Beach County, Pratt and Whitney makes jet engines; Motorola, pagers; and Siemens, communications equipment. Miami-Dade, the home of the University of Miami, is a major center for health care, fashion, and entertainment. Fort Lauderdale's Broward County has more workers employed in education than in direct goods production. Orange County is, of course, a major entertainment center with Walt Disney World and Universal Studios, but it also a home for computer services. In these areas, college-educated women and white working-class voters both tend to vote Democratic as they do in the more advanced ideopolises. For example, white working-class voters in the Miami area supported Gore 51–47 percent, while college-educated white women backed him 68–30 percent.[48]

During the 1990s, Democrats have also benefited from the growth of Florida's minority population, which accounted for about 2 million of the 3 million additional residents of the state. The Hispanic population went from 12 to 17 percent, African-Americans from 13 to 15 percent,

Democratic Margin in Five Largest-Growth Florida Counties, 1988–2000 (in percentages)

County (increase in population)		1988	1992	1996	2000
Broward	(368,000)	0	+21	+35	+36
Miami-Dade	(316,000)	-11	+4	+19	+6
Palm Beach	(268,000)	-11	+12	+25	+27
Orange	(219,000)	-37	-11	0	+2
Hillsborough	(165,000)	-20	-6	+2	-3

Source: Authors' analysis of 1988–2000 county election returns and 1990 and 2000 census data.

and Asians from 1 to 2 percent of the state.[49] Most of the new Hispanics were from Central America and Puerto Rico and, unlike Cubans, have tended to vote Democratic. The influx of Puerto Rican voters into Orange County—Hispanics went from 10 to 19 percent of the county's population during the decade—was clearly a factor in that county's shift toward the Democrats.

The Republicans remain strong in rural Florida—exactly where the Democrats used to get their votes.[50] Escambia County, in the panhandle near the Alabama border, and Nassau County, near the Georgia border, formerly went heavily for Democrats. In 1960 these counties went for Kennedy by almost two to one even though Nixon won Florida. But these voters, angered by national Democratic support for civil rights, would support Goldwater in 1964 and Wallace in 1968. Since then, both counties have become increasingly Republican. In 2000, Bush carried Escambia 63–35 percent and Nassau 69–29 percent. Needless to say, however, the votes in these small, rural counties are eclipsed by those in Orange or Palm Beach. In Florida, growth is very definitely on the side of the Democrats.

North Carolina and Virginia

North Carolina and Virginia have voted Republican in presidential elections since 1980 but, because of the influx of minorities and the growth of postindustrial metropolises, could turn Democratic in the next decade. Three decades ago, North Carolina led the nation in low-wage manufacturing. Since then, its tobacco and textile industries have shrunk, but it has become a national leader in banking, biotechnology, pharmaceuticals, environmental services, and in computer research and development. These new industries are centered in Charlotte's Mecklenburg County and in the Raleigh-Durham–Chapel Hill Research Triangle, the centers of population growth in North Carolina during the 1990s. Once primarily a small-town rural state, North Carolina is increasingly organized around these new postindustrial areas.[51]

Like other Southern states, North Carolina was traditionally Democratic, although there were always Republicans in the Appalachian regions to the west. But in the sixties, many of the state's white working-class voters abandoned the Democrats over the national party's support for civil rights and began to vote Republican, helping to elect conservative Republican Jesse Helms to the Senate in 1972. But in contrast to neighboring South Carolina, where the Democrats became identified with blacks and with political corruption, North Carolina whites continued to back moderate Democrats like Jim Hunt, who was elected governor in 1976, and after serving for two terms, was elected for another two terms in 1992. Since Hunt's election, Democrats in North Carolina have increasingly relied not only on votes from minorities but also from the professionals, women, and other relatively liberal whites in the state's growing postindustrial areas (see map). Since 1988, all these areas have become more Democratic. Dukakis lost Mecklenburg County 59–40 percent in 1988, but Gore lost it only 51–48 in 2000, even though he did not campaign in the state. The Democrats' edge in Durham County increased from 54–45 percent to 63–35 percent over the same period. In the Raleigh metro area, Gore won with 50 percent, including 55–42 percent among college-educated white women voters.[52]

State Democratic candidates have done even better in these high-tech areas. North Carolina democratic senator John Edwards, who defeated incumbent Lauch Faircloth in 1998, won Raleigh's Wake County 51–48 percent. In 2000, Democratic gubernatorial candidate Mike Easley won it 55–43 percent. Edwards and Easley also won Charlotte's Mecklenburg County. Significantly, Edwards did not repudiate the national party, but ran in 1998 on national Democratic issues such as the patients' bill of rights. It's not hard to envision a Democrat who could establish a rapport with the state's voters winning North Carolina's electors.

Like North Carolina, Virginia has gone Republican in presidential elections, but has alternated between Democrats and Republicans in Senate and gubernatorial elections. Who wins these latter elections has depended on who carried the increasingly vote-rich northern Virginia suburbs of Washington, D.C. In the late seventies, alienated by liberal Democratic spending and criticisms of the military, these suburban voters swung the state Republican. In the eighties, alienated by the rise of the religious right, which was headquartered in Falwell's Lynchburg and Robertson's Chesapeake, they backed Chuck Robb for governor and the Senate and Doug Wilder and Gerald Baliles for governor. In the nineties, wooed by "compassionate conservatism" and tax cuts, they elected George Allen to the governorship and Senate and James Gilmore as governor.

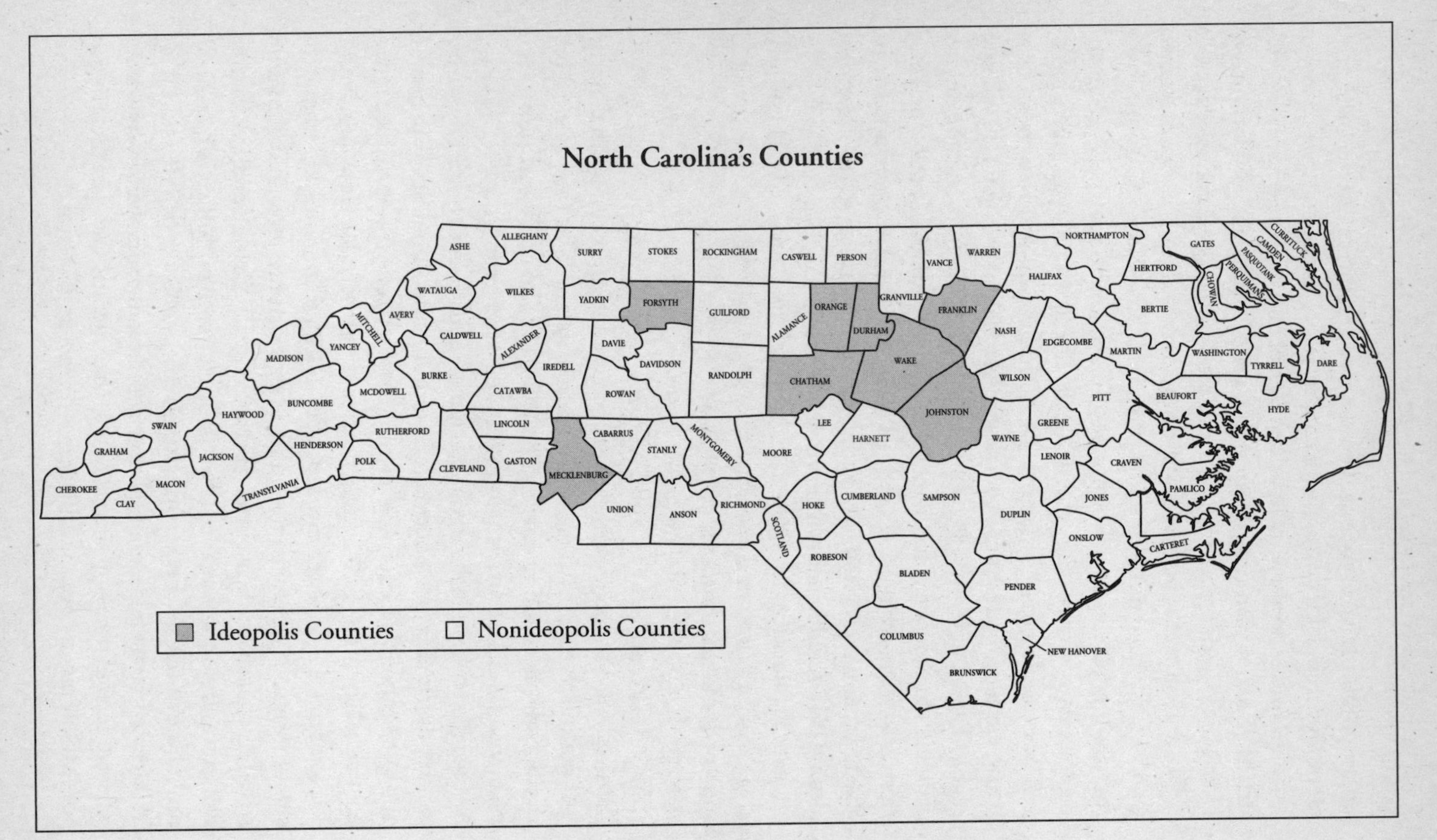
North Carolina's Counties
ASHE
ALLEGHANY
SURRY
STOKES
ROCKINGHAM
CASWELL
PERSON
VANCE
WARREN
NORTHAMPTON
GATES
CURRITUCK
CAMDEN
PASQUOTANK
PERQUIMANS
CHOWAN
HERTFORD
HALIFAX
WATAUGA
WILKES
YADKIN
FORSYTH
GUILFORD
ALAMANCE
ORANGE
DURHAM
GRANVILLE
FRANKLIN
BERTIE
MITCHELL
AVERY
CALDWELL
ALEXANDER
IREDELL
DAVIE
DAVIDSON
RANDOLPH
CHATHAM
WAKE
NASH
EDGECOMBE
MARTIN
WASHINGTON
TYRRELL
DARE
MADISON
YANCEY
BURKE
MCDOWELL
CATAWBA
ROWAN
WILSON
PITT
BEAUFORT
HYDE
BUNCOMBE
HAYWOOD
SWAIN
RUTHERFORD
LINCOLN
LEE
JOHNSTON
GREENE
GRAHAM
JACKSON
HENDERSON
POLK
CLEVELAND
GASTON
CABARRUS
STANLY
MONTGOMERY
MOORE
HARNETT
WAYNE
LENOIR
CRAVEN
CHEROKEE
CLAY
MACON
TRANSYLVANIA
MECKLENBURG
UNION
ANSON
RICHMOND
SCOTLAND
HOKE
CUMBERLAND
SAMPSON
DUPLIN
JONES
PAMLICO
ONSLOW
CARTERET
ROBESON
BLADEN
PENDER
COLUMBUS
BRUNSWICK
NEW HANOVER
Ideopolis Counties
Nonideopolis Counties

But Virginia may be swinging back to the Democrats. In the 2001 state elections, Democrats won two out of three of the major offices. Democratic gubernatorial candidate Mark Warner carried northern Virginia's Fairfax County, also the state's largest, 54–45 percent. And in spite of Democratic indifference to Virginia in presidential elections, a clear trend toward the Democrats exists in these same high-tech suburbs, which contain the second-greatest concentration of computer firms in the country. Fairfax has gone from a 61–38 percent Republican margin in 1988 to a 49–47 percent Bush margin in 2000, with 3 percent to Nader. Loudon County went from a 66–33 Republican margin to a 56–41 percent Republican advantage. Arlington went from a 53–45 Democratic edge to a 60–34 percent Democratic advantage, with 5 percent to Nader, over the same period. If these suburban voters keep increasing their proportion of the Virginia vote, and if they continue to trend Democratic, they could very well tilt Virginia back to the Democrats, even in presidential elections. Certainly, Democrat Mark Warner's victory suggests this is a real possibility.

The Republican South

Republicans are strongest in some of those states, such as Mississippi, Alabama, and South Carolina, with the largest percentage of black voters. In these states, race is not just one political issue, but the most important issue, by far. Mississippi and South Carolina have recently had raging controversies over whether to fly a Confederate flag, a symbol of Southern racism, over their state capitols. In South Carolina, a Republican governor lost his bid for reelection in 1998 partly because he favored taking down the flag. "The intensity of the debate over the flag reveals that the economic issues that have dominated South Carolina's political discourse in recent years have yet to displace racial concerns at the core of South Carolina's political culture," wrote Glen T. Broach and Lee Bandy in a perceptive study of the state's politics.[53] In April 2001, Mississippi voted by two to one to retain the flag.[54]

In these states, there remains a close correlation, dating back to the Wallace era, between the Republican vote and white racial concerns. Mississippi's DeSoto County, which voted six to one for the flag, went for

Wallace by three to one in 1968 and for George W. Bush by a similar margin in 2000, giving him 71 percent of the vote. All the other Mississippi counties where Bush's vote exceeded 70 percent were also lopsided for Wallace in 1968.

The strongest Republican states are also those that have lagged behind Northern and Western states in developing a postindustrial economy. Mississippi's principal innovation over the last two decades has been riverboat gambling. Oklahoma is still dependent on a declining oil industry. The standard of living in these states is well below the national average. Taking 100 as the national norm in per capita income, Oklahoma's fell from 89 in 1978 to 80.3 in 1997. Mississippi's per capita income is at 71.6 and Alabama's at 81.7. Democrats can still win elections in these states, but generally only if they repudiate the national party and tailor their message to the state's voters. Democratic gubernatorial candidates in Alabama, Mississippi, and South Carolina have won elections this way, but national Democrats face an uphill battle.

In two of the states with lagging development, Louisiana and Arkansas, Democrats still have a good chance of winning the state's presidential electors. Democrats won both states in 1992 and 1996. Clinton's favorite-son status was certainly a factor in Arkansas, but by the same token Clinton's popularity in that state over two decades showed that its white voters, who make up 87 percent of the voting electorate, will support a progressive centrist Democrat. White workers in Arkansas and Louisiana—and particularly in Cajun country—still respond to New Deal Democratic appeals. But in 2000, Gore failed to win these voters. Clinton had won Jefferson Davis parish in Cajun country 53–33 percent in 1996. Even Dukakis won it in 1988. But Gore lost it to Bush 55–41 percent. Just as in southeast Missouri, these voters were probably heavily motivated by cultural considerations in their 2000 vote choice; they felt more comfortable with Bush, a Texas oilman, than with Gore. With a different set of candidates, the result could have been quite different.

Over the next decade, a Democratic presidential candidate could also win the electoral votes of Georgia, Tennessee, and yes, even Texas. In all three of these states, the same conditions obtain, though to a lesser degree, that might make it possible for the Democrats to win North Carolina and Virginia. All three have large minority populations that, in the case of Georgia and Texas, are getting larger at a rapid clip and that vote primarily Democratic. In Georgia, the Hispanic population increased from 2 to 5 percent and blacks from 27 to 29 percent during the 1990s. (The increase in black population was primarily a product of a reverse migration back from the North to the South.) In Texas, the Hispanic population increased from 26 to 32 percent in the 1990s, while the black population remained at 12 percent.

Each of these states also has postindustrial areas where the Democrats are doing well. Dukakis lost Nashville's Davidson County by 5 points in 1988, but Gore won it by 17 percent in 2000. In Texas, Clinton won Austin's Travis County in 1996 by 52–40 percent, and the county elects a Democratic congressman. But the other postindustrial areas in these states are not culturally and politically integrated. They and their white voters begin from an overwhelmingly Republican base, so even though the Democrats have been doing better in most of them, Republicans generally remain far ahead.

Texas's ideopolises in the Dallas and Houston metro areas and Georgia's Atlanta metro area are constructed around the model of St. Louis. Most high-tech economic development has taken place outside the core urbanized area, and the residents of many primarily white suburbs that surround the minority-dominated central area define themselves politically and economically against it. The professionals in these suburbs are likely to identify with managers and to vote Republican rather than Democratic. Even white college-educated women in these suburbs, a strong Democratic group in most ideopolises, tend to vote Republican. In the primarily white suburbs that form the outer ring of the Atlanta metro area, college-educated white women were only marginally less Republican than their male counterparts, preferring the Republican Bush 70–26 percent, while in the racially integrated suburbs immediately adjoining Atlanta, college-educated white women voted Democratic 59–39 percent.

In all three of these states, white working-class voters began moving away from the Democrats in the sixties, and while they have fitfully come back when Republicans appear to be responsible for a recession, many of them abandoned the Democrats in 2000—probably for the same reasons that rural Democrats in Missouri or Cajun Louisiana did. In Georgia, Gore got only 23 percent of the white working-class statewide vote. In Tennessee he did better with 34 percent, but a Democrat would probably need close to 40 percent to carry the state.

Still, the Democrats have a chance in all three of these states if the minority vote continues to grow, if white voters eventually experience the same kind of cultural change that residents of other ideopolises have, and if white working-class voters become convinced (as they do periodically) that their jobs, social benefits, and general quality of life depend on having Democrats in office.

A warning: This survey is not intended to show that a Democratic majority is inevitable. What it shows is that over the next decade, the Democrats will enter elections at an advantage over the Republicans in securing a majority. Whether Democrats actually succeed will depend, in any given race, on the quality of the candidates they nominate and on the ability of candidates and their strategists to weld what is merely a potential majority into a real one. Whether they can do that will depend upon the politics of the new majority.

Summary: Democratic Prospects in the South in the Next Decade

Leaning Democratic	Leaning GOP, Very Competitive	Leaning GOP, Competitive	Solid GOP
Florida	Virginia	Georgia	Alabama
	North Carolina	Tennessee	Mississippi
		Texas	South Carolina
		Louisiana	Oklahoma
		Arkansas	
27 electors	28 electors	75 electors	30 electors

CHAPTER FOUR

The Politics of the Emerging Democratic Majority

> It should be constantly borne in mind that a coalition is just that—it is not a consensus. Both the opportunities of Johnson and Nixon—after massive victories—were lost when the responsible people came to believe that they could achieve consensus and basically ignore politics. A coalition is composed of many different factions of people who basically don't like each other much and are competing for various rewards and favors that a government can offer. The trick is finding a mixture of rewards and factors that will hold 51 percent of the voters together in a reasonable stable block.
>
> —Pat Caddell, 1976[1]

Political majorities are always coalitions. They combine different, and sometimes feuding, constituencies, interest groups, religions, races, and classes often united by nothing other than greater dislike for the opposing party, candidate, and coalition. What, after all, united the white Southern Bourbon and the Northern black who voted for Roosevelt in 1940, or the upscale suburbanite from Bergen County and the white working-class evangelical from Greenville who voted for Reagan in 1984? Like these past majorities, the new Democratic majority will be made up of disparate groups and voters—from the autoworker from Jefferson County, Missouri, concerned, above all, about his job and wages, to the Boston corporate lawyer concerned about her daughters' right to choose. To unite these disparate groups and voters is the role of politics and politicians—and of the political strategists that they rely on.

The strategy, or worldview, that unites these disparate groups has not consisted of a simple formula or commitment. Only small third parties such as the Libertarian or Natural Law Party boast a unified, homogeneous appeal. Instead, the political strategies of major parties resemble the heterogeneous groups that they are attempting to unite. From 1912 to 1920, Woodrow Wilson's Democrats stood for progressive economics, a foreign policy based on national self-determination, and white Southern racism. In the 1980s, Reagan conservatives advocated a libertarian economic policy and an authoritarian social ethic. What seemed like inconsistencies to the political philosopher reflected attempts to unite politically divergent constituents behind a common set of candidates.

The search for a new Democratic majority began after the debacle of 1968. Over the next decade, Democrats would search for a strategy and a set of constituencies that would make up a majority. Three alternatives would emerge that would frame the debate over Democratic strategy: first, a *New Left liberalism* that fused a Johnsonian–New Deal optimism about government intervention with a commitment to the social movements of the sixties; second, a *restorationist* strategy that tried to re-create the status quo ante of New Deal and Cold War liberalism; and third, a *revisionism* that tried to rebuild a new majority primarily on college-educated suburbanites. The proponents of each of these political alternatives insisted that only their own held the path to success for the Democrats. But as it turned out, success did not lie in traveling only one of these paths, but all three simultaneously. The Democrats needed a strategy, and a worldview, that could accommodate the white working class, the political remnants of the sixties, and the suburban baby boomers and yuppies.

I. MCGOVERN, CARTER, CADDELL, AND KENNEDY

In 1972, George McGovern drew upon the social movements of the sixties and the broader parts of society that they would eventually represent. His candidacy was based not only on ending the war, but on the assumption that the social ills facing the country, including those unearthed by the environmental, consumer, and civil rights movements, could be cured through large-scale government intervention, financed by taxes on the wealthy and by the diversion of funds from the military. He advocated, among other things, a national health insurance system and a guaranteed annual income (a "Demogrant") to replace welfare. With Johnson, he became the model of the "tax and spend liberal" that Republicans would later attack.

The counterreaction to McGovern's candidacy set in even before the election was over. A group of Democrats led by Washington senator Henry "Scoop" Jackson and former Johnson administration speechwriter Ben Wattenberg formed the Coalition for a Democratic Majority (CDM). The CDM's purpose was to reclaim the Democratic Party for Jackson, Hubert Humphrey, and other Cold War liberals who believed that it had been hijacked by McGovern and sixties New Leftists. Their lodestar was Wattenberg and Richard Scammon's *The Real Majority*, which recounted how the white working class had abandoned the Democrats over what Wattenberg and Scammon called "the social question."[2] Their book was the Democratic equivalent of Phillips's *Emerging Republican Majority* and proved no less prophetic. What they described as the prototypical Democratic defector of the 1970s—a "forty-seven-year-old housewife from the outskirts of Dayton, Ohio, whose husband is a machinist"—became the Reagan Democrat of the 1980s. But as strategists, they were as blind to reality as the McGovernites they opposed. The constituency they championed was a dwindling part of the electorate, and at least some of the voters they coveted—white Southerners who had left the Democratic Party over race issues—simply weren't ready to come back unless the party was willing to repudiate its commitment to civil rights.

In 1976, CDM members backed Jackson for president, while many of the former McGovernites supported Congressman Morris Udall. But neither proved any match for former Georgia governor Jimmy Carter. There was plenty about Carter that McGovern supporters could like. He had been a "new South" governor who prided himself on his support for civil rights; he was a conservationist and environmentalist; he had reservations about the Vietnam War; and he favored extensive campaign finance and lobbying reform. But Carter rejected the McGovernites' "big government" utopianism. Among other things, he refused to endorse the New Left and liberal Democrats' cause célèbre, the original Humphrey-Hawkins Full Employment bill, which would have required government to guarantee every American a job.

Carter, of course, would go on to win—but only by a slim margin, particularly given the long shadow Watergate had cast over the country. Which is one reason that just a month after Carter's election, his pollster, Pat Caddell, drafted a memo spelling out how Carter could create a new realignment out of his majority. Caddell, who had also served as McGovern's pollster in 1972, produced an astute piece of analysis—the first tract of post–New Deal revisionism. While the CDM had urged Democrats to focus on blue-collar Midwesterners, Caddell argued that if Democrats wanted to create a new "political realignment," they had to reach "the younger white-collar, college-educated, middle-income suburban group that is rapidly becoming the majority of America."[3] Wrote Caddell, "If there is a future in politics, it is in this massive demographic change. We now have almost half the voting population with some college education, a growing percentage of white-collar workers, and an essentially middle-class electorate." These "white-collar and professional" voters, Caddell warned, were "cautious on questions of increased taxes, spending, and particularly inflation."

Caddell also urged Carter to pay attention to twenty-five-to-thirty-five-year-old baby-boom voters. Like white-collar, suburban voters, Caddell said, these voters, too, couldn't be expected to fall in line behind traditional Democratic appeals. "Younger voters," Caddell wrote, "are more likely to be social liberals and economic conservatives. More importantly, they perceive a new cluster of issues—the 'counterculture' and issues such as growth versus the environment—where the old definitions don't apply. . . . We must devise a context that is neither traditionally liberal nor traditionally conservative, one that cuts across traditional ideology." But Caddell couldn't tell Carter what that new ideology was. "What we require is not a stew, composed of bits and pieces of old policies, but a fundamentally new ideology. Unfortunately, the clear formulation of such an ideology is beyond the intellectual grasp of your pollster."

Caddell had grasped, if imperfectly, what the electorate of the future would look like, particularly the impending dominance of the suburbs, the rise in educational levels, the shift away from blue-collar work, and the importance of professionals. But during Carter's term, he failed to devise a political appeal and set of policies for winning over this future electorate. Carter and his political consultant were ahead of their time. They were presiding over what by then was the inexorable wreck of the New Deal coalition, from which a new progressive centrist coalition was not yet ready to emerge. Carter was faced with continuing racial tensions that divided whites from blacks in the Democratic Party and rising unemployment, along with inflation, that the traditional Democratic tool of deficit spending would only exacerbate. To stem inflation, Carter had the impossible choice of wage-price controls, which had not worked for Nixon, and a Federal Reserve–induced recession, which his own party rejected. Politically, he was pinioned on one side by a rising Republican conservatism, augmented by Washington's business lobbies, that frustrated his attempt to enact even modest reforms, and on the other side by a New Left and labor bloc within the Democratic Party that blamed him for his failure to enact even more ambitious reforms, such as the original Humphrey-Hawkins bill.

As the 1980 election approached, liberals, including some leaders of industrial unions, rallied behind the presidential candidacy of Massachusetts senator Edward Kennedy. Kennedy advocated exactly what Carter refused to champion—a massive government jobs program, comprehensive national health insurance (even though Congress had blocked Carter's modest plan for hospital cost containment), and mandatory price controls. In the primaries, Carter defeated Kennedy—not only because of voters' initial support of Carter during the hostage crisis and their disapproval of Kennedy's abandonment of a drowning woman off Chappaquiddick Island a decade earlier, but also because of public skepticism about Kennedy's programs. Public support for Great Society–style social engineering had disappeared, but Kennedy acted as though it were still there.

Carter's popularity, which was initially buoyed by Kennedy's challenge, began to sag, however, once the fall campaign began. The Iranian hostage crisis raised doubts about the Democrats' willingness to confront third world militants and a Soviet Union that had just invaded Afghanistan. The growing misery index (inflation plus unemployment), combined with higher taxes and deficits, raised doubts, particularly among the white working and middle class, about the Democrats' ability to manage the economy and fed fears that Carter was giving precedence in his policies to minority interests. Reagan's campaign took ample advantage of these fears and doubts. Carter's defeat that fall by Reagan ended the first attempt to build a new kind of Democratic majority.

II. HART, MONDALE, AND JACKSON

After Reagan's victory and the Republican capture of the Senate in 1980, Democratic strategists once again confronted the question of how to regain a majority. In Congress, a group of Democrats—dubbed Atari Democrats for their interest in the "information revolution"—advanced a strategy that would define Democrats as the party of economic growth rather than of economic redistribution and that would remove the label of "tax and spend liberal" that Johnson's presidency, McGovern's candidacy, and Kennedy's primary challenge had hung around the party's neck. A leading member of this dissident group was Colorado senator Gary Hart.

Hart was a product of the politics of the sixties who had learned the hard political lessons of the seventies. After graduating from Yale Law School, he had helped draft environmental legislation for the Johnson administration.[4] In 1972, he managed McGovern's campaign and hired Caddell as McGovern's pollster. McGovern's crushing defeat chastened him. In 1974, when he ran for Senate, his stump speech was entitled "The End of the New Deal." The title was more interesting for what it suggested politically than for its historical accuracy. In his speech, Hart argued against a standard sixties bugaboo, big government, and the alliance between business and government, which characterized at best the first New Deal of 1933–34. In the Senate, Hart became a champion of military reform and of an industrial policy that would encourage new high-tech industries rather than rescue older factories.[5]

In October 1983, Caddell produced another grand analysis, "The State of American Politics." He described a division within the Democratic Party between "its younger baby boom cohort, who came to politics through the antiwar movement and are now coming of age as elected and party leaders, and its older traditional leadership."[6] He noted that "unlike their parents, these people tend to be far more liberal on social issues, more concerned about the environment, skeptical about institutions, but also more conservative on economic issues, e.g., government. . . . The party, ideology, or individual who could mobilize the bulk of this cohort as a base support group could dominate politics for well into the twenty-first century." Caddell called for the creation of "new ideas" that would "eschew the current instinct toward incrementalist problem-solving." These ideas would not be Johnsonesque expansions of government, but "the most vigorous departure from statist government since Franklin Roosevelt's first and second New Deals." What they would actually look like Caddell didn't say.

Caddell's emphasis on generation rather than social group was off-target, as would become obvious in the 1990s. What was important was not just when people were born and what they had experienced growing up, but also the kind of jobs they were filling in the new postindustrial economy. His rejection of the New Deal, like Hart's, was also aimed at the Humphrey-Hawkins advocates of the seventies, but was silent on key programs such as social security or medicare, which were also part of the New Deal tradition. This made his rejection of the New Deal somewhat incoherent and susceptible to misinterpretation. But these failings aside, Caddell, like Hart, was trying to adapt Democratic politics to a new postindustrial society. Caddell's paper provided a framework for Hart's political campaign. Hart, who enlisted Caddell as his adviser, became the candidate of new ideas and of the baby-boom generation.

Hart's main opponent was former vice president Walter Mondale. Initially, Mondale had feared that he would have to face Kennedy in the primaries, so he had cultivated some of the same unorthodox thinkers that Hart had. But when Kennedy declared he would not run, Mondale hastily locked up the endorsement of party regulars and of the AFL-CIO. Emboldened by Democratic victories during the 1982 congressional election, Mondale eschewed new proposals and adopted a standard liberal attack against the unfairness of Reagan conservatism. He promised a jobs program and government aid to Midwestern smokestack industries. And he would later attack Hart for criticizing the government bailout of Chrysler and for rejecting the United Auto Workers' plan to require foreign automakers to produce their cars in the United States. Hart, in turn, attacked Mondale as the candidate of special interests rather than the public interest—which was a key postsixties theme and one that Reagan would later use effectively against Mondale.

Mondale deployed his support from labor-union and party regulars to win the nomination by defeating Hart in the crucial Southern and Midwestern primary states where organization mattered, but the final primary results bore out Caddell's thesis. While the overall electorate was certainly changing, so, too, was the Democratic primary electorate. In the 1984 primaries, over half of the Democrats interviewed in exit polls had at least some college—a figure that is probably too high, but even if substantially discounted, is indicative of serious change in the electorate—and these voters supported Hart over Mondale 39–32 percent.[7] Almost half the voters made $25,000 and over, and this relatively affluent group, too, had preferred Hart to Mondale.[8] And Hart had obliterated Mondale among voters under thirty by 39–26 percent. Mondale's most loyal voters had been those over sixty, union members, and those who did not possess a high school diploma—the voters least likely to be part of the new postindustrial economy. To make matters worse, while Mondale had defeated Hart in the Deep South, Hart had easily defeated Mondale in California, winning two-thirds of its convention delegates. (In northern California, the vanguard of postindustrial society, Hart had won ninety-one delegates to four for Mondale.)

Once Mondale had secured the nomination, he tacked back to the center to lure Hart's voters and the independents who had been attracted to Anderson in 1980. In his convention speech, Mondale focused on the threat of growing deficits and called for a tax increase. Mondale's newfound moderation may have helped him with upscale professionals, among whom he actually did better than Carter in 1980. But pressured by NOW president Eleanor Smeal, who had boasted that "Reagan can be defeated on the woman's vote alone," he gambled by picking an untested woman running mate, Congresswoman Geraldine Ferraro, rather than Hart.[9] Mondale and Smeal were certainly correct in perceiving a shift in women's voting, but their strategy for exploiting it underestimated women's intelligence. Ferraro was not particularly qualified to succeed Mondale as president—she was a second-tier congresswoman with no experience in foreign policy. Ferraro also quickly became embroiled in a scandal concerning her husband's business associations.

The third candidate in 1984 was the Reverend Jesse Jackson, a former Martin Luther King lieutenant who had backed McGovern in 1972 and had co-led the Illinois delegation that had ousted Chicago mayor Richard Daley and the party regulars. Jackson, whose following was largely confined to the black community and the campuses, attempted to craft a New Left message. He wanted to build a "rainbow coalition," but it would not be based on what Kennedy in his 1980 convention speech had called "the cause of the common man and woman." Instead, it would represent what Jackson called "the damned, the desperate, [and] the dispossessed."[10] Jackson's candidacy in 1984—initially fueled by Harold Washington's victory in Chicago—would founder on racial divisions (which he exacerbated in 1984 through his alliance with Nation of Islam head Louis Farrakhan) and on white voters' unwillingness to endorse a radical expansion of Johnson's Great Society that they perceived to be aimed primarily at blacks and inner cities.

In 1988, Jackson ran again, but this time sought to broaden his coalition to include small farmers threatened with foreclosure, gay rights activists, and Midwestern industrial workers whose plants were moving overseas. His platform was again reminiscent of McGovern's—one of his main appeals was to convert military spending into social spending—but he also advocated trade protection against Asian imports. Jackson would ask audiences how many of them owned MX missiles and how many owned Japanese VCRs.[11] Jackson won five primaries in the Deep South, then scored a surprising victory in the Michigan Caucus in March, garnering some support from white UAW members. But once Jackson began to be seen as a genuine presidential candidate and not merely as a protest candidate, his white support deserted him. After Michigan, he would lose every succeeding primary except for predominately black Washington, D.C., to eventual nominee Michael Dukakis.

Jackson's candidacy failed because he was seen as a black activist whose primary allegiance was to African-Americans rather than as a Democratic politician (such as Los Angeles mayor Tom Bradley) who happened to be African-American. Jackson was, as Amiri Baraka wrote in July 1988, "the chief spokesman of the African-American people."[12] White Americans might have reconciled themselves to a politician who was black, but they would not accept a candidate who they believed gave priority to blacks over whites. Jackson was a victim not only of the legacy of racism, but of the identity politics that the American left had encouraged over the prior two decades. And his defeat in 1988 marked his own last attempt at the presidency—and the end of any similar effort to be both a black protest candidate *and* a credible candidate for the nomination. It cleared the way for a candidate who could try to unite black and white working-class Democrats around common objectives.

III. THE FOUNDING OF THE DEMOCRATIC LEADERSHIP COUNCIL

In the 1980s, the task of developing a new strategy eventually fell to an organization of moderate Democrats, the Democratic Leadership Council (DLC), that had been founded in 1985 to counter the embattled Democratic National Committee. The DLC would try to craft a politics and a platform that could overcome the obstacles that Democrats had faced in the 1980s. And the DLC leaders would look for a candidate who could carry out this politics.

The initial impetus for the DLC came from Louisiana congressman Gillis Long, the head of the Democratic Caucus and of its Committee on Political Effectiveness (CPE).[13] The CPE brought together Atari Democrats like Gore, Colorado's Tim Wirth, and Missouri's Richard Gephardt (who would not move sharply left until late 1987) with Southern Democrats like Long who were worried that the party was abandoning the South. Long stressed the importance of gearing Democratic politics to the "national interest" rather than "special interests." He wanted to downplay Democratic support for abortion rights and gun control and emphasize Democratic vigilance on crime and support for basic New Deal reforms and for a strong national defense. The positions of CPE were an interesting hodgepodge of CDM-style restorationism on defense and economics with the Atari Democrats' attention to high technology, free trade, and white-collar workers.

At the 1984 Democratic convention in San Francisco, Long held meetings with Georgia senator Sam Nunn, Arizona governor Bruce Babbitt, Virginia governor Chuck Robb, Gephardt, and others to work out a long-term strategy that could allow the party to survive the coming disaster. After the November election, the talks began to focus on the idea of a new organization that would parallel and rival the Democratic National Committee. When Long died of a heart attack in January 1985, leadership over the project passed to his chief aide, Alvin From. From had backed liberal Democrat Ed Muskie in 1972, but in 1984, disenchanted with the party's direction, he had supported Hart against Mondale. Working with another former House aide, Will Marshall, From pulled together a new organization, the Democratic Leadership

Council, that the two of them staffed, but that was composed of elected officials and financed primarily by Washington business lobbyists who were sympathetic to congressional Democrats. The DLC got going in March of 1985 with forty-three members and with Gephardt as its chair, but almost from the beginning its direction was in the hands of From, Marshall, and Robb, who succeeded Gephardt as chairman in 1986, and of Nunn, who would succeed Robb in 1988.

In a memo to the future DLC members, From had expressed his concern about the Democrats' decline, which he blamed on the "consistent pursuit of wrongheaded, losing strategies."[14] From was particularly critical of Mondale's strategy of "making blatant appeals to liberal and minority interest groups in the hopes of building a winning coalition where a majority, under normal circumstances, simply does not exist." He worried that with union membership declining the Democrats "are more and more viewed as the party of 'big labor,'" and that with liberalism in disrepute, Democrats are "increasingly viewed as the 'liberal' party." From was most at home with Southern Democrats like Nunn, Robb, and Long. He supported social security and other basic New Deal reforms, was concerned about poverty, was committed to civil rights, and wanted a strong defense, but he was also sympathetic to business's view of its problems, hostile or indifferent to labor unions, and opposed to any ambitious new government social programs.

Yet in the DLC's first years, the organization did not seek to sell this politics publicly. Instead, From and the DLC adopted an insiders' factional strategy. They attempted to alter the way presidential nominees were chosen so that someone like Robb would be nominated for president in 1988. Robb could then transform the party in his image. And the DLC did take the first step in its strategy. It got the Democratic Party to schedule an early "Super Tuesday" of Southern primaries that would, presumably, allow a Southern moderate to compete for the party's presidential nomination. But the DLC's strategy completely backfired. Robb didn't run, and Gore, the other Southerner who did, wasn't ready for prime time. Indeed, the big winner on Super Tuesday was the DLC's ultimate political nemesis, Jesse Jackson, who captured five Deep South states, one more than Gore.

The DLC, as well as New Left Democrats, had seen the 1988 election as a prime opportunity to recapture the White House. The Reagan administration was mired in the Iran-contra scandal and financial scandals. Republican nominee George Bush was a weak candidate presiding over what was already becoming a divided party. But the Democrat field, dubbed "the seven dwarfs," was even weaker. Massachusetts governor Michael Dukakis finally won the nomination only because he was the most credible alternative to Jackson. A fiscal moderate, he had no experience in foreign policy at a difficult time when the Cold War looked as if it could be ended through skillful diplomacy. And because of his opposition to capital punishment, his strong civil rights record, and his reliance on Jackson in the fall campaign, Dukakis was vulnerable to the Bush campaign's subtle use of the race card.

After the 1988 fiasco, From, Marshall, and the DLC decided to develop a philosophy and a platform for the Democratic Party. With money raised primarily by Wall Street Democrats, the DLC set up the Progressive Policy Institute (PPI), with Marshall at the helm, and hired policy experts to draft papers and proposals.[15] The most important of these was an 1989 paper entitled "The Politics of Evasion," written by William Galston, Mondale's former issues director, and PPI fellow Elaine Kamarck, who would later become Gore's policy adviser in the first Clinton administration. Galston and Kamarck argued that in the late sixties, the liberalism of the New Deal had degenerated into a "liberal fundamentalism," which "the public has come to associate with tax and spending policies that contradict the interests of average families; with welfare policies that foster dependence rather than self-reliance; with softness toward the perpetrators of crime and indifference toward its victims; with ambivalence toward the assertion of American values and interests abroad; and with an adversarial stance toward mainstream moral and cultural values."[16]

Galston, Kamarck, and the DLC advocated fiscal conservatism, welfare reform, increased spending on crime prevention through the development of a police corps, tougher mandatory sentences, support for capital punishment, and policies that encouraged traditional families. Another PPI fellow, David Osborne, developed a strategy for "reinventing government" by contracting out services while retaining control over how they were performed. Government should "steer, not row" in Osborne's formulation.[17]

The DLC wanted to counter the reputation of the Democrats as the party of "big government" and "tax and spend liberalism" and also as the party that took its cues from black militants. Opposition to capital punishment and to increased spending on police and public safety, for instance, was part of the cluster of issues around race that had driven white voters out of the Democratic Party. Bush had cleverly exploited this cluster during the 1988 campaign against Dukakis. By abandoning these positions, Democrats would be preventing Republicans from using these issues to distract working-class voters from those areas of economic policy where they might agree more with Democrats than with Republicans. Galston and Kamarck spelled this objective out clearly: "All too often the American people do not respond to a progressive economic message, even when the Democrats try to offer it, because the party's presidential candidates fail to win their confidence in other key areas such as defense, foreign policy, and social values. Credibility on these issues is the ticket that will get Democratic candidates in the door to make their affirmative economic case. But if they don't hold that ticket, they won't even get a hearing." From referred to this strategy as "inoculating" Democrats from criticism on other fronts so that they could make their economic case.

But what was that economic case, and to whom would it be made? The DLC's advice about inoculation applied to just about any Democratic economic proposal—from the defense of social security to a proposal for a single-payer national health care system.* Instead, the DLC and PPI argued, the Democratic Party should develop programs that achieved traditional goals, while avoiding charges of "big government." They advocated, for example, using market incentives and penalties to enforce environmental regulation; they wanted to use "managed competition" to hold down health-care costs while broadening access to insurance; they favored charter schools and public school choice (as opposed to private school vouchers) to improve education; they didn't call for large jobs programs, but they wanted more money for worker training; they wanted increases in government spending targeted at creating growth and limited to increases in per capita income.[18]

If the DLC had one overarching ideological creed, it was something like

*Massachusetts congressman Barney Frank would make arguments similar to Galston and Kamarck's in his book *Speaking Frankly* (New York: Thunder's Mouth Press, 1992), but Frank did so in the interests of gaining an audience for the Democrats' more liberal economic proposals.

the communitarian, "national interest" approach first favored by Long. The DLC expressed its proposals in terms of a "new social compact that demands individual responsibility from everyone and ties public benefits to public service." Welfare recipients should seek education and work; students who receive government aid should enroll in a new national service program; and corporations that receive government subsidies should invest in competitiveness and "treat their workers as assets who are partners in productive enterprises."

The DLC and PPI strategists didn't detail the constituencies they were trying to reach. But they were implicitly targeting Caddell's middle-class, white-collar suburbanites, as well as the blue-collar Reagan Democrats that Wattenberg and Scammon had described. They also didn't talk about how a majority would appear on a map, but their focus seemed to be primarily on winning the Midwest and the South for Democrats. The DLC was skeptical about California being the anchor of a new majority—Galston and Kamarck derided this idea as "the California dream." The DLC also didn't put stock in the power of the women's vote to deliver a new majority. Galston and Kamarck wrote that "the gender gap that has opened up in the past twelve years is not the product of a surge of Democratic support among women, but rather the erosion of Democratic support among men."[19] The DLC's 1990 platform didn't even explicitly support abortion rights.

In other words, the DLC didn't yet understand the special role that professionals, women, and minorities would play in the new Democratic majority, nor the central role that California and the Northwest would play. But the DLC and PPI's post-1988 strategy nevertheless represented an enormous step forward for the Democrats. While other Democrats were putting their faith in increased voter turnout or a steep recession to alter their national prospects, From, Marshall, and the organization's members boldly confronted the image of the Democrats as the party of big government and racial favoritism that had led to a string of embarrassing defeats for the party's presidential candidates. And they tried to advance proposals that altered that image but that did not compromise the party's commitment to economic justice and civil rights.

IV. THE THREE FACES OF BILL CLINTON

In March 1990, From succeeded in convincing Bill Clinton to succeed Nunn as chairman of the DLC. From saw Clinton as the DLC's chance to have its own candidate and platform in the 1992 presidential race. A year and a half later, Clinton fulfilled From's wishes—he resigned as DLC chair to run for president, taking several DLC advisers with him and incorporating parts of the DLC's strategy and its themes into his campaign. He championed welfare reform, increased spending on police and public safety, and capital punishment to inoculate himself against Republican attacks. He spoke of a "new covenant" between the people and the government—"a solemn agreement between the people and their government, based not simply on what each of us can take, but what all of us must give to our nation."[20]

But as From had recognized, Clinton's commitment to the DLC was only one part of his complex political makeup. Like many successful politicians, he was a combination of disparate and seemingly contradictory influences that allowed him to appeal to a wide range of constituencies. Clinton was a Southern politician, but of an entirely different lineage from Robb and Nunn.* Raised in humble circumstances and brought up politically in the Democratic Party of a poor state, Clinton was the heir of a Southern-Southwestern populism that had also claimed Lyndon Johnson, Albert Gore Sr., Dale Bumpers, and Oklahoman Fred Harris. He envisaged Democrats as the representatives of the people against the powerful, even if, at times, he acted on behalf of the powerful. When he was first elected to office in 1976 as Arkansas's attorney general, he made his reputation fighting utility-company rate increases.

At the same time, Clinton, who graduated from Georgetown and Yale Law School and attended Oxford as a Rhodes scholar, was a product of the sixties' student movements. In 1972, he volunteered for the McGovern campaign and was sent by Hart to Texas. He remained close to a group

*Robb and Nunn were heirs of the Southern Whig tradition, which had flourished briefly before the battle over slavery and the creation of the Republican Party forced Southerners to embrace the Democratic Party. Even then, the Whigs were the party of business and of class harmony rather than conflict. Nunn was an admirer of Georgia Whig Alexander Stephens. See John B. Judis, "Nunn of the Above," *The New Republic,* October 30, 1995.

of liberal intellectuals who included Robert Reich, Ira Magaziner, Taylor Branch, Eli Segal, and Derek Shearer. And, of course, Hillary Clinton had been part of the same circles. Veterans of the sixties, they brought to the Clinton campaign not only an emphasis on consumer rights, civil rights, the environment, and women's rights, but also a New Left penchant for big government proposals that would cure major social ills. They wanted large-scale public investments in infrastructure and a national health insurance program. They disdained the DLC's concern about deficits and big government.[21] They thought they could use the power of government to transform and revive.

Clinton expressed these different sides of himself during the campaign, but circumstances led to his giving more prominence to the populist, New Deal side than From and the DLC would have wished. Clinton had expected that his main foe in the Democratic primaries would be New York governor Mario Cuomo, a proponent of New Left liberalism. Clinton had expected to parry Cuomo's politics with the DLC's "new Democrat" politics, but Cuomo decided not to run, and the other unreconstructed liberal, Iowa senator Tom Harkin, quickly fell by the wayside. Clinton's main opponent turned out to be former Massachusetts senator Paul Tsongas.

Tsongas's views resembled those of the nonpopulist Clinton. He embraced the DLC's experimental approach to economics and the New Left's commitment on social issues and foreign policy. A Peace Corps veteran, Tsongas had been elected to the House in 1974 from a suburban Massachusetts district that included Route 128's electronics and computer firms. He moved up to the Senate in 1978, but retired in 1984 after he was diagnosed with cancer. Tsongas was, perhaps, the original neoliberal and Atari Democrat. In 1980, he had shocked the audience at an Americans for Democratic Action gathering by urging them to focus on economic growth rather than the redistribution of wealth and by advocating the deregulation of natural gas prices. Tsongas was a strong, almost ideological, fiscal conservative who believed in using market incentives rather than government control to solve economic problems, but he was also an ardent environmentalist and outspoken defender of abortion rights, gay rights, and affirmative action and was a human rights internationalist. Claiming that he had been cured of cancer, Tsongas ran for president in 1992.

Tsongas was running second to Clinton in New Hampshire until the uproar over Clinton's affair with Gennifer Flowers and his exemption from the draft caused the Arkansas governor's popularity to fall. Tsongas won New Hampshire and battled Clinton for the nomination over the next six weeks. To defeat Tsongas, Clinton emphasized his populist streak. Like Mondale in 1984 against Hart, Clinton also ran as a champion of the New Deal. He charged Tsongas with a lack of faith in social security; Clinton promised a large middle-class tax cut, massive public investments, and national health insurance. He avidly courted unions, blacks, and senior citizens. As a result, Clinton won the primaries against Tsongas.

Naturally, this move to the left had made him vulnerable in the general election, as more conservative voters began to see him as another liberal Democrat who would squander their tax money. By mid-June, potential third-party candidate Ross Perot was running ahead of Bush and well ahead of Clinton in national polls. So, during the summer, Clinton set about righting his campaign—first by distancing himself symbolically from Jesse Jackson, then by choosing the more explicitly centrist Gore as his running mate. Clinton still trumpeted his support for women's rights and for the environment, and with the country mired in recession, he continued to promise ambitious new programs in a first "hundred days" that would rival FDR's. But Clinton also emphasized his support for reducing government bureaucracy and for "ending welfare as we know it." In the end, Clinton's campaign was a blend of Caddell revisionism, the DLC, seventies-style Humphrey-Hawkins liberalism, and old-style populism, epitomized by his platform statement, "Putting People First." With a strong assist from Perot's candidacy, which in 1992 took more votes from Bush than from Clinton, the former Arkansas governor reclaimed the White House for the Democrats.

Of course, Clinton had actually gotten a smaller percentage of the popular vote than Dukakis. But Clinton did not heed it as a warning—a mistake for which he, and the party, would pay dearly. The first stumble came over gay rights, as Clinton got drawn into supporting a controversial proposal to allow gays to serve openly in the military. Gay rights did not enjoy the popular support of women's rights, particularly in conjunction with military service. Clinton also backed an economic stimulus package weighted toward poor city neighborhoods, which allowed Republicans to paint Democrats as busting the budget to pay off New York City's

African-American mayor, David Dinkins, for his campaign support. And Clinton postponed welfare reform in favor of a complex, almost unintelligible, plan for national health insurance, which, while relying on the existing health-care system, evoked fears of an overweening government bureaucracy. These proposals did much to alienate voters who had backed either Clinton or Perot in 1992, an alienation that was deepened by the continued sluggishness of the economy. In November 1994, many of them abandoned the Democrats and voted for Republicans, giving the GOP control of the Congress for the first time since the 1953–54 session. (In 1992, almost half of Perot voters had backed Democratic congressional candidates. In 1994, only 32 percent did.[22])

After November 1994, Clinton changed course. Prompted by political consultant Dick Morris, he reverted to the DLC's inoculation strategy. He invoked the "new covenant" in his 1995 State of the Union, and in his 1996 address declared that "the era of big government is over." He committed himself to backing welfare reform and a balanced budget and tried to co-opt the Republican "family values" agenda through supporting school uniforms and a proposal that an antiviolence V-chip be installed in television sets. At the same time, he and the Democrats advanced proposals for raising the minimum wage, extending health insurance coverage, and protecting the environment. These proposals were of a piecemeal, incremental nature that could not easily be labeled "big government."

Clinton's change of course might have proved too little too late, but he was aided by the conservative Republicans who took over Congress after November 1994. They introduced legislation to gut the EPA and the Occupational Safety and Health Administration; to abolish cabinet departments, including the Department of Education (which enjoyed public support except among the religious right); to crack down on immigration; and to cut medicare expenditures while reducing taxes for the wealthy. In the fall of 1995, the Republicans shut down the government to force Clinton to accept these proposals. This action did for Clinton and the Democrats what they might not have been able to do on their own: it united liberal and moderate Democrats, independents, and moderate Republicans behind Clinton and his administration.

In Clinton's 1996 campaign, he was able to bring together all the different sides of his complex political character—and by extension the different strategies for a Democratic majority that had swirled around

Washington for a decade or more. The campaign, buoyed by the strong economic growth that began in early 1996, was a success on multiple fronts, which foreshadowed a Democratic majority. Its strategy and worldview was that of progressive centrism. Clinton the populist—reinforced by an AFL-CIO reinvigorated politically under its new president, John Sweeney—flayed the Republicans for cutting medicare to pay for a tax cut to the wealthy; Clinton the former DLC chairman boasted of reforming welfare and advanced incremental, not "big government" reforms to make higher education affordable, put computers in classrooms, and provide child care and increased access to health care. Clinton the child of the sixties campaigned earnestly for civil rights, women's rights, and the protection of the environment. And Clinton, the tribune of postindustrial America, promised to "build a bridge to the twenty-first century."

The results bore out the strategic insight of Clinton's campaign. He increased his proportion of the vote from 1992 among all the key groups of the emerging Democratic majority: by 9 percent among women, by 4 percent among professionals, by 5 percent among the white working class, by 13 percent among Asians, by 11 percent among Hispanics, and by 10 percent among eighteen-to-twenty-nine-year-olds.[23] In Ohio, Clinton bettered his vote among college-educated whites by 12 percent. In New Jersey, he improved among white working-class voters by 10 percent.[24]

At the beginning of his second term, Clinton set about solidifying Democratic support among these constituencies through a series of reforms in education, health care, child care, and housing. These reforms were incremental, but like Clinton's proposal for extending medicare to younger retirees, they could represent steps toward major reforms. "Quantity would lead to quality," explained Clinton aide Sidney Blumenthal, harking back to Hegel's theory of the dialectic.[25] The new majority seemed there for the taking.

But it was not to be. In January 1998, as Clinton was about to unveil a raft of proposals in his State of the Union address, federal prosecutor Kenneth Starr revealed that Clinton had been having an affair with a White House intern. Clinton, facing calls for resignation from Republican conservatives, was kept off-balance for the next thirteen months and lost what chance he had to put the political synthesis of 1996 into permanent programmatic form. Clinton survived impeachment, thus avoiding Nixon's fate, but on the eve of the 2000 elections Democrats found themselves in precisely the same situation as the Republicans of a generation before. Instead of handing down to his successor a solid majority, Clinton had bequeathed to him a shadow of scandal that dogged his campaign and contributed to his defeat.

V. GORE, GREENBERG, AND PENN

Al Gore was a product of many of the same influences as Bill Clinton. He had been a founding member of the DLC and was the choice of some of its leaders for president in 1988. As a student at Harvard, he had become familiar with, and participated in, the social movements of the sixties, and particularly the environmental movement, for which he later wrote a book, *Earth in the Balance.* And he had inherited his father's populist convictions. But there was an important difference between Clinton and Gore as politicians. Gore had populist convictions, but having been raised as a child of wealth and power in Washington, D.C., he did not come naturally to the style of Jacksonian Democratic populism. He was an intelligent, diligent, but uninspiring congressman, and a wooden campaigner who sounded scripted even when he was extemporizing. Like Clinton, he had different sides and faces, but in public he could only exhibit them over time, and in a manner that made his audience question whether they were seeing the real Al Gore or a campaign contrivance.

In his presidential campaign, which began in early 1999, he shifted every few months from one face and strategy to another. During the first phase of his campaign, Gore relied heavily on New York pollster Mark Penn. Penn had been brought into Clinton's 1996 campaign by Dick Morris. Afterward, Penn had gone back to working for corporations, but the DLC had hired him to do polls and provide strategic analysis. As Gore began running, Penn advised him not to worry about the effect of the Clinton scandals on his campaign. Penn helped to craft a message aimed at white-collar suburbanites, or what he and the DLC now called "wired workers." This message stressed the threat of "suburban sprawl" to a better "quality of life." And it eschewed any hint of populism or class conflict, which Penn argued was antithetical to the spirit of wired workers.

The DLC and Penn had gotten the idea of wired workers from Morley Winograd, an AT&T executive in California who was close to the DLC and would later go to work for Gore. They defined them as workers who "frequently use computers that are part of a network and work together in teams."[26] The DLC claimed these workers had become "the dominant force in the new economy." According to From and Marshall, they "are optimistic about their economic prospects; they are for choice and competition in education and against race and gender preferences; they are impatient with the ideological ax-grinding of the left-right debate; and they favor a smaller, nonbureaucratic form of government activism that equips people to help themselves." From and Marshall also insisted that these workers took umbrage at a politics of "class warfare." "Outdated appeals to class grievance and attacks on corporate perfidy only alienate new constituencies and ring increasingly hollow to the modern workforce."[27]

Like Caddell and Hart, the DLC understood that as the workforce and population were changing, so, too, was the Democratic electorate. And the concept of wired workers was an advance upon Caddell's theory of the baby-boom generation. It described the new constituency not in terms of its age or date of birth, but in terms of its relation to the postindustrial economy. And it also suggested that the Democrats should align themselves with the country's future rather than its past. But the category itself had little explanatory value because there was no evidence that "wired workers"—who ranged from a telemarketer in West Virginia to an airline clerk in Springfield, Missouri, to an insurance executive in Hartford to a computer programmer in Redmond—were making political judgments based on their using computers, being part of a computer network, or working together as part of a team. If anything, the term blurred the important distinction between professionals and managers—and between workers who were inclined to question the imperatives of the market and those who were not.

By October 1999, Gore believed that Penn's strategy was not working. He trailed Bush by 19 percent in one opinion poll and had lost his lead to his Democratic challenger, former senator Bill Bradley, in Iowa and New Hampshire. And to make matters worse, Bradley and Bush seemed to have hurt Gore by linking him repeatedly to the Clinton scandals. Gore fired Penn and hired Harrison Hickman, a more conventionally liberal pollster. Gore also enlisted former Kennedy speechwriter Bob Shrum, who had written Kennedy's paean to New Left liberalism at the 1980 Democratic convention.

Gore now adopted the same strategy against Bradley that Mondale had used against Hart and that Clinton had used against Tsongas. He defended Democratic orthodoxy and the party's most loyal constituencies. His campaign manager, Donna Brazille, described these groups as "the four pillars of the Democratic Party . . . African-Americans, labor, women, and what I call other ethnic minorities."[28] Gore adopted a highly mannered populism, repeating the verb *fight* and looking stern and determined. Gore declared that he would "fight for the people against the powerful." He described "the presidency" as "a long, resolute, day-by-day fight for people." He accused Bradley of undermining medicaid and tried to outbid him in his support for gay rights and gun control. The strategy worked for Gore, as it had for Mondale in 1984. He secured the AFL-CIO's endorsement in October and, with solid support from union members and blacks, defeated Bradley for the nomination.

But having vanquished Bradley, Gore found himself once more trailing Bush. And so, like Mondale and Clinton before him, his initial reaction was to grasp for the center. He attacked Bush's tax program as a "risky" threat to the fiscal health of the country and promised to maintain the budget surplus even in the face of a recession. In June 2000, he launched a "prosperity and progress" tour to remind voters of what two terms with Clinton and Gore had brought. But this time the trick didn't work. A month had passed and Gore was still consistently trailing Bush, with a double-digit deficit in many opinion polls.

That's when Gore brought Stan Greenberg on board.[29] Greenberg, a former Yale political scientist, had been the pollster for Clinton's 1992 campaign. He remained with Clinton and the DNC until after the 1994 November election, when Clinton fired him—reportedly because he blamed Greenberg for not warning him about the looming public opposition to his health-care bill. Afterward, Greenberg went to work for foreign candidates, including Britain's Tony Blair and Israel's Ehud Barak, but he continued to write about American politics and what the Democrats should do. Greenberg's priority for the Democrats was winning back the white working class. He recognized that Democrats would win votes among minorities, professionals, and women, but he thought that without substantial support from the white working class, Democrats could not win elections. Greenberg had written, "Democrats cannot aspire to dominate this period and lead the country unless they can reinvent their links with and regain the confidence of downscale voters—working- and middle-class voters—who want nothing more complicated than a better life."[30]

Greenberg, who had done polling for the DLC, agreed with Galston and Kamarck that to reach white working-class voters, Democrats had to counter the perception of the party that Republicans had fostered and some Democrats had reinforced. Greenberg believed that Clinton's victory in 1992 was due in large part to his support for "values" issues such as welfare reform, but he worried that Clinton's affair with Monica Lewinsky had "once again identified" the party with "1960s-style irresponsibility."[31] Greenberg also believed that to reach these voters, Democrats had to embrace a populist message that identified Democrats as the party that stands up for workers "who are vulnerable to the whims of more powerful forces in society."[32] Greenberg certainly had history on his side. Democrats from Andrew Jackson to Franklin Roosevelt to Bill Clinton had effectively used such populist appeals to win the support of working-class voters.

Greenberg advised Gore to use his biography, particularly his service in Vietnam, to counteract voters' identification of him with the Clinton scandals, to steer clear of Clinton himself, and to underplay his support for issues like gun control and abortion that could alienate working-class voters.[33] Gore followed this strategy. Given the opportunity in the debates to attack Bush's support in Texas for carrying concealed weapons or his cavalier administration of the death penalty, Gore held back and equivocated. Gore also made a point of distancing himself from Clinton and even from the administration's accomplishments. Gore's reluctance to use Clinton as a campaigner may have won him votes in some parts of the country, but probably lost him at least Arkansas.[34]

Greenberg also recommended that Gore resume the populist rhetoric of the primary campaign, but without committing himself to any large government programs. Gore's convention speech did exactly this. He said of the Republicans, "They're for the powerful, and we're for the people." Gore promised to "stand up and say no" to "big tobacco, big oil, the big polluters, the pharmaceutical companies, the HMOs." After the convention speech, Gore suddenly sped past Bush in the opinion polls and remained ahead for more than a month—until the fateful debates, when his personal limitations as a candidate shone through.

Gore's defeat was the narrowest ever—and made even more so by the third-party candidacy of the Green Party's Ralph Nader. Nader, who played a key role in founding the modern consumer and environmental movements, decided to run in 2000 as the candidate of the tiny Green Party. Unlike Jackson in 1988 or Perot in 1992, Nader was not running to win, but to register his disapproval of Clinton and Gore, whom he believed had betrayed the left liberal cause. He also hoped to gain the Green Party ballot status in the 2004 election by securing 5 percent of the vote nationally. Nader succeeded at least partially in his first objective. He not only won attention from the media, but he actually cost Gore the election by providing Bush's margin of victory in Florida and New Hampshire and by forcing Gore to divert precious resources in the last weeks of his campaign to states like Minnesota and Oregon that, in the absence of Nader, Gore would have been assured of winning easily.

In the end, though, Nader failed to attain the 5 percent that he and the Green Party sought, getting only 2.7 percent of the vote. Which is one reason why Nader's campaign in 2000 probably spelled the end of his political career and of similar efforts by his supporters. Many of Nader's youthful followers did not understand how American politics worked. They believed that they could build an American Green Party similar to the European parties. But the American presidential system has always encouraged two major parties and discouraged third parties, except as spoilers. The major parties do not represent a single unified philosophy. They are coalitions of constituencies and views. Those who attempt to build a party of uniform conviction invariably suffer disillusionment, as Nader's followers did in 2000, and either withdraw from politics or adopt a more realistic view of how change is made.

VI. THE NEW SYNTHESIS

In his December 1976 memo, Caddell described the need for a "synthesis" of views and strategies: "I think it can be argued clearly that we are at one of those points in time, when—as Marx or Hegel would have argued—neither the thesis nor the antithesis really works. We need a synthesis of ideas."[35] In the wake of Gore's defeat, Democratic strategists brought forward thesis and antithesis, but not a new synthesis. They insisted that the Democrats were faced with stark and opposing choices in what direction to take. But behind these polarities lay a rough kind of synthesis.

The DLC and Penn blamed Gore's loss on his adoption of a populist appeal in the last months of the campaign. "Gore chose a populist rather than a New Democrat message," From wrote. "As a result, voters viewed him as too liberal and identified him as an advocate of big government. Those perceptions . . . hurt him with male voters in general and with key New Economy swing voters in particular. By emphasizing class warfare, he seemed to be talking to Industrial Age America, not Information Age America."[36]

Penn wrote that Gore "missed the new target of the twenty-first century: the wired workers." He failed to reach "middle-class, white suburban males, many of whom had voted for Clinton in the past." Gore's "old-style message sent him tumbling in key border states . . . they were turned off by populism."[37] According to Penn, "Clinton fatigue" was not a "key factor that cost Al Gore the presidency . . . postelection polls showed little evidence of such a phenomenon." In other words, the legacy of the Clinton scandals did not hurt Gore's candidacy. What hurt him was his populist rhetoric, which cost him votes among wired workers, and in particular middle-class, white suburban males.

Greenberg took the antithesis. He blamed Gore's defeat primarily on the decline of the Democratic vote among white working-class voters, particularly white working-class men. According to Greenberg, they backed Bush rather than Gore because they didn't trust Gore—a sentiment traceable to the Clinton scandals—and because they rejected Gore's stands in favor of gun control and abortion. They were not put off by Gore's populism. On the contrary, it was a major reason that many of them backed him.[38]

Who was right? In explaining Gore's defeat, Greenberg's analysis was much closer to the truth. In the border states like Missouri and West Virginia, and in the states like Ohio, Arkansas, and Louisiana that Clinton had won in 1996, but Gore lost in 2000, Gore lost votes compared to 1996 primarily among the white working-class rather than among "middle-class, white suburban males." For instance, in Missouri, Clinton won working-class white men by 3 percent in 1996, while Gore lost the same voters by 25 percent, a swing of 28 percent against the Democrats. In contrast, Clinton lost college-educated white men by 8 percent in 1996, while Gore lost the same voters by 15 percent, a much smaller anti-Democratic swing of just 7 percent. Gore lost Missouri in the working-class north and southeast, not in the affluent St. Louis or Kansas City suburbs.

Gore didn't lose support among these voters because of his populist rhetoric. In some states, such as West Virginia and Kentucky, Gore lost votes because of his specific stands on the environment, tobacco, and coal. Many rural and small-town voters objected to Gore's support for gun control. And in most of the states, the single most important reason for voting against Gore was distrust of him stemming in large part from the Clinton administration scandals.

Greenberg backed up this analysis with an extensive postelection poll conducted among 2,036 respondents. When he asked respondents their three main reasons for not voting for Al Gore, 29 percent cited his "exaggerations and untruthfulness," 20 percent his "support for legalizing the union of gay couples," 19 percent his "pro-abortion position," and 17 percent his "being too close to Bill Clinton." Among white, non-college-educated male voters, 31 percent cited Gore's untruthfulness, 29 percent cited his "antigun positions," and 21 percent cited his being too close to Clinton. In other words, their doubts stemmed from the Clinton scandals and Gore's position on gun control. When Greenberg asked these voters what three factors most contributed to their voting, or considering voting, for Gore, the one that far outnumbered all the others—mentioned by 49 percent of these respondents—was his New Deal–style "promise to protect social security and add a prescription-drug benefit for seniors."[39]

Moreover, there is little evidence that white, suburban, college-educated voters were put off by Gore's populist rhetoric. According to Greenberg's poll, only 10 percent of white, college-educated male voters said that Gore's populist attacks had contributed to their doubts about him—an even lower percentage than the 13 percent of working-class white men who said they were put off by Gore's populist attacks. These figures seem paradoxical until you remember that many of these college-educated voters are white-collar professionals whose positions have put them in conflict with market imperatives—a fact that is entirely obscured by categories like "wired workers." What primarily drove these voters away from Gore was distrust of him stemming from the scandals. Gore's "untruthfulness" was cited by 38 percent of white, college-educated male voters as a reason for not voting for him; no other reason came close.

Greenberg was mostly right about why Gore lost, and the DLC and Penn were mostly wrong, and Greenberg was also right earlier in his insistence that populism—understood broadly to be the party's identification with the "common man and woman" and its defense of their interests against the powerful—was essential to the Democratic majority. Indeed, it has been a defining difference between Democrats and Whigs, and then Democrats and Republicans, since the 1830s.

But while the DLC and Penn were wrong about 2000, they were ultimately right about where the party's future lies. It may not lie in "wired workers," which is much too vague an appellation, but it does lie in the new workforce of postindustrial America and in the fast-growing metropolitan areas where they live and work. The key for Democrats will be in synthesizing Greenberg and Penn—in discovering a strategy that retains support among the white working class, but also builds support among college-educated professionals and others in America's burgeoning ideopolises. To do that, they don't have to choose between a populist politics and a politics that emphasizes the "quality of life." They can do both, as Clinton began to demonstrate in 1996, but as Gore failed to in 2000, largely because of factors that had nothing to do with the appeal of his politics. The Democrats' future, and the promise of its new majority, lies in the rough synthesis represented by this progressive centrism.

CHAPTER FIVE

The Tenuous Case for a Republican Majority

Some political strategists argue that what is most likely over the next decade is a new Republican majority. Karl Rove, Bush's political director, has compared the Bush presidency to that of William McKinley and the election of 2000 to the election of 1896:

> Under Rove's theory, America is experiencing a "transformational" era comparable to the Industrial Revolution more than a century ago. He sees parallels to the election of 1896, when Republican governor William McKinley of Ohio—"a natural harmonizer," according to one admirer—rode to victory on a belief that the GOP could no longer base its appeal on old divisions from the Civil War because the nation had utterly changed. Today, Rove argues, the "new economy," based on technology, information, and entrepreneurship, is again transforming America, along with a new wave of immigrants from Latin America, Asia, and elsewhere. And the country is eager for a new leader who will, in Bush's inelegant phrase, be a "uniter, not a divider"—just like McKinley was.[1]

Rove sees Bush as the candidate of the "new economy," and his victory in 2000 as a harbinger of the kind of thirty-four-year Republican majority that McKinley initiated.

What are the grounds for believing that this kind of a new Republican majority is imminent? And are any of them valid? The most widely cited proponent of Rove's view is journalist Michael Barone, the lead author of the biannual *Almanac of American Politics.* Barone makes a case that while Republicans and Democrats currently divide up the electorate evenly, the country is moving toward what he calls the "Bush nation."

Barone sees religious observance as a primary difference between Republicans and Democrats. The Bush and Gore voters, he writes, represent "two nations of different faiths. One is observant, tradition-minded, moralistic; the other is unobservant, liberation-minded, relativist."[2] He sees a parallel difference in the two parties' view of markets, choice, and government. The 2000 election, he writes, was "a contest between more choice and more government." Barone argues that in both respects, Bush's views will eventually prevail. "Demography is moving, slowly, toward the Bush nation," he writes.

Barone's argument and those of like-minded Republican strategists can be broken down into three assertions: first, that the growth of the population, based on the 2000 election and census, will favor the Republicans rather than the Democrats; second, that the trends in religious observance and belief favor the Republicans rather than the Democrats; and third, that the trends in economic philosophy and practice favor the Republicans rather than the Democrats. We will consider each of these arguments in turn.

The September 11 terrorist attack has produced a fourth argument for a Republican majority. Most Democrats, as well as Republicans, have acknowledged that the administration's success in prosecuting the war against terror has benefited Bush, and by extension, Republicans in Congress. But some Republican conservatives argue that the war against terror has permanently altered the policy agenda in Washington and has created the opportunity for Bush to redraw the boundaries between the parties. David Brooks wrote in *The Weekly Standard* that Bush had gained an opportunity to turn the Republicans into the "party of patriotism" and to occupy the political center by relegating the party's "cultural warriors" and business lobbyists to the sidelines.[3] By doing this, Bush could regain the moderates and independents who deserted the party in the 1990s. If he could also retain the religious conservatives, he could have a version of the Reagan majority, but with a somewhat different center of gravity.

I. THE PARTIES AND THE POPULATION

Barone argues that demography favors the "Bush nation" because Republicans enjoy an advantage in "the fastest-growing parts of the United States." Barone is absolutely right: in the fifty counties that grew the fastest during the 1990s, Bush averaged 62 percent of the vote compared to 33 percent for Gore. But the Republican advantage in these counties doesn't suggest that there will be a growing Republican advantage in the electorate as a whole. Most of these pro-Bush counties are relatively small, and their rate of growth is less significant than their actual numbers, which pale before the growth of larger metropolitan counties. And as they become more densely populated over the decades, these "edge" or "collar" counties, initially populated by rural émigrés, will tend to become more Democratic and less Republican.

Barone's argument takes advantage of a simple mathematical fact: it is easier for a county to grow fast when it starts from a smaller base. Elbert County, Colorado, which was the third-fastest-growing county, doubled in size in the nineties from under 10,000 to just under 20,000. It went for Bush 69–26 percent. The fifth-fastest-growing county was Park County, Colorado, which doubled from 7,000 to 14,000, and supported Bush 55–36 percent. Boise County, Idaho, the ninth-fastest-growing, went from 3,500 to 6,700, and Bush won it 66–24 percent. But the picture changes completely if you consider the fifty counties with the largest population growth. In these counties, Gore won 54–42 percent overall, with 3 percent going to Nader. These large-growth counties average 1.46 million in size compared to an average of 109,000 for the fifty fastest-growth counties. This difference in size means that Gore came out of the fifty largest-growth counties with a 2.7-million-vote lead, compared to Bush's margin of half a million from the fifty fastest-growing counties.

Moreover, the Democrats are also gaining ground in a number of still-Republican large-growth counties that are losing their rural character and becoming more tightly integrated into metropolitan areas. The elder George Bush carried California's San Bernadino County, the eleventh-largest-growth county, by 21 percent in 1988; his son carried it by only two points, 49–47. In 1988, George Bush carried Maricopa County, Arizona, the largest-growth county in the United States, by 65–34 percent;

in 2000, his son's margin was down to just 53–43, a swing of 21 percentage points toward the Democrats. Bush senior carried Clark County, Nevada, the thirteenth-fastest-growing county, and the third largest in actual population increase, 56–41 percent in 1988. Gore defeated George W. Bush 51–45 percent in Clark County in 2000. The trends in these large-growth counties are the likely future of many fast-growth counties as they become larger and go through the same metropolitan integration process.

What Barone's numbers really show is that Bush and the Republicans enjoy an advantage in rural areas and in counties that are being formed primarily by white émigrés from rural areas. And because nonmetro or rural counties make up about three-fourths of all counties, and occupy about four-fifths of the land area in the United States, this creates an impression of Republican geographical dominance. But these counties don't include enough people, and when they do, they start to become less Republican. If American history were running in reverse, and if the country were becoming a primarily rural nation again, then the Republicans would enjoy a distinct demographic advantage. But history continues to run in the exact opposite direction. Rural America is shrinking—its share of the country's population down a hefty 17 percent over the last four decades—and densely populated metropolitan America is growing.[4] And so are Democratic chances.

As we already noted in chapter 2, Democrats benefit from other prominent population trends. Two of the fastest-growing parts of the population are Hispanic and Asian minorities, both of whom have tended to vote Democratic. The major occupations projected to grow the fastest in this decade are professionals and low-level service workers, both of whom have tilted Democratic. Among women, the proportions of working women, single women, and highly educated women, all of whom tend to vote heavily Democratic, are growing, while the least Democratic group, married homemakers, is shrinking. All in all, demography is moving toward a Democratic majority.

II. OBSERVANT REPUBLICANS

Barone also argues that religious observance separates Republicans from Democrats and implies that this division favors Republicans over the next decade. According to exit polls, Bush won the support of voters who say they attend church more than weekly by 63–36 and voters who say they attend church weekly by 57–40. And these voters make up 43 percent of the electorate. According to a study by John C. Green and other political scientists, Bush defeated Gore among "more observant" evangelical Protestants 84–16 percent and among "more observant" Roman Catholics 57–43 percent.[5] If one assumes that these groups are growing as a percentage of the electorate, then Bush and the Republicans should be in good shape for years to come.

But this assumption is not warranted. Surveys of religious attitudes and church attendance are notoriously inaccurate. As sociologists Penny Long Marler and C. Kirk Hadaway have demonstrated, Americans exaggerate their church attendance when asked by pollsters.* But even leaving aside the question of exaggeration, there is reason to believe that Americans as a whole are not as strongly devout as conservative evangelicals

*In a 1993 article for the *American Sociological Review,* "What the Polls Don't Show: A Closer Look at U.S. Church Attendance," Marler and Hadaway, along with Mark Chaves, found that Protestants in an Ohio county and Catholics in eighteen dioceses around the country were exaggerating by almost 100 percent their church attendance. In Ohio's Ashtabula County, they found, for instance, that "among Protestants, 19.8 percent attended a church workshop . . . during a typical week in 1992, compared to 35.8 percent who said they attended." Challenged and heavily criticized, Marler and Hadaway repeated the experiment at a large Protestant evangelical congregation in the Deep South. This time, they literally counted who attended and found the same results ("Testing the Attendance Gap in a Conservative Church," *Sociology of Religion,* 1999). While 70 percent of the church's parishioners said they attended a service, only 40 percent actually did. In a communication with the authors, Hadaway suggested on the basis of several studies they have done that the gap in reporting wasn't as wide forty or fifty years ago as it is now. This suggests that the decline in church attendance from that period to the present is probably even steeper than it appears. It also sheds light on a problem in current polling. In exit polling, the VNS survey, which asks cursory and limited questions in a public space where normative influences can be particularly strong, seems much more likely to have elicited exaggerated responses about attendance than the more careful and detailed questions asked by the National Election Study and the National Opinion Research Center. For this reason, we attach more credence to the latter than the former in assessing the level of religious observance in the United States.

claim and that over the last decades they have become less rather than more devout. While Bush did better than Gore among those who said they attended church weekly or more, even according to the unusually high VNS figures, they made up only a bit over two-fifths of the electorate in 2000.[6] Each of the groups in the less observant three-fifths of voters—those who said they attended church a few times a month, a few times a year, or never—preferred Gore over Bush, with support particularly strong among never-attenders, who gave Gore a 61–32 percent margin.

Moreover, in surveys taken over the last thirty years, it is the ranks of those who never or rarely attend church that have grown the most. According to a National Opinion Research Center (NORC) study, those who said they never attended church or attended less than once a year went from 18 percent in 1972 to 30 percent in 1998. Confirming this latter figure, the National Election Study found that those who say they never attended was at 33 percent of the citizenry and 27 percent of voters in 2000.[7] This group is about twice the size of those who identify themselves as members of the religious right and has tended to vigorously support Democrats rather than Republicans.

Some of the growth in the nonattenders came out of the mainline Protestant churches. In the seventies and eighties, white evangelical Protestants, the group out of which the religious right came, grew considerably in both numbers and proportion. But in the nineties, this group did not grow as a percentage of the electorate. According to an extensive survey by John C. Green and other political scientists, white evangelicals accounted for 25 percent of the electorate in 1992 and 26 percent in 2000, a statistically meaningless difference.[8] Those who identify themselves as members of the religious right (another highly subjective, but suggestive, designation) fell from 17 percent of the electorate in 1996 to 14 percent in 2000. And according to sociologist David Leege, the proportion of observant Catholics—one of the Bush campaign's targeted groups—also dropped during the 1990s.[9] In other words, trends among the religious do not favor Republicans over Democrats. If anything, they favor Democrats.

Republican strategists don't like to say so aloud, but Republicans have paid a heavy price for their avid support from the religious right. As members of the Christian Coalition and other groups have gained strength and controlled nominations or taken over state parties, they have tended to drive out old-guard and moderate Republicans. Divisions among Republicans in some congressional and state races have allowed Democrats to win seats that had long been held by Republicans. Perhaps the most vivid example is in Kansas's third congressional district, which until 1998 had always been held by Republicans. The district is dominated by the suburbs outside Kansas City, which includes upscale moderates from Overland Park, many of whom work for high-tech firms like Sprint, and ex-rural religious conservatives from the edge city of Olathe.[10] In 1996, a conservative Republican backed by the Christian Coalition won the seat. He quickly alienated the moderate Republicans in Overland Park, who were up in arms over an attempt by the religious right to impose the teaching of creationism on Kansas's public schools. In 1998, these voters, along with the voters from Lawrence, where the University of Kansas is located, swung the election to a moderate Democrat, Dennis Moore. In 2000, Moore was reelected when Republicans nominated another religious-right candidate over a moderate in the primary.

Even in the Deep South, where the religious right has bolstered the Republican Party, moderate Democrats have sometimes been able to defeat Republicans who were closely identified with the religious right. In 1996, Democrat Jim Hunt easily won the North Carolina gubernatorial election after the Republicans, in a bitter primary battle, chose Christian Coalition candidate Robin Hayes over a moderate. In Georgia, Democrat Zell Miller won the governor's office in 1994—a heavy Republican year—after a Christian right candidate won the Republican nomination in a primary against a moderate. In Alabama, Democrat Don Siegelman won the governor's office in 1998 against Christian right Republican Fob James. In all these cases, Democrats were able to create a coalition that included upscale white moderates who had been voting Republican, but who were unwilling to back a candidate of the religious right.

III. THE FREE MARKET PARTY

Conservative Republicans from Goldwater to Mississippi senator Trent Lott have always championed a laissez-faire theory of the government and the economy. They have blamed government intervention for whatever economic ills the country suffers. As Reagan put it in his 1981 inaugural address, "Government is not the solution to our problems; government is the problem." Conservative Republicans have called for the deregulation of industry, the privatization of government functions, including social security, and the dispersal of government funds to the private sector through tax cuts. Republican strategists believe that this laissez-faire philosophy could still be the basis of a new majority. Barone thinks such an approach is "in line with the increasingly decentralized character of American society."[11] Republican speechwriter Daniel Casse, writing in *Commentary* after the 2000 election, concurs, arguing that Republican proposals to privatize social security and to eliminate federal control of medicare will eventually be the basis for a new majority. Asks Casse, "For how long will voters abide Democratic leaders who remain steadfastly against any use of private accounts for social security?"[12]

Barone, Casse, and the Republican strategists really raise different kinds of questions. First, are these free market policies of deregulation and privatization as popular as the authors make out? Are Americans increasingly supportive of proposals for privatizing social security or reining in the Environmental Protection Agency? Second, will these proposals, if enacted, accomplish what their proponents claim? Will privatization rescue the social security system from the threat of insolvency and put more money in retired Americans' pockets? A policy need not work to get politicians elected; but it has to show results to get them reelected and to secure more than a fleeting majority for their party. Yet on both of these counts, the Republican argument for a laissez-faire majority fails to be convincing.

American support for laissez-faire rather than interventionist government policies has gone in cycles like the economy. By the late 1970s, continued stagflation and rising tax bills had undermined support for the interventionist policies advocated by the Carter administration and the even more ambitious programs advanced by liberal Democrats like Ted Kennedy. A growing number of Americans had come to believe that government intervention had caused the stagflation of the late 1970s. The change in opinion was captured in the Harris Poll. In September 1973, only 32 percent of Americans agreed that "the best government is the government that governs the least"; by February 1981, 59 percent agreed (see chart). They were willing to give Reagan's program of privatization and deregulation a chance to work.

"The Best Government Is the Government That Governs the Least"

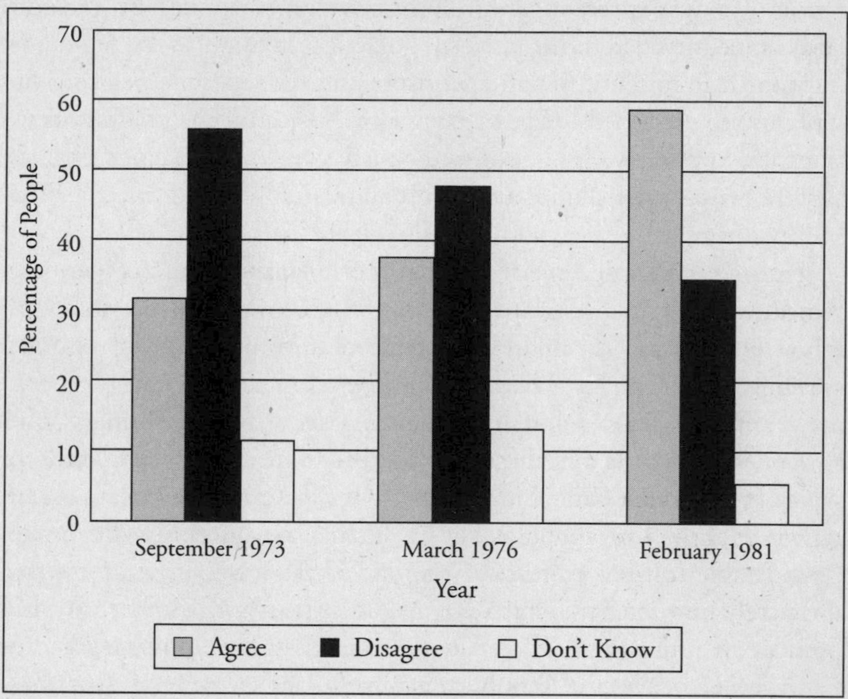

Source: William G. Mayer, *The Changing American Mind: How American Public Opinion Changed Between 1960 and 1988* (Ann Arbor, Mich.: University of Michigan Press, 1992).

The Reagan-era policies—if those of the Federal Reserve are included—did finally end the stagflation and helped restore business's incentive to invest, but by the end of Reagan's second term, these policies had also led to massive budget and trade deficits and to a series of squalid business scandals, topped off by the savings-and-loan collapse. By the late eighties, the public had become disillusioned with the conservative Republican approach. The reaction showed up most clearly in a dramatic increase in how many people thought the government was doing "too little" to protect the environment, improve the nation's health, and the country's educational system. In 1980, for instance, 48 percent thought the government was doing too little to protect the environment; by 1988, after two terms of conservative Republican rule, 65 percent believed the government was doing too little.[13] In 1980, 53 percent thought we were spending too little on education; by 1988, it had climbed to 64 percent. In 1988, 66 percent thought we were spending too little on "improving and protecting the nation's health," up from 55 percent in 1980. The reaction also showed up in a growing identification of conservative laissez-faire policies with subservience to business lobbyists—a perception that Perot and Clinton would exploit in the 1992 campaign.*

The precipitous decline in popularity of Reagan-era policies began a five-year comedy of political errors. In 1993, Clinton misread the public's opposition to laissez-faire conservatism as strong support for public spending and enthusiastic backing for an extensive health-care program. Some simpleminded polling questions did show overwhelming public support for a national health insurance program. But other questions, which included the kind of drawbacks that were eventually raised about the program—from higher taxes to greater bureaucracy—did reveal considerable softness in public support. These misgivings, of course, ultimately undermined Clinton's health-care plan and, quite nearly, his presidency. Similarly, after voters repudiated Clinton and the Democrats in November 1994, the Republicans misread the victories of their congressional candidates as enthusiastic support for laissez-faire conservatism. They soon discovered they, too, were sorely mistaken.

By the 1996 election, it had become abundantly clear that the public opposed both a revival of Great Society–style social engineering and laissez-faire conservatism. Instead, as the Clinton administration recognized, the public backed a more incremental approach to improving health-care delivery and insurance and to strengthening existing environmental and consumer regulations. They wanted more money spent on social needs, but they wanted it spent carefully. Indeed, in an extensive

*Lee Atwater, George Bush's campaign manager and later chairman of the Republican National Committee, recognized the problem as early as 1985. In a symposium on "baby-boom politics," Atwater warned that the Republicans were in danger of losing this generation of voters. "What we as Republicans have always got to be aware of is that they're also anti-big-business, and if we once again become viewed as the party that caters solely to big business, we would be in trouble with this group," Atwater said. See David Boaz, ed., *Left Right and Baby Boom: America's New Politics* (Washington, D.C.: Cato Institute, 1986).

1998 poll, 73 percent of the public thought the government was not spending enough on education, 70 percent thought it was spending too little on health care, and 65 percent thought it was unduly ignoring the environment.[14]

Perhaps the clearest public endorsement of regulatory capitalism came in the 2000 campaign when Republican candidates discovered that they, too, would have to profess support for new government regulations even if they had no intention of enacting them. When Gore accused George W. Bush at the last presidential debate of not supporting "a strong national patients' bill of rights," Bush responded, "Actually, Mr. Vice President, it's not true. I do support a national patients' bill of rights. As a matter of fact, I brought Republicans and Democrats together to do just that in the state of Texas, to get a patients' bill of rights through." In point of fact, the Texas bill had passed over Bush's opposition, and once in office as president Bush would oppose a similar bill.

Even the most conservative Republicans embraced regulatory capitalism. Missouri Republican senator John Ashcroft had fought attempts to regulate HMOs and to include prescription-drug coverage in medicare. He was a darling of the health and drug industry lobbyists. Yet in his campaign for reelection in 2000, facing a moderate and popular Democratic governor, Ashcroft ran as a *proponent* of a patients' bill of rights and a foe of the drug companies. "John Ashcroft stood up to the drug companies for unfair drug prices," one campaign commercial intoned. Ashcroft recognized that the public itself no longer supported the conservatives' laissez-faire agenda.

Casse and other Republicans insist that the public does support privatization of social security, but they couldn't be more mistaken. They are relying on the same kind of misinterpretation of polling data that convinced Clinton and the Democrats in 1993 that they could press ahead with a bold national health-insurance plan. For example, the Cato Institute, which is funded by the same securities firms that would enjoy a windfall from privatization, has conducted surveys that purportedly show Americans back privatization by more than two to one. But these surveys simply ask questions like "How likely would you be to support social security privatization if it allowed you to take your social security money and invest it in a retirement account of your choosing?"[15] Such surveys fail to ask respondents the questions other surveys do: whether they would support privatization if it resulted in reduced guaranteed benefits, lower overall benefits, or higher taxes—all of which could happen because of reduced payroll tax revenues, the transition costs of a new system, and the vagaries of the stock market. In just one recent example, when the American Association for Retired Persons asked respondents whether they would favor the chance to invest part of their payroll taxes, 54 percent said that they would; when asked if they would still favor privatization if that meant lower guaranteed benefits from the government, only 42 percent backed privatization.[16]

The Republicans also contend that there is widespread public support for a voucher-based system for medicare. Under such a system, seniors would get a set amount from medicare and then have to shop around among a number of basic plans for their health insurance. If they wanted a better plan than the ones available at the base amount, they would have to pay extra to get it. But advocates, who say that consumers will embrace the system because it gives them more choice, use the same kind of tendentious polling evidence to make their case. They cite questions such as this one, which Republican pollsters John McLaughlin and Associates asked: "Should senior Americans have the right to choose between different health-care plans with different benefits just like members of Congress and federal employees?" Unsurprisingly, the public is overwhelmingly supportive of such an idea.

But any attempt to put this proposal in a realistic context that mentions something besides choice—that turning medicare into a voucher system would strictly limit the amount medicare would contribute to recipients, that recipients might be financially penalized if they wanted to continue standard medicare fee-for-service coverage and not move into an HMO, and that they might have to pay more money out of pocket for their health expenses—results in a precipitous drop in support.[17] Indeed, it is difficult to find realistic descriptions of the medicare choice idea that elicit more than about one-third support from the public. The laissez-faire agenda is no more popular in the area of health—probably less—than it is in the area of retirement.

If support for laissez-faire and regulatory capitalism goes in cycles, we are, if anything, at the end of a period in which laissez-faire has reigned, and at the beginning of a new period in which greater government intervention will occur. Barone argues that the onset of postindustrial capitalism inspires laissez-faire approaches, but in the late nineties, the contrary was true. In Bush's first eighteen months, the onset of a recession and of a war against terrorism has strengthened support for government spending, while the electricity crisis in California and the Enron scandal have put Republican proponents of continued deregulation and privatization on the defensive.

That has become evident even for tax cuts—always a key part of the Republican argument for shrinking government. Bush's tax cut that passed in August 2001 contributed to his falling popularity prior to the war. In the November 2001 gubernatorial elections in New Jersey and Virginia, the Republican candidates promised to cut taxes while accusing their Democratic opponents of being tax-and-spenders. In Virginia, Mark Earley promised to continue eliminating the state's car tax and to veto a referendum in the northern-Virginia suburbs to determine whether local taxes should be raised to improve the area's transportation system. In New Jersey, Bret Schundler promised to eliminate the tolls on the Garden State Parkway. But in the light of falling revenues and growing social needs, voters repudiated both candidates. A *Washington Post* poll showed four-to-one support in northern Virginia for a tax referendum.[18]

In the late 1970s, many citizens believed that they were paying high taxes for programs they didn't want. In the early part of this new century, many citizens believe that their states are suffering from insufficient revenues to pay for programs in health care, transportation, and education that they do want. In the 2001 elections, eleven of twelve states passed referenda approving infrastructure spending proposals.[19]

IV. THE PARTY OF PATRIOTISM

George W. Bush and the Republicans can't build a new majority by trying to revive the conservatism of Newt Gingrich, the U.S. Chamber of Commerce, and the Heritage Foundation. In 2000, Bush would not have won the presidency, even against a tarnished opponent, if he had not disguised his own conservative convictions on environmental and health-care issues. During his first nine months, governing within a conservative framework, except on education, Bush found himself and the Republicans sinking in popularity. On the eve of September 11, a Zogby poll found his job approval rating at 50 percent—a historical low for a first-year president.[20] It looked likely that, with the recession deepening, Bush and the Republicans would be routed in November 2002, giving birth prematurely to a Democratic majority. But the terrorist attack on September 11, and Bush's effective response to it, boosted his popularity and that of his party.

Even before September 11, Bush and Republicans had enjoyed greater public support than the Democrats on handling foreign policy and national security. The war against terror made national security the most important issue in the country, completely overshadowing and even redefining the recession in the immediate post-9/11 period. Prior to September 11, much of the public had blamed Bush for the flagging economy; after September 11, many shifted blame to the terrorists and saw whatever privation they suffered as a necessary sacrifice to defeat terror. As long as the war continues, and as long as the administration is seen to prosecute it effectively, Bush's popularity should remain unusually high, and the Republicans should benefit (although it is not clear by how much) in the polls. But the question for the future of American politics is, what will happen once the obvious imperative for war abates. Will Bush and the Republicans be able to sustain their popularity? Or will the trends that have led toward a Democratic majority reassert themselves?

David Brooks and some other Republican conservatives argue that Bush has been using the post–September 11 mood of national emergency to reposition the Republicans as a more centrist party of patriotism—to distance it from business and religious conservatism and to move closer to his former rival John McCain. While such a move might not create what Brooks calls a "reemerging Republican majority," it could create a continued stalemate in American politics—what W. D. Burnham has called an "unstable equilibrium"—over the remainder of the decade.[21] But there is not a great deal of evidence that Bush has moved closer to the center and distanced Republicans from their older base.

In national party affairs, the Bush administration has been willing to countenance a more politically diverse Republican Party. Bush befriended New York mayor Michael Bloomberg, even though Bloomberg remains at heart a liberal Democrat, and Bush and his political director, Karl Rove, encouraged liberal, pro-choice former Los Angeles mayor Richard Riordan to seek the Republican nomination in California's 2002 gubernatorial race. But Bush has continued to govern domestically from the right rather than the center, and the Republican leaders in the House and Senate have, if anything, hardened their own conservative convictions. Rather than using his newfound popularity to reposition the party, he and other Republicans have used it to deflect opposition to their continued conservative direction on taxes, the environment, social security, and worker protection.

Bush has had numerous opportunities since September 11 to reposition himself and his party politically, but has not done so. His first chance came in the debate over how to improve the nation's private and notoriously incompetent airport security system, which had failed to detect a terrorist threat on September 11. Instead of backing a coalition of Democrats and moderate Republicans who favored federalizing the airport security force, Bush backed the House Republican leadership, which had been heavily lobbied by the security firms. Republican Marshall Wittmann, who had backed McCain in 2000, commented about the president's decision to back the House Republicans: "While the president enjoys stratospheric poll ratings, these numbers will eventually return to earth. That is why it is surprising that the administration has displayed little political imagination in building a broader governing coalition that is sustainable for the long haul. They were presented with a golden opportunity to rebuke DeLay and assume a law-and-order position on airport security. But, no, the White House continues to slavishly adhere to pre-9/11 'base' politics."[22]

Since then, Bush has continued to tack right. He used the threat to national security to justify rolling back environmental regulations and pressing for his plan to turn the Arctic National Wildlife Refuge over to oil companies.[23] Facing criticism for withdrawing from the global-warming treaty, he introduced a plan, backed by business, to limit voluntarily the carbon dioxide emissions that are causing global warming. Even the most moderate environmental groups denounced it. He also opposed a continuation of corporate taxation for Superfund cleanup efforts, shifting these costs onto the taxpayer.

Bush has tried to appeal to white working-class Democrats in Pennsylvania and West Virginia by making concessions on steel and coal production, but these are dwindling constituencies. On the broader economic and social issues, he has failed to advance the kind of themes or proposals that would attract the constituencies that would potentially compose a new Democratic majority. Bush's stimulus program was filled with additional tax breaks for the wealthy and for corporations, including a plan to eliminate the alternative minimum tax on businesses that might otherwise pay no taxes at all to the government. He presented a ten-year budget at the beginning of 2002 that was heavy with tax cuts for business supporters and that cut money for job training and environmental enforcement. He abandoned any attempt to protect the social security fund surplus, guaranteeing the emergence of budget deficits, and at the same time reintroduced a plan to privatize part of social security.

Bush responded to the Enron debacle with a cosmetic reform in securities regulation that stressed self-regulation. Brooks and the McCain Republicans wanted him to champion reforms in corporate governance, but faced with alienating his corporate support, Bush balked at doing so. He also continued to cultivate social conservatives by appointing conservative judges and taking every opportunity to inject evangelical Christian discourse into politics. And he abandoned his effort to win over Hispanic voters by liberalizing immigration rules. Of course, congressional conservatives proved to be even more intractable. During the recession, for instance, House Republicans even opposed extending unemployment benefits for the jobless unless they could be tied to tax cuts for business and the affluent. And the Republican primary electorate, which chose conservative over moderate gubernatorial candidates in New Jersey in 2001 and California in 2002 (over Bush's own choice of Riordan), has proven equally inflexible.

In the wake of 9/11, Bush and the Republicans did fashion a party of patriotism, but one as conservative on social and economic issues as the pre-9/11 party. As long as the war was at its height, Bush and the Republicans did not have to pay a political price for continuing to back bigger tax cuts for the wealthy or reductions in environmental enforcement. But these kind of positions, and the Republican association with firms like Enron, are likely to resurface—like early childhood traumas—once the public ceases to be preoccupied with the war against terror. When that happens, American politics is likely to turn toward a new Democratic majority rather than a reemerging Republican one.

* * *

There is one last possibility, which hinges on the outcome of the war against terror. By December 2001, the United States had defeated the Taliban government in Afghanistan and destroyed most of al Qaeda's bases there. The war itself appeared to be devolving into an international police action, punctuated by the use of American Special Forces and military advisers and by less frequent terror alerts from the attorney general. But in George W. Bush's January 2002 State of the Union speech, he suggested that the United States would expand the war from Afghanistan to an "axis of evil" in Iraq, Iran, and North Korea. That would mean using American forces and troops against those of other foreign governments whose militaries are far more powerful than those of the Taliban. Some Bush advisers advanced a strategic argument that the United States needed to pursue such a wider war to protect its citizens from future threats, but it remains unclear as of this writing whether Bush will act on their arguments.

If the United States were to score relatively easy victories, such as occurred before in Kosovo or Afghanistan, then this success would redound to the popularity of the Bush administration. But if the expansion of the war were to lead to protracted fighting and military occupation, and to terrorist reprisals, then it could spark the kind of sharp debate within the country and the parties that occurred during the Korean War, the Vietnam War, and the later stages of the Cold War. Here the Republicans would probably benefit immediately, but over a lengthier period, support for Republican foreign policy could erode, leading to a Democratic advantage. Thus, in the event of a wider war, either party could gain a temporary majority for reasons having little to do with the long-term trends toward a progressive centrist politics. These trends would be likely to reassert themselves, however, and give birth to a new Democratic majority, once peace was secured and Americans could look toward the pursuit of happiness rather than the prevention of terrorist assaults.

CONCLUSION

The Progressive Center

These are turbulent and unusual times. In the 1990s, America saw its longest peacetime economic expansion, including a half decade of spectacular economic performance, led by computer automation and the Internet. Although superficially identified with twenty-something millionaires making a killing on dotcom stocks, the period presaged a postindustrial society in which advanced electronic technology would progressively liberate human beings from repetitive drudgery and toil; in which knowledge and intelligence would displace brute physical power as the engine of economic growth; and in which citizens could increasingly devote their lives to the pursuit of knowledge and happiness. The boom of the nineties was followed, of course, by a recession and by the onset of a war against radical Islamic terrorists who, if successful in their jihad, would have undermined the promise of postindustrial society and plunged the world back into the dark uncertainty and otherworldly fanaticism of the Middle Ages.

In the midst of these tumultuous times, the United States has been undergoing a significant political transition from a conservative Republican majority, which dominated American politics during the 1980s and maintains a weak grip on national power, to a new Democratic majority, which began to emerge during the Clinton presidencies of the 1990s. This new majority is intimately bound up with the changes that America began to go through in the last part of the twentieth century: from an industrial to a postindustrial society, from a white Protestant to a multiethnic, religiously diverse society in which men and women play roughly equal roles at home and at work, and from a society of geographically distinct city, suburb, and country to one of a large, sweeping postindustrial metropolises.

The conservative Republican realignment of the 1980s was in large part a reaction to the turmoil of the sixties and seventies. It sought to contain or roll back the demands of civil rights protesters, feminists, environmentalists, welfare rights organizers, and consumer activists. It was also a reaction to the changes wrought in family structure, work, neighborhood, and ethnic composition by the transition to postindustrial capitalism. And it was a protest against government programs that cost too much and accomplished too little in the midst of a stagnating economy.

Much of that political reaction was inevitable and understandable. Some government programs did waste resources and did little to promote better citizens and a better society. Welfare, as originally devised, did encourage family breakup; much public housing fostered ghetto crime. And the intersection of war and social protest gave the movements of the sixties an apocalyptic edge. The civil rights movement degenerated into ghetto riots and gun-toting militants; feminists ended up challenging the utility of the family and of marriage; consumer activists looked down upon the tastes and habits of average Americans; the counterculture championed drugs and mocked traditional religion in favor of fads and cults; and community organizers encouraged the poor to depend on government handouts.

But the conservative reaction has ranged to extremes of its own. It exploited white Southern resistance to racial desegregation; it denigrated single mothers and working women while stigmatizing homosexuals; it rejected any government intervention into the market and called for abolishing whole sections of the federal government; and it sought to impose the strictures of sectarian religion on education and scientific research. The emerging Democratic majority is a corrective to this Republican counterrevolution—an attempt to come to terms with what was positive and enduring in the movements of the sixties and in the transition to postindustrial capitalism. It does not represent a radical or aggressively left-wing response to conservatism, but a moderate accommodation with what were once radical movements. Like the Republican realignment of 1896, it seeks to ratify and consolidate progressive views that increasingly dominate the center of American politics.

I. SECURITY, STABILITY, AND FREE MARKETS

In the early twentieth century, Republican progressives pioneered the idea of a regulatory capitalism that stood between laissez-faire capitalism and socialism. This kind of public intervention through government attempted to reduce the inequities and instability created by private growth without eliminating the dynamism of markets. It preserved private ownership of farms, factories, and offices, but subjected them to regulation on behalf of the public interest. Franklin Roosevelt's New Deal expanded the scope of government regulation and intervention, creating a system that worked well for many decades. By the 1970s, however, the system was breaking down and became mired in a crippling stagflation that government seemed helpless to correct. Many liberal Democrats came to believe that measures like nationalization of the energy industry, the control of wages, prices, and even investments, and publicly guaranteed full employment were necessary to get the system back on track.

At that point, Republican conservatism provided a useful corrective, a reassertion of the importance of markets and entrepreneurial risk to economic growth. But the Republican support for markets became hardened into a laissez-faire dogma. By the midnineties, the economy was booming, aided by technology-driven productivity growth, but it was also generating new kinds of inequity, instability, corruption, and insecurity—problems that would become even more apparent during the downturn that began in late 2000. Yet Republican conservatives continued to argue for reducing regulations and for cutting taxes for corporations and the wealthy even further. They were motivated partly by laissez-faire ideology, but also by alliances with business lobbies in Washington that heavily funded their campaigns.

By the nineties, the Republican approach put them at odds not only with public opinion, but with the demands that the new postindustrial economy was putting on Americans. For one thing, Republicans seemed oblivious to Americans' concern about their quality of life. Air pollution continued to pose a risk to public health and, through global warming, to the planet's future. But after winning the Congress in 1994, Republicans tried to virtually close down the EPA. When Democrats tried to toughen air standards in 1997, Republicans and their business allies blocked the new rules through a court suit.[1] A decade before, Democrats had used the same legal tactics to block Republican attempts to weaken regulations. What was a sign of political weakness in the Democrats of the eighties was equally a sign of political weakness and desperation in the Republicans of the nineties.

When George W. Bush became president, he undid Clinton administration environmental regulations and pulled the United States out of negotiations for a global-warming treaty. Bush equally ignored popular concern about product quality and safety, appointing regulatory foes to head the Federal Trade Commission and the Consumer Product Safety Commission. Bush's moves were so controversial that he eventually had to back off on some of them, including the reduction of clean water standards. Mindful of potential public opposition, the administration resorted to eliminating regulations by quietly negotiating them away in response to industry suits that were brought against them.[2]

Republicans also ignored public concerns with the corruption of the campaign finance system. In the aftermath of 1996 campaign finance scandals, Democrats and a few moderate Republicans, including John McCain, backed a modest measure—well short of public financing of elections—that would have eliminated unlimited "soft money" contributions by corporations, unions, and wealthy individuals to candidates. But conservative Republicans, led by Kentucky senator Mitch McConnell, blocked the legislation. After George W. Bush took office, a campaign finance bill passed the Senate over Bush's objection, but conservative Republicans were able to stop it in the House. Finally, in the wake of the Enron scandal, moderate Republicans in the House banded together with Democrats to pass the campaign bill and Bush, facing a public revolt, finally signed it, though with a conspicuous lack of enthusiasm.

Republicans seemed equally oblivious to the insecurities created by the postindustrial economy. In the older industrial economy, a blue-collar worker at an automobile or steel factory could expect to hold his job until he retired and to enjoy health insurance and a pension. So could a white-collar worker at a bank or insurance company. In the postindustrial economy of global competition and automation, these kinds of jobs declined in number and could also suddenly disappear as companies moved overseas or reorganized or automated at home. Many of the newer jobs in low-wage services and professions were without the kind of fringe benefits that American workers of the 1950s had enjoyed. From 1979 to 1998, the percentage of private sector workers with employer-provided health insurance went down 7.3 percent. The drop was the sharpest among the lowest-paid workers. Of those in the bottom fifth of wage earners, coverage went down by 11.1 percent.[3] Americans also lacked the kind of job protections they had enjoyed earlier. Their sense of insecurity rose, even during a period of recovery. In 1978, 29 percent of workers believed they were in some danger of losing their job; by 1996, the percentage had risen 10.7 percent to 39.7 percent.[4] During the recession, these figures rose still further. In 2001 alone, 1.2 million Americans lost their health insurance.[5]

Democrats sought to respond to this new insecurity through a national health insurance program, but when the public balked at that level of government intervention, they began considering a series of incremental measures. These included extending medicare downward to Americans fifty-five years and older and to children under eighteen; providing prescription drug coverage as part of medicare; eliminating abuses by health maintenance organizations; making health insurance and pensions portable; and providing universally available retirement accounts that workers can use to increase their old-age pensions. By contrast, Republicans have insisted that Americans would be best off in the hands of private markets and with government removed entirely from the economy. "We do have an economic game plan," the House Republicans declared in *Restoring the Dream,* "and its central theme is to get bureaucratic government off of America's back and out of the way."[6] They advocated turning medicare into a voucher system and partially replacing social security with private investment accounts. Only in the face of widespread public support for the Democratic programs did they sponsor their own version of a patients' bill of rights or medicare prescription drug coverage—and in both cases, their proposed alternatives were intentionally so full of loopholes as to be virtually ineffective.

The rise of postindustrial capitalism and the increase of global competition has also put a premium on educated workers. Over the last three decades, only workers with a four-year college degree or more have seen their real wages increase, while workers with less than a college degree have seen their real earnings actually decline. Workers with a high school degree, for instance, made $13.34 an hour in 1973 and $11.83 an hour in 1999 (in 1999 dollars). In the same period, workers with advanced degrees saw their income rise from $23.53 an hour to $26.44 an hour.[7] The clear message to workers was to acquire more education. That message was reinforced by changes in the global economy in which manufacturing work—the most remunerative of noncollege occupations—increasingly shifted from the United States to less developed capitalist countries.

Democrats have advocated more money for job retraining and early childhood education and to allow every high school graduate to attend a two-year college. They have also called for more money for school buildings, science and computer equipment, and teacher salaries. By contrast, Republicans, after taking control of Congress in 1994, tried unsuccessfully to shut down the Department of Education. In many states, Republicans, led by the religious right, have promoted home schooling or exotic theories of education. Nationally, Republicans have made a special priority of vouchers—a program with particular appeal to some white Catholic and evangelical Protestant voters, but remarkably unpopular with much of the electorate. Republicans have deservedly criticized some Democratic efforts as merely "throwing money at problems" and correctly emphasized the need for high standards, but they have used these deficiencies in the Democrats' approach as an excuse to neglect needed spending. Even in a recession, the Bush administration cut funds for worker training—a key component of any education program—in the fiscal year 2002 budget.

Democrats, reflecting their New Deal heritage, have also tried to use government policy to reduce the income inequality created by the new postindustrial economy. In 1993, the Clinton administration dramatically raised the earned income tax credit (EITC) for low-wage workers, while raising the top rate for upper-income Americans. According to the Harvard political scientist Jeffrey B. Liebman, the increase in the EITC worked wonders for low-income workers: "As recently as 1993, a single-parent family with two children and a full-time minimum-wage worker made $12,131 (in today's dollars) with the EITC. . . . Because of the expansions of the EITC during the 1990s, that family now makes $14,188—a 17 percent boost above the poverty line. The Census Bureau estimates that the EITC lifts 4.3 million people out of poverty, including 2.3 million children."[8]

By contrast, the Republican efforts of Reagan, the Republican Congresses of the 1990s, and the George W. Bush administration have widened income inequality by bestowing tax breaks disproportionately on the most wealthy and on corporations. In the Bush plan that Congress passed in August 2001, the tax cuts, phased in over ten years, will primarily benefit the top 10 percent of income earners. After 2001, they will receive 70.7 percent of the tax benefits, while the bottom 60 percent will get 6.5 percent of the benefits.[9]

These broad differences between the parties became even more apparent after the September 11 terrorist attacks. With the economy slumping, Democrats wanted to give the bulk of money in a stimulus package to unemployed workers who would spend it immediately, with some extra money thrown in to help the newly jobless buy health insurance. By contrast, Republicans in the House, with the Bush administration's support, passed a bill that would primarily have provided tax benefits to corporations and wealthy individuals. Under the bill, almost three-quarters of the tax benefits would have gone to the top 10 percent of income earners, and incredibly, no benefits whatsoever would have gone to a typical family of four with an income of $50,000.[10] In addition, *Fortune* 500 companies would have gotten a $25-billion windfall through the retroactive elimination of the corporate "alternative minimum tax." Almost all of the tax measures in the Republican bill would have taken effect too late to help the economy.[11]

Democrats blocked the Republican stimulus package in the Senate, but in its 2002 budget, the Bush administration was back at redistributing the country's wealth to the wealthy. With deficits rising, the administration actually proposed accelerating when the ten-year tax cuts that Congress had passed would take effect. The administration also proposed making them permanent after ten years rather than subject to congressional review.

II. RACE AND REALIGNMENT

Republicans were the original party of racial equality. In the 1950s and early 1960s, leaders from both parties attempted to come to terms with the new Southern civil rights movement. But after 1964, the Democrats embraced, and the Republicans rejected, the cause of civil rights. The new conservative movement took root in opposition to the federal civil rights acts of 1964 and 1965. It gained a wider following and credibility in the 1970s and 1980s—attracting many whites without any animus toward black civil rights—because of the extremes to which some black militants, such as New York's Reverend Al Sharpton, the author of the infamous Tawana Brawley hoax, went and because of the corruption and venality of some black Democratic officials, such as Washington, D.C.'s Marion Barry. The backlash was also sustained by white voters' frustrations with 1970s stagflation and by the utter inadequacy of many of the civil rights remedies proposed by liberal Democrats. School busing, for instance, often had the effect of encouraging white flight rather than integrating schools. Some public housing programs put the entire onus of integration on working-class white neighborhoods. But Republicans used the corruption of the black officials and the inadequacy of these programs to stigmatize the Democrats and to avoid offering any constructive remedies of their own.

Republicans, particularly in the South, sought to build a new majority by wooing the whites who had backed segregationist George Wallace in 1964 and 1968. South Carolina Republican Hastings Wyman, a former aide to Strom Thurmond, recalled the tactics by which Republicans built this new majority in the South: "I was there, and I remember denouncing the 'block vote'; opposing busing so long and so loud that rural voters thought we were going to do away with school buses; the lurid leaflets exposing 'the integrationist ties' of our Democratic opponents—leaflets we mailed in plain white envelopes to all the white voters in the precincts that George Wallace had carried. . . . Racism, often purposely inflamed by many Southern Republicans, either because we believed it, or because we thought it would win votes, was a major tool in the building of the new Republican Party in the South."[12]

In 1980, when the realignment finally occurred, it was based to some extent on disenchantment with Democratic economics and foreign policy. But opposition to the civil rights movement and to a cluster of race-based or race-identified policies was particularly important in the South and in the ethnic suburbs of the Midwest and Northeast. In many of those areas, the two parties became identified with their different racial compositions—the Republicans as the "white party" and the Democrats as the "black party." Such an identification was inimical to the cause of racial reconciliation. It created a dynamic by which the Republicans, to maintain their majority, sought to divide whites from blacks. It also created an incentive for Republicans to ignore black economic inequality in their policy proposals and legislation.

Some Republican politicians, such as former congressman Jack Kemp, tried to develop a multiracial Republican Party and strategy, but they were ignored. (Kemp was popular among Republicans because of his outspoken advocacy of tax cuts, not because of his support for racial equality.) Most Republican politicians were swept away by the racial logic underlying the Republican majority. Faced with the prospect of defeat at the hands of a Democratic opponent, Republicans from Jesse Helms to the elder George Bush used racial wedge issues to win over erstwhile white Democrats. And while Bush's son avoided these sorts of tactics in his own run for president, as recently as fall 2001 two other Republicans—both of whom, interestingly, had reputations for racial reconciliation—pulled out the race card once they found themselves trailing in the polls.

Early on in his run for the governorship of Virginia, Republican attorney general Mark Earley had boasted of his membership in the NAACP and vowed that he would not ignore the black vote. But by the summer's end, Earley was trailing Democrat Mark Warner by 11 percent in the polls. Warner was even ahead in Southside Virginia, where small-town white voters had deserted the Democrats for Wallace in 1968 and had subsequently backed Republican presidential candidates. To win back Southside whites, who were drawn to Warner's message of encouraging high-tech growth, Earley and the Virginia Republican Party ran radio ads and passed out leaflets in the area accusing Warner and the Democratic candidates for lieutenant governor and attorney general of supporting gun control, same-sex marriage, and the abolition of capital punishment. The charges were false, and without foundation. And they grouped together the candidates in spite of the fact that they had been nominated separately, disagreed on a range of issues, and were running entirely separate campaigns. What was most striking about the leaflets, however, was not what they said about the candidates' positions, but what they showed: a photograph of Warner with that of attorney general candidate Donald McEachin. Warner is white and McEachin is African-American. Such a technique, pioneered by Helms's political machine in

North Carolina, was designed to demonstrate to these white Southside voters, who had a history of racial voting, that Warner was the candidate of the "black party."

In New Jersey, Republican Bret Schundler had captured the mayor's office in Jersey City twice, winning substantial black votes each time. But, as he fell far behind Democrat Jim McGreevey in the race for governor, Schundler increasingly resorted to issues with a strong racial component. In New Jersey, these issues pivot around the differences between the primarily black cities and primarily white suburbs. In his first debate with McGreevey, Schundler, without any prompting, raised his opposition to the New Jersey Supreme Court's Mount Laurel decision. This 1975 decision forced developers in affluent suburbs to devote a "fair share" of their new properties to affordable housing. Schundler said he wanted to "get rid of" the decision because it increased "suburban sprawl."[13] Although people tend to worry about suburban sprawl because they're concerned about pollution or want to ease congestion on the roads, the link to the Mount Laurel decision made it obvious that Schundler had something other than the environment or traffic in mind: Schundler was proposing to curb the movement by the poor—overwhelmingly black and Hispanic—into more affluent, mostly white suburbs.

In the closing month of his campaign, Schundler also highlighted his plan to provide vouchers. Some conservatives have advocated vouchers so that ghetto children could afford to go to private schools as an alternative to failing public schools. But in his campaign, Schundler brazenly appealed to Catholic and religious right parents who already send their children to private schools. He attacked spending on public education as a subsidy to urban—that is, minority—schools and presented vouchers as a way of rewarding suburban parents who send their children to private schools. Schundler charged that McGreevey, who opposes vouchers, "wants to just throw more money into urban school districts and cut money for suburban and rural school districts." McGreevey, in Schundler's coded words, was guilty of favoring primarily black cities over primarily white suburban and rural school districts.

Earley and Schundler, like the elder Bush, showed no sign of personally being racist. But as Republicans, they inherited a coalition and a strategy that divided the parties along racial lines and that encouraged Republicans, when in trouble, to stress their opposition to race-based or race-identified programs. In the seventies and early eighties, these tactics frequently worked. But as Democrats abandoned programs like busing, and as a new generation of black leaders, including Washington, D.C., mayor Anthony Williams and Detroit mayor Dennis Archer, replaced the old, race-baiting began to backfire on Republicans, particularly among professionals and women voters who were raised in the sixties ethos of racial tolerance. In Virginia's 1989 gubernatorial race, African-American candidate Douglas Wilder's standing in the Washington, D.C., affluent suburbs shot up after a Virginia Republican attempted to paint Wilder as a black militant. And in the 2001 Virginia and New Jersey races, Republicans had no success whatsoever using these kinds of tactics.

III. STEM CELLS, GAY RIGHTS, AND THE RELIGIOUS RIGHT

In 1980, when Ronald Reagan called on Americans to affirm the values of "family, work, and neighborhood," he was drawing a distinction between these values and those that the extremes of the sixties counterculture had embraced. Republicans became the party opposed to the drug culture, bra burning, sexual promiscuity, teenage pregnancy, and the New Age denigration of religion. And they won elections on this basis. But in the 1980s, as Republicans embraced the religious right of Falwell and Robertson, they went well beyond repudiating the most extreme movements of the sixties. They rejected the new values and social structure that postindustrial capitalism is creating and nourishing.

Most important among these are women's equality at home and at work. The transition to postindustrial capitalism has profoundly altered family structure and the role of women, as the public sector and private industry have increasingly absorbed tasks at home that women traditionally performed. The imperative to have large families has disappeared. Women, no longer consigned to the home, have entered the workforce and many have taken up professional careers. The numbers of divorced women and single mothers have risen; so has the number of college-educated women professionals. *Father Knows Best* has given way to *An Unmarried Woman.* Modern feminism arose in response to these changes. Like other political movements, it included apocalyptic and utopian extremes, but at its core, it represented an attempt to remove the contradiction between an older patriarchal ideology and the growing potential for equality between men and women.

The Republicans, prodded by the religious right and by conservatives who sought its support, rejected the Equal Rights Amendment and the right of women to have an abortion. They balked at federal money for child care and held up the older ideal of the family. (Pat Robertson stated the case in 1992: "I know this is painful for the ladies to hear, but if you get married, you have accepted the headship of a man, your husband. Christ is the head of the household and the husband is the head of the wife, and that's the way it is, period."[14]) Republicans highlighted the most extreme aspects of the women's movement in order to reject the whole. By contrast, Democrats absorbed the mainstream of the new feminist movement, exemplified by the abortion rights organizations and the National Organization for Women. Democrats also advanced proposals for child care and paid family leave to accommodate the reality that so many mothers were now working outside the home.

Democrats and Republicans have similarly parted ways on encouraging sexual education among teenagers and on preventing discrimination against homosexuals in housing or employment. Like the controversies about prohibition in the 1920s, these seem peripheral to the heart of politics, but in fact arise directly from the transition from one way of life to another. Prohibition was the cause of the small town against city, the ordered life of the farmer and craftsman against the chaos and squalor of the factory city, and of Anglo-Saxon Protestants against ethnic immigrants. Similarly, the Republicans, goaded by the religious right, have become the defenders of the mores of Middletown against those of the postindustrial metropolis.

Republicans, as the party of the religious right, have upheld the older ideal of sexual abstinence and of family life as not merely the norm, but as a moral imperative. They have opposed sexual education, if not sex itself, for teenagers. In December 1994, congressional Republicans forced the Clinton administration's surgeon general, Jocelyn Elders, to resign because she responded favorably to an off-the-cuff question at a press conference about the advisability of discussing masturbation as part of sexual education. Republicans have also adopted the religious right's attitude toward homosexuals as purposeful sinners who represent a threat to public morals. They opposed not only Clinton's unpopular proposal to allow gays to serve openly in the military, but also began to mount initiative campaigns to deny gays protection from discrimination in housing and employment. In Congress, Senate Republicans even refused to confirm a Clinton administration choice for ambassador to Luxembourg because he was a homosexual. They have also indicted homosexuals for causing the AIDs epidemic. In Virginia's 2001 contest for lieutenant governor, the Republican candidate, Jay Katzen, declared that AIDs "is the product, sadly, in most cases of a choice that people have made. . . . We recognize that homosexuality is a choice. It's a lifestyle with public health consequences."[15]

These Republican attitudes were common, of course, fifty and a hundred years ago, but they have lost ground in postindustrial America. Americans today see sex not simply as a means to procreation, but as a source of pleasure and enjoyment. Many still cringe at the sight or prospect of homosexuality, but recognize it as a possibly inherited form of sexual expression that, if denied and closeted, could prevent a person's pursuit of happiness. They may not want gays to be honest about their sexual preference in the military, but they see conservative attempts to punish and stigmatize gays as bigotry and intolerance.

Conservative Republicans and Democrats also part ways on the relationship of religion to science. Here, there was little provocation by the Democratic left or even from the counterculture, unless the arch-Victorian Charles Darwin is seen as representative of the left-wing counterculture. In search of votes, the conservative Republicans of the 1980s made a devil's pact with religious fundamentalists that entailed their indulgence of crackpot religious notions. While Democrats have opposed the imposition of sectarian religious standards on science and public education, the Republicans have tried to make science and science education conform to Protestant fundamentalism. Throughout the South and the Midwest, Republicans have promoted teaching creationism instead of or in competition with the theory of evolution. Creationists hold that the Bible is the literal truth and that the world began several thousand rather than billions of years ago. One leading creationist, for instance, holds that dinosaurs roamed the earth in the twentieth century.[16]

Prominent Republican politicians and intellectuals, including Irving Kristol, William Bennett, and Robert Bork, have refused to repudiate these notions.[17] Instead, they have sanctioned the idea that creationism and Darwinian evolution are merely two competing theories. In the 2000 presidential campaign, George W. Bush endorsed this view: "I believe children ought to be exposed to different theories about how the world started." Later Bush's official spokeswoman said, "He believes both creationism and evolution ought to be taught. He believes it is a question for states and local school boards to decide but he believes both ought to be taught."

The Republican rejection of modern science reached an apogee during Bush's first year in office when he became embroiled in a controversy over whether the government should fund stem-cell research. Stem cells were finally isolated and reproduced for research purposes in 1998 by a University of Wisconsin scientist. These cells could provide the basis for a new "regenerative medicine" that would aid, and even cure, victims of Parkinson's, Alzheimer's, heart disease, stroke, diabetes, and some forms of cancer by replacing or regenerating cells. Stem cells have been garnered from embryos at fertility clinics. Some one hundred thousand embryos are currently frozen and, if not used, will eventually be discarded. Scientists want to use them for scientific research, and the Clinton administration agreed to fund research on new stem cells.[18]

But Republicans sided with the religious right who argued that these embryos are living beings that cannot be "murdered" for the sake of scientific research.* This notion of life prompted journalist Michael Kinsley to ask in *Time* magazine, "Are we really going to start basing social policy on the assumption that a few embryonic cells equal a human being?"[19] But Bush, after claiming to spend months pondering the issue of life in a petri dish, finally announced in a nationwide address that researchers could only use stem cells that had already been created from embryos. They could not use new embryos. Such a decision bore out the degree to which conservative Republicans had become hostage to the religious right's campaign against modernity and postindustrial America.

On many of these economic and social issues, conservative Republicans initially won support by standing resolutely against the excesses of

*Bush also solicited the views of the pope and other Catholic leaders on whether to fund stem-cell research. Bush was not similarly concerned about Catholic views on capital punishment or on government aid to the poor. His interest in Catholic views seemed to flow from the interest of his political adviser Karl Rove in winning votes for 2004.

the sixties and of post–New Deal liberal Democrats. But clearly they have gone to extremes of their own. They are putting forth remedies for problems that no longer exist and ignoring problems that do. They are fighting the future on behalf of the past. In the meantime, Democrats, chastened by defeat during the eighties, have repudiated their own extremes and moved to the political center, which itself has gravitated in a broadly progressive direction. Ironically, the party that the Democrats most clearly resemble is the one that Bush and Rove claim for themselves—the progressive Republicans of the early twentieth century. Like the progressive Republicans, today's Democrats stand between the extremes of right and left and at the gateway at the end of one era of capitalism and the beginning of another. They are the new party of progressive centrism.

Today's Americans, whose attitudes have been nurtured by the transition to postindustrial capitalism, increasingly endorse the politics of this progressive centrism. They want government to play an active and responsible role in American life, guaranteeing a reasonable level of economic security to Americans rather than leaving them at the mercy of the market and the business cycle. They want to preserve and strengthen social security and medicare, rather than privatize them. They want to modernize and upgrade public education, not abandon it. They want to exploit new biotechnologies and computer technologies to improve the quality of life. They do not want science held hostage to a religious or ideological agenda. And they want the social gains of the sixties consolidated, not rolled back; the wounds of race healed, not inflamed. That's why the Democrats are likely to become the majority party of the early twenty-first century.

AFTERWORD

"The Enemy Is Coming"

If the November 2002 elections had been held on September 10, 2001, the Democrats would have made impressive gains, increasing their one-seat edge in the Senate and probably winning back the House of Representatives. At the time, George W. Bush was seen as a weak and ineffective leader, who was most comfortable reading *The Very Hungry Caterpillar* to kindergartners. His approval rating was at 51 percent, dangerously low for a president in his first nine months.[1] In addition, the Clinton boom had given way to a pronounced economic slowdown. Combine these factors with popular support for Democratic positions on social security, health care costs, the environment, and the economy, and you had a recipe for a Republican disaster. But nothing of the kind occurred. In the wake of the September 11 terrorist attacks, Bush and the Republicans boosted their popularity and actually gained seats in both houses, narrowly winning back the Senate.

The GOP successes in November 2002 gave rise to new theories about a long-term Republican realignment. In the conservative *Weekly Standard,* Fred Barnes described an emerging 9/11 majority. "We are no longer an equally divided, 50–50 nation," Barnes wrote. "America is now at least 51–49 Republican and right of center, more likely 52–48, maybe even 53–47. The terrorist attacks on September 11, 2001, created a new political era, and the midterm election on November 5 confirmed it."[2] Barnes was certainly right about the Republican tilt of the election, but not about the "new political era." The November 2002 elections represented the temporary revival of the older conservative realignment of the 1980s. September 11 brought to the forefront national security issues on which Republicans have enjoyed an advantage since the election of 1980; and Bush's sure-handed performance in the months that followed ensured that this advantage would accrue to him and the Republicans in

November 2002. But this advantage will persist only as long as Americans feel under attack and also feel that the Republicans are best able to protect them from attack. The 2002 election did not begin a new era but unexpectedly prolonged an older one.

In the 1980s, the conservative Republican majority was based on supply-side economics, opposition to civil rights advances, social conservatism, and militant opposition to communism. The Democrats' division over the Vietnam War and the setbacks overseas during the Carter administration, culminating in the Iranian hostage crisis, had convinced many voters that Republicans were better able to meet threats from abroad. But by the early 1990s, most of these Republican advantages had disappeared, lost some of their power, or become irrelevant. Supply-side economics and social conservatism no longer enjoyed majority support; the Democrats' support for welfare reform had partially blunted Republican racial appeals, even in parts of the white South; and with the Cold War's end, foreign affairs and national security no longer held the public's attention, except for trade and economic relations. By 1996, there wasn't a hint of interest in foreign affairs. In 2000, Bush ran on a promise to withdraw the United States from foreign involvement. But September 11 changed all that.

September 11 infused foreign affairs with a threat to Americans' security at home, making concern about foreign policy paramount in a way that it had been only during the Vietnam War and World Wars I and II. Public-opinion polling bore this out. Just before September 11, thirty-nine percent of the public had cited some economic problem as the most important facing the nation. Terrorism was not mentioned at all. One month later, the percentage of people citing economic problems was cut in half and the number targeting terrorism as the most important problem had soared to 46 percent.[3] And this concern didn't merely overshadow domestic issues—it reshaped Americans' perception of them. The recession that finally took hold was widely seen as a result of September 11, and the party in power mostly escaped blame for it. In a mid-December poll, 79 percent said that the September 11 attacks deserved a great deal or some of the blame for the recession.

Bush responded to September 11 by abandoning his own indifference to world affairs. His initial performance, leading to the ouster of the Taliban regime in Afghanistan in December 2001, strongly enhanced his reputation. Bush's approval rating hit 90 percent in late September and did not fall below 80 percent until March of the following year.[4] The rising approval of Bush, along with the importance attached to national security, cast a glow on the Republicans themselves, increasing their public support at the expense of the Democrats. In August 2001, a Harris Poll had found only 37 percent of the public saying that the Republicans in Congress were doing an excellent or pretty good job; by mid-October, that number had soared to 67 percent.

The newfound Republican support after September 11 was concentrated among the white middle- and upper-middle-class voters who had probably backed Ronald Reagan in 1980 and 1984 but who supported Clinton and Gore. These converts back to Republicanism included some suburban professionals and managers who rejected the Republicans because of the party's identification with the religious right. Even so, by the late summer of 2002, as popular concern with terrorism began to abate, the Democratic advantages that had been growing in the 1990s began to reappear. As voters became more concerned about the flagging economy and about a spate of corporate corruption scandals, the Democrats began pulling ahead of the Republicans in the generic congressional polls and in the individual state races. In a late-August Gallup poll, registered voters preferred Democratic over Republican House candidates by 50–42 percent.

In the November 2001 gubernatorial races, which the Democrats swept, the White House had intervened hesitantly in the campaigns, but the White House threw itself energetically into the November 2002 races. Over the next two months, under White House leadership, Republicans sought to refocus Americans on national security and presidential leadership, and to deflect Democratic charges that Republicans had mishandled the economy or favored programs that would throw widows out in the snow. The Democrats, for their part, sought to maintain the public's focus on unmet social needs, the flagging economy, and the growing scandal over corporate corruption. The final results were very close, but the Republicans, who enjoyed the advantage of White House visibility, did a far better job of enhancing their advantages than the Democrats. By brilliantly exploiting the special circumstances created by September 11, they were sufficiently successful in reviving the older Republican coalition to offset the trends toward a Democratic electorate.

* * *

To shift the public's focus from domestic social and economic issues to the war on terror and national security, the Republicans, guided by Bush political advisor Karl Rove, used the closing months of the campaign to launch a debate on whether to go to war with Iraq. The Bush administration had decided earlier to attempt to oust the Iraqi dictator Saddam Hussein. But the White House staged the congressional debate about the war during the height of the election rather than before or after it. Rather than remove the issue of war from political partisanship—as Bush's father had done in 1990 by postponing the congressional debate about whether to forcefully oust Iraq from Kuwait until after the election—the Bush White House sought to use the issue for its political ends.

Bush presented the Iraqi threat as "imminent" and cataclysmic and as part of the war against terror and Al Qaeda. He and other administration officials warned that Saddam would soon have nuclear weapons to potentially use against American cities and that he already possessed massive arsenals of chemical and biological weapons he could use himself against Americans or transfer to Al Qaeda, with whom, the administration claimed, the Iraqi regime was allied. The administration's warnings either ignored existing intelligence about Iraq or grossly exaggerated what was known, but they had a dramatic effect on the electorate.[5] By November, 59 percent of Americans favored an invasion of Iraq, and only 35 percent were opposed.[6] By even larger majorities, Americans thought Saddam was acquiring nuclear weapons and was linked to Al Qaeda. Most astonishing of all, by the end of October, 79 percent of the public believed that it was "very or somewhat likely" that Saddam was involved in September 11, in spite of the fact that American intelligence agencies had failed to find any evidence of it.[7]

The administration also used the first anniversary of September 11 to heighten public fears of a terrorist attack from Al Qaeda. The Justice Department raised the terror alert that week, explaining later that it had been justified by what the FBI learned of the threat posed by an Al Qaeda "sleeper cell" in Lackawanna, New York. Over the next week, federal officers arrested six Yemeni-Americans in Lackawanna. In response, major news magazines and television networks featured lurid stories of sleeper cells operating under cover of darkness in American cities. *Newsweek* ran a cover story in September headlined "The Hunt for Sleeper Cells," featuring the Lackawanna Six. But the administration had no evidence, and none surfaced over the next year, that the Lackawanna defendants had been organizing a terrorist plot against the United States. The six, motivated in part by religious reasons, had attended an Al Qaeda camp in Afghanistan in June 2001, but since returning home, had not been engaged in any kind of plotting or conspiracy. The administration used the publicity around the arrests largely for political ends—to sharpen the public's focus on the administration's war against terror.

The administration coupled the terror alerts about sleeper cells with an attack on the Democrats for blocking passage of the Homeland Security Bill. Democrats had initially proposed the new department, and the passage of the measure had actually been held up by Republicans who insisted that it contain a measure allowing administrations to prevent labor unions from organizing department workers, a proposal the Democrats refused to include. The resulting administration charge of Democratic obstruction, reinforced by the terror alerts and the exaggerated or false claims about the Iraqi threat, worked to the party's advantage. In the months before the election, Americans became more fearful of attack, and they looked to Republicans to protect them. In one October poll, likely voters favored Republicans over Democrats on the issue of terrorism by an astonishing 72–17 percent margin.[8]

Taking their cue from the White House, Republican candidates repeatedly charged their Democratic opponents with ignoring national security and the war on terror. In the New Hampshire Senate race, Republican John Sununu charged Democrat Jeanne Shaheen with accepting a contribution from the Council for a Livable World, an antiwar organization. In the Georgia Senate race, Republican Saxby Chambliss, who had never served in the military, attacked incumbent Max Cleland, a war hero who had lost his legs and an arm in Vietnam, for not supporting the Republican plan for the Homeland Security Department. The Republicans even went so far as to run an add linking Cleland to images of Saddam Hussein and Osama Bin Laden.

At the same time, the Republicans sought to neutralize Democratic appeals on domestic issues by co-opting their approach. After initially opposing any measure to strengthen securities and accounting regulation, the Bush administration signed on to a Democratic bill, and its candidates, including antireform conservatives like Colorado senator Wayne

Allard, ran as corporate reformers, charging their opponents with being lax on the issue. Supporters of social security privatization like Missouri Senate candidate Jim Talent swore that they had always opposed privatization and would defend the integrity of the social security system. Talent, who as a congressman sponsored legislation to divert 16 percent of social security taxes to retirement accounts managed by private managers, declared during the campaign that he had "not voted and will not vote to fully or partially privatize Social Security." Republicans also produced their own expensive and limited bill to provide prescription drug coverage to seniors, which they trumpeted (with the help of drug-company lobbying organizations) as being superior to the Democratic alternative. These efforts were not necessarily designed to win support, but rather to cloud and neutralize the Democrats' appeals.

In the South and border states, the Republicans also quietly revived racial appeals that they had used decades ago to lure white Democratic voters. In Georgia, party chairman Ralph Reed, the former director of the Christian Coalition and a public proponent of racial inclusion within the Republican party, sent to rural Georgians fliers attacking the Democrats for having replaced Georgia's state flag, which had celebrated the Confederacy and the state's defiance of civil rights for blacks. In other states, the Republicans conducted campaigns intended to hold down black voting. In Arkansas' Jefferson County, Republican poll watchers, including two staffers from Republican Senate candidate Tim Hutchison's campaign, confronted black voters who went to the county courthouse to cast their early ballots, photographing them and demanding that they show identification, even though Arkansas law stipulates that poll watchers cannot ask voters to show identification.[9]

The Democrats, guided by Senate Majority Leader Tom Daschle, House Minority Leader Dick Gephardt, and Terry McAuliffe, the chairman of the Democratic National Committee, adopted a deeply flawed strategy to counter the Republicans. They focused on prescription drugs and social security. Democrats did maintain an advantage on these issues through the final results. According to postelection polls by Greenberg Quinlan Rosner (GQR), Democrats enjoyed a 19 percent edge on health care, 18 percent on prescription drugs, and 9 percent on social security over Republicans. But Republican efforts to co-opt the Democrats succeeded at least partially. By the election, the GQR survey found that only 34 percent of voters thought that the Democrats and Republicans disagreed about a prescription drug benefit for seniors.

Most notably, the Democrats did not offer any economic program to combat growing unemployment in the country. Daschle and the Senate Democrats were inhibited by the fact that some Democrats, vulnerable to Republican challenges in states that Bush had won, had supported the main Republican economic program of tax cuts. But the result was that voters perceived the Democrats as not having an alternative to the Republican program. A CBS/*New York Times* survey before the election, for example, found that the public, by 41–37 percent, believed that Republicans were "more likely to make sure the country is prosperous." That view was reflected in the Voter News Service (VNS) exit poll results, in which voters who said the economy was their most important issue voted Republican for the House by 52–48 percent.[10]

Many of the Democrats, led by Gephardt, adopted a strategy of simply accepting the administration case for war, with all its attendant falsehoods and exaggerations, in the hope of getting the vote over quickly so that voters would focus on the domestic issues on which the Democrats had an advantage. In early October, Gephardt cut short an attempt at a bipartisan counterresolution on the war by agreeing to an administration proposal. Daschle and other Democratic leaders, fearing that they would suffer isolation and defeat if they opposed the war resolution, dropped their efforts at forcing a compromise and supported the Bush proposal. Four days after the vote on Iraq, Gephardt gave a major speech heralding the Democrats' social and economic programs but omitted any discussion of the prospect of war with Iraq. His ill-conceived strategy allowed Bush free reign in rallying the country against the threat to its national security during the last two weeks of the campaign.

Nevertheless, with three weeks to go in the election, Democrats were actually leading in generic polls and many of the individual races. They looked as if they would hold or increase their margin in the Senate, while narrowing the Republican edge in the House. During those last weeks, Bush undertook a whirlwind national tour that highlighted the war on terror and the threat from Al Qaeda and Saddam Hussein. In the last week alone, Bush made seventeen stops in fifteen states. At each stop, after briefly trying to allay voters' fears about Republican economic policies, he would launch into a jeremiad about the threat from abroad. As he put it during a stop in Columbia, South Carolina:

> You've just got to understand there's an enemy out there that hates America because of what we love. We love every aspect of our freedom, and we're not changing. We're not backing down, and the enemy can't stand that. No longer can we assume oceans will protect us. As a matter of fact, quite the contrary. We must assume that the enemy is coming, and we've got to do everything we can to protect the homeland. That's why I started talking about the issue of Iraq.[11]

Bush's final tour turned a dead heat into victory for the Republicans by generating a pro-Republican surge among likely voters.* Republicans had trailed Democrats by three points in Gallup's poll of likely voters on October 21 through 22. By election weekend, twelve days later, the Republicans led by six points.[12] The Republicans gained two Senate seats, creating a 51–48 margin, with independent James Jeffords voting with the Democrats. Their margin in the House increased to 229 seats to 205, with one Democratic-voting independent.

The results showed how Bush and the Republicans' strategy had worked. Voters believed that in supporting Republicans they were endorsing Bush's leadership in the war against terror. According to the GQR poll, the two top reasons for voting Republican in 2002 were to support President Bush and to support the war on terrorism and a strong military. By election time, the Republican advantage over the Democrats on the issue of which party could do the best job "keeping American strong" had increased from 25 percent on October 24 to 39 percent. Voters did worry about the economy, but their perception of it was shaped by the war on terror. In one late-October poll by Fabrizio, McLaughlin and Associates, 23 percent of respondents blamed the business cycle for the bad econ-

*The Republicans were also aided when friends and supporters of Minnesota senator Paul Wellstone turned his nationally televised funeral on October 30 into a tasteless, partisan affair that inflamed Republicans and turned off independents. Wellstone's funeral might have cost the Democrats both the Minnesota and the Missouri Senate seats—the latter because the funeral turned what would have been a sympathy vote for Jean Carnahan, who lost her husband in a plane crash in October 2000, into an anti-Democratic backlash.

omy, 21 percent the September 11 attacks, 15 percent former president Clinton, and only 14 percent Bush.[13]

In a study of the election based upon the University of Michigan's post-election surveys in 2000 and 2002, political scientist David Gopoian tried to determine what distinguished the 19 percent of voters who had backed Vice President Al Gore in 2000 but expressed greater support for Bush in 2002 from those voters who still favored Gore.[14] According to Gopoian, these "floating" pro-Bush voters remained critical of Republican domestic approaches but, unlike the 2002 Gore loyalists, were strongly supportive of Bush's conduct regarding the war against terror and the coming war against Iraq. "The issues that matter" in distinguishing these voters, Gopoian wrote, "are foreign policy and terrorism."

The picture of who backed which party in November 2002 recalls that of the Reagan-era presidential elections. Republicans did well among white rural and suburban, particularly exurban, voters. Some of the suburbanites who had crossed over to the Democrats in the late 1980s and 1990s because of the Republicans' social conservatism appear to have turned back to the Republicans because of what they saw as Bush's leadership in the war against terror. Also, just as in the 1980s, the male gender gap overshadowed the female. In ths VNS exit poll, Democrats broke even among women, but lost among men by 12 points.

The Democrats clearly lost ground, especially in key states, among white working-class voters who had once been loyal Democrats but had backed Reagan in 1980 and 1984 and George H. W. Bush in 1988. These voters probably moved back to the Republicans for one of the reasons they had first done so in 1980: their perception that Republicans could better handle threats to national security. Macomb County, Michigan, was the home of the Reagan Democrats, but Clinton won Macomb in 1996 as Gore did in 2000, and Democrat David Bonior had continued to win elections as its congressman. But in the 2002 election, Republican Candice Miller, aided partly by redistricting, won Bonior's seat. The national campaign even spilled over into the governor's race. Macomb backed the Republican gubernatorial candidate, Dick Posthumus, against Democrat Jennifer Granholm. Granholm won Michigan by 51–48 percent, but lost Macomb County by 52–47 percent.

The Democrats also lost ground among white voters in more upscale suburban areas. Republican Norm Coleman dramatically reduced the Democrats' advantage in Hennepin County, which includes Democratic Minneapolis, but which also includes well-to-do suburban areas that have swung between Democrats and Republicans. In 2000, Democratic Senate candidate Mark Dayton won Hennepin by 53–37 percent, and Gore defeated Bush there by 54–39 percent, but in November 2002, Coleman's challenger, Walter Mondale, won it by only 51–47 percent. In Missouri, suburban voters helped to elect Talent in his race against Democrat Jean Carnahan. In 2000, Carnahan's late husband Mel had won St. Louis County, the predominately white upper-middle-class area that borders St. Louis on the west, by 8 percentage points. In 2002, Jean Carnahan carried it by only 3 points. That alone cost her sixteen thousand votes in a state she lost by only about twenty-one thousand votes. Throw in reduced margins of victory in nearby Jefferson County, the Jackson County suburbs of Kansas City, and in Boone County, where Columbia and the University of Missouri are located, and there's easily enough lost votes to account for her statewide defeat.

In Georgia, Republicans did well among white rural voters to whom state chairman Reed made racial appeals. Racism still works in the rural South, but the Republican victory was based heavily on suburban areas that still go Democratic in some state elections. For example, in upscale, white Cobb County north of Atlanta, Republican Chambliss defeated Cleland by 59–40 percent while Democratic candidate Zell Miller had defeated the Republican Senate opponent Matt Mattingly by 52–45 percent in 2000. That's a swing of 26 points. Cleland had been well ahead of Chambliss in polls until the very end, but Bush's visit to the state, combined with Chambliss's assault on Cleland for opposing the Department of Homeland Security, moved many of these suburban voters into the Republican column.

The other factor in 2002 was turnout. Republican voters appeared to go to the polls at a significantly higher rate than in other midterm elections. In fact, according to the VNS exit poll, fully 40 percent of voters were self-identified Republicans, a level higher than at any time in the last decade.[15] They were moved by the party's "72-Hour Project," which did an outstanding job of boosting turnout in conservative areas, but they were also inspired by Bush's last-minute appeals. In contrast, some loyal

Democratic voters appeared to stay away from the polls—the result, in part, of the Democrats' inability to counter the Republican message on the economy and foreign policy. According to the VNS exit poll, for example, blacks constituted a lower percentage of the vote than in either 1998 or 2000.[16] More broadly, county-level voting returns suggest that turnout in Democratic-leaning large cities and inner suburbs, even where it did not decline, did not keep pace with increases in Republican-leaning exurban and rural areas. With higher pro-Democratic turnout, particularly among blacks, Democrats would have been more competitive in a number of states and might have won close races like the Senate contest in Missouri.

After the election, Republicans wanted to make the case that their strong showing in 2002 reflected deeper, long-term trends at work. Pollster Matthew Dowd argued that the Republicans won not because of Bush's response to September 11, but because voters trusted them more to improve the economy. If that were true, the election might have augured a new political era. But the war on terror completely overshadowed and, in the end, defined the terms of the campaign, including the public's understanding of the economy. The key factors in the Republicans' success—the higher turnout among Republican and conservative voters; the defection to the Republicans of male, white working-class and middle-class voters, particularly in suburban areas; the reduced turnout among blacks and other loyal Democrats—were all traceable to the peculiar post-September 11 circumstances of this election. If these circumstances persist with the same strength into 2004, the Republicans will do well again, but once they begin to recede, the trends toward a Democratic majority should reassert themselves.

The trends toward the Democrats were apparent in polling before September 11, in the November 2001 elections, and again during the late summer of 2002, when the campaign had begun, but before the Bush White House had nationalized the campaign around the war on Iraq and against terror. These trends were also somewhat apparent in the governor's races. These races were still affected by the national political climate, but probably less so than Senate or House races. Democrats gained three seats and would have done much better had they not lost races in solidly Democratic Massachusetts, Rhode Island, and Maryland because of poor candidates. (In Maryland, for instance, the Democrats picked up two House seats, while losing the governor's race.) Democratic victories in Pennsylvania, Illinois, Michigan, and Wisconsin confirmed Democratic trends in the Mid-Atlantic and the Midwest. Janet Napolitano's victory in Arizona against former congressman Matt Salmon showed that Democrats can be competitive in the Southwest.

On domestic issues, Republican candidates had to mimic Democratic approaches precisely because they are more popular with voters. Republicans had to claim they opposed corporate corruption and wanted to reduce seniors' drug costs. They had to promise to protect social security, expand spending on education, and defend environmental and consumer regulations. Outside the deep South, few Republicans appealed directly to the religious right and its agenda. Those candidates who did, like Kansas Republican gubernatorial candidate Tim Shallenburger, went down to defeat for that very reason.

Other Republican pundits, following Michael Barone's analysis of the 2000 election in *The Almanac of American Politics,* cited the party's strong showing in exurban counties as a harbinger of an emerging Republican majority.[17] The party did benefit from increased turnout in some places like Douglas County outside of Denver or St. Charles County outside of St. Louis, but Republican margins in these areas were similar to Bush's margins in 2000. Where Republicans enjoyed an unexpected advantage in 2002 were in some of the more populous working-class and upscale suburban areas that had been trending Democratic in the 1990s, and—leaving aside September 11—would have continued to do so.

In his essay on the November 2002 election, the *Weekly Standard*'s Barnes rests his case for a new Republican realignment on the effect of September 11 and Bush's leadership. Wrote Barnes, "The September 11 attacks produced a new political climate. Bush recognized it. Democrats still don't." That was certainly true enough during the November election, but the effect of September 11 is not likely to be lasting.

What was distinctive about September 11 was that it was a direct attack on the United States. It was a terrorist Pearl Harbor that depended on total surprise and a lack of vigilance by federal authorities for its success. During the 2002 election, the Bush administration, guided by neoconservatives, convinced American voters that by going to war with Iraq, the country would be safer not only against another terrorist assault but against an Iraqi nuclear attack. In other words, they presented the invasion of Iraq as an extension of the war against terror. But the war and occupation did not confirm the administration's case. No weapons of mass destruction or links to Al Qaeda were discovered—raising questions about the administration's credibility. And instead of proving to be a "cakewalk," as the administration had promised, the war turned into a low-intensity guerrilla war sustained by the resistance of the American occupation. By the second anniversary of September 11, popular support for Bush's leadership—based in part on trust in his word—had begun to erode, and with it the Republican's chances of sustaining the special political circumstances of September 11 through the remainder of the decade.

There are two factors that will help the Republicans over the rest of this decade, but they have nothing to do with the party's innate appeal. One is money, an advantage that could be exacerbated if the campaign finance reform bill passed in 2002 gets through the Supreme Court unscathed. Historically, Republican voters, who have been more concentrated among the wealthy, have been more likely to give money as individuals than Democrats. Working-class voters tend to give money, if at all, through the organizations to which they belong. But the new campaign finance legislation would ban "soft money" contributions from labor unions—a prime source of working-class contributions—while raising the limit on what wealthy individuals can contribute to campaigns. In April 2003, with the new campaign law in effect but still under court review, Republican campaign organizations outraised Democratic organizations by almost four to one.[18] This advantage in money will translate into electoral advantage, especially in close House contests. In November 2002, Republicans won close House races in Alabama and Colorado largely because their Democratic opponents ran out of money. Conversely, Janet Napolitano's victory in Arizona's gubernatorial race was partly made possible by public financing that equalized her and Salmon's spending.

But money can still be overrated as a determinant of election outcomes. It is most effective in scaring off competition or in pushing one side over the finish line in an otherwise close race. But it cannot defeat a candidate who is reasonably well-funded and whose politics are clearly more popular than their opponent. And even the advantages money bestows can cut two ways in elections. In low-turnout congressional elections, it can benefit the big spender in a tight race, but in high-visibility elections, it can dramatize the Republican dependence on wealth and on big business.

Republicans will also enjoy an advantage from redistricting, which the GOP handled more effectively than the Democrats. Too many Democratic votes are concentrated in House districts with overwhelming Democratic strength, while Republican votes are scattered around more effectively to produce House districts with substantial, but not overwhelming, Republican advantages.

The 2000 redistricting made this pattern worse and creates a difficult challenge for Democrats. But difficult does not mean impossible or even improbable in the right circumstances. And redistricting will affect House races, but not races for the Senate or the White House. Republican advantages in money and redistricting are important, but at best they will delay or soften the realignment that began to occur a decade ago.

The pressures for a Democratic realignment, driven by the growth of postindustrial metropolitan areas and by demographic change, are certain to grow over the decade. The electorate's movement from right to center, which began in the early 1990s, has continued, evidenced in the Republican attempts in 2002 to co-opt Democratic domestic positions. Just as happened in the last Republican realignment of 1980, it could finally take a crisis in foreign policy or continued economic stagnation to end what W. D. Burnham called the "unstable equilibrium" between the parties and to create a new majority. But barring the entirely unforeseen, there is little reason to doubt that before this decade is over, the Democratic majority, which began to emerge clearly in the 1990s, will finally succeed the conservative Republican majority that Ronald Reagan created.

APPENDIX: DATA SOURCES

NATIONAL ELECTION STUDIES (NES)

The National Election Study is a biennial academic survey about politics conducted in every election year by the University of Michigan's Center for Political Studies. The survey has been conducted since 1948 and collects a wide range of data about attitudes, opinions, and voting behavior. The continuity of the survey and the richness of the data make it the premier data source used by academics in the study of American politics.

These factors also made the survey useful for some of the research conducted for this book. In fact, to the extent we were interested in political attitudes and the demographics of voting behavior going back to the 1960s, there was really no choice. The NES is the only survey that allows you to go back that far and investigate these issues.

The NES has interviewed from 1,200 to 2,700 respondents over the years. In recent years, the totals have been 2,485 (1992), 1,795 (1994), 1,714 (1996), 1,281 (1998), and 1,807 (2000). Since the NES surveys the adult citizen population, the actual number of (self-reported) voters is less than these numbers would indicate, since some adults choose not to vote. However, even with this diminution of the sample, the survey is still quite adequate for looking at broad political and attitudinal trends among voters. For more elaborate analysis of smaller subgroups of the voting electorate (e.g., Hispanics, married working-class whites with children), the NES sample does start to have limitations due to the small number of respondents in such subgroups. Fortunately, an alternative with a much larger sample size, exit polls (discussed below), allows us to perform more elaborate analyses for recent elections.

BUREAU OF THE CENSUS DATA

We use three different Bureau of the Census data sources. First, of course, we use the decennial censuses of 1990 and 2000 to track demographic changes in the 1990s. This was particularly useful in looking at changes in population and race/ethnic distribution nationally, by state, and by counties within states.

In doing so, we faced the difficulty common to all who have used these data to compare 1990 and 2000 race/ethnic distributions: the change in race coding in the 2000 census made it possible for respondents to check more than one race. This creates the problem of comparing a distribution from 1990, where it was only possible to check one race, with a distribution from 2000, when two or more races could be selected.

The solution we used, as outlined in a paper by geographers James P. Allen and Eugene Turner, was to assign race fractionally based on other data that showed how likely a biracial individual was to have designated a given race as his or her primary race. Individuals who selected three, four, or five races were simply divided up equally among the races in question.

We also linked the 1990 and 2000 census data to a database of county-level presidential voting results going back to 1960. This allowed us, for example, to look at how counties that had added the most people in the 1990s voted in recent presidential elections.

Second, we used the Current Population Survey (CPS) Voter Supplement data to look at the demographics of voters. The CPS is the Bureau of the Census's large-scale monthly survey to track changes in the labor market, particularly unemployment rates. In addition, the CPS periodically collects supplementary information about selected social and economic topics. One such effort is the Voter Supplement, administered as part of the November CPS in every election year (presidential and off-year). The Voter Supplement collects basic information about whether respondents voted, whether they were registered, and a small number of other items (for example, what time of day the respondent voted). No information is collected about whom the respondent voted for or what the respondent's political attitudes and partisan preferences are.

The lack of political information means the Voter Supplement is useless for examining what any given election is about. But its huge size—90,000 to 100,000 respondents eighteen and over—combined with the rich demographic information always collected by the CPS, makes it a superb source for analyzing how the demographics of the voting pool have changed over time.

The Voter Supplement data are particularly useful as a corrective to the exit polls' apparent tendency to overstate the educational credentials of voters. For example, in the 2000 election, the exit polls said that 42 percent of voters had a four-year college degree; in contrast, the census data said that only 31 percent had a four-year college degree. Similarly, in 1996, the exit polls said 43 percent of voters were college-educated; the census data said only 29 percent. This is quite a substantial difference and suggests the exit polls should be used mostly for what they were intended for: to project the results of elections and, secondarily, to compare the political attitudes and preferences of different voter groups.

The question has been raised, most forcefully by political scientists Samuel Popkin and Michael McDonald,[1] whether this is a fair judgment, since the census data are based on self-reports of voting, whereas the exit polls, with all their flaws, are at least based directly on voters. Therefore, perhaps it is the exit poll data that are accurate and the census data that are biased.

A number of things are wrong with this argument.[2] Most importantly, if one believes the exit poll data, implied turnout levels by education are literally unbelievable. For example, according to the 1996 VNS exit poll, 43 percent of voters were college graduates. Based on the total number of votes cast and the education composition of the population, this implies a turnout rate for college-graduate citizens of 102 percent. This is impossible and clearly indicates a serious problem with the exit polls.

Popkin and McDonald's main reply has been that the exit poll question on education is flawed, and that this, not education bias in the exit poll sample, mostly accounts for the difference between the two surveys. They pointed out that the education question on the exit poll, until recently, typically listed the some-college category as "some college but no degree." Given this wording, it seemed a reasonable assumption that some unknown proportion of those with a two-year AA degree didn't check this category but selected the "college graduate" category instead. But this didn't make the exit polls right; it merely meant they overstated the proportion of four-year college graduates for a different reason (question wording instead of sample bias).

More seriously—and fatally for the substance of their question-wording thesis—VNS *did* change their question wording in 2000 so that voters with associate degrees were included in the some-college category. But the 41.7 percent in the 2000 VNS college category still translates into an implied turnout rate for college-educated citizens of 99 percent—a preposterously high figure, though a slight improvement on 1996's absurd implied rate of 102 percent. Thus, there does appear to be a serious exit-poll-sample education-bias problem, and it seems prudent to rely on the CPS voter supplement data for estimates on the education distribution of voters.

The third census data source we used was the CPS Outgoing Rotation Group (ORG) files. These files are particularly useful for looking at labor force characteristics such as occupation and union membership. When collected for an entire year, the large number of labor force cases (about 150,000) allows for good estimates of these characteristics in the nation, individual states, and selected metropolitan areas.

NATIONAL EXIT POLLS

A consortium of television networks and newspapers sponsors large national exit polls during every presidential and off-year election, currently conducted by Voter News Service (VNS). The number of questions asked is small compared to the NES, but the sample size is much larger (11,000 to 16,000 voters in recent years, compared to just 800 to 2,000 for the NES). This makes it an ideal data source for looking at recent trends in voting support among various demographic subgroups (though not for looking at the demographic composition of voters, particularly education, as discussed in the previous section).

Since VNS conducts exit polls in every state, it is possible to use their surveys to look at voting patterns in various states, rather than just nationally, as is the case with the NES. In addition, since the VNS state data sets typically include a variable that indicates roughly where in the state a respondent was interviewed, it is possible to use these "geocodes" to look at voting patterns among various demographic groups in different regions of states.

We should point out that only some of the VNS geocodes are clear enough in terms of their geographic coverage to be useful. We should also stress that the VNS data are not really designed for this kind of substate analysis, and in fact, the VNS cautions against it. However, we elected to use the data anyway in selected instances because no alternatives exist if one is interested in asking certain questions about substate voting behavior.

COUNTY PRESIDENTIAL ELECTION RESULTS

We made extensive use of presidential voting results by county going back to 1960. We copied most of these data from Dave Leip's excellent Web site of presidential election results. Data we took from Leip's Web site was carefully cross-checked against hard-copy data in the *America Votes* series of election data compilations. We also used the *America Votes* volumes to fill in gaps in the data on Leip's Web site.

Finally, we took these data and linked them by county FIPS (Federal Information Processing Standards) code to an extensive set of 1990 and 2000 county-level data from the decennial censuses of those years. We also created a special county-level variable for whether a county could be considered part of an ideopolis. A footnote in chapter 3 explains our procedure for doing this.

NOTES

Introduction

1. See E. J. Dionne, *They Only Look Dead* (New York: Simon & Schuster, 1996).
2. See David Osborne and Ted Gaebler, *Reinventing Government* (New York: Plume, 1993).

Chapter 1

1. See Walter Dean Burnham, "Party Systems and the Political Process," in *The American Party Systems,* ed. William Nisbet Chambers and Walter Dean Burnham (New York: Oxford University Press, 1975). V. O. Key first described a theory of realignment in "A Theory of Critical Elections," *Journal of Politics,* 1955.
2. See Key, "Theory of Critical Elections."
3. Kevin Phillips, *The Emerging Republican Majority* (New York: Arlington House, 1969).
4. The University of Michigan's authoritative National Election Study confirmed what these patterns imply: an overwhelming proportion of Wallace voters who voted in 1972 cast their votes for Nixon.
5. These and other figures on changes in the House and Senate by party for different elections are taken from *National Journal,* November 11, 2000, pp. 3557, 3562.
6. Norman J. Ornstein, Thomas E. Mann, and Michael J. Malbin, *Vital Statistics on Congress, 1995–96* (Washington, D.C.: CQ Press, 1996).
7. See Thomas Edsall with Mary Edsall, *Chain Reaction* (New York: Norton, 1991).
8. Authors' analysis of National Election Study data.
9. Stanley Greenberg, "Report on Democratic Defection," The Analysis Group.
10. Authors' analysis of 1980 National Election Study data; figures based on white voters only.
11. *New York Times*/CBS News exit polls.

12. Ibid.
13. Ibid.
14. Edsall, *Chain Reaction.* Senator Phil Gramm, who would switch parties in 1982 to become a Republican, talked about some Americans who "rode in the wagon" and others who "pulled the wagon" and put himself and other conservative Republicans clearly on the side of the latter.
15. See Sidney Blumenthal, *Pledging Allegiance* (New York: HarperCollins, 1990).
16. *New York Times*/CBS News exit polls.
17. See Stanley Greenberg, *Middle Class Dreams* (New York: Random House, 1995).
18. Quoted in Alexander P. Lamis, ed., *Southern Politics in the 1990s* (Baton Rouge: LSU Press, 1999).
19. Authors' analysis of county-level election returns, 1960–2000.
20. See "Clinton's Revolution," *Newsweek,* March 1, 1993.
21. Grover Norquist, *Rock the House* (Fort Lauderdale: Vytis, 1995), 2.
22. Ornstein, Mann, and Malbin, *Vital Statistics,* tables 1-5 and 2-3.
23. See Taylor E. Dark, *The Unions and the Democrats* (Ithaca, N.Y.: Cornell University Press, 1999).
24. On third parties, see Micah L. Sifry, *Spoiling for a Fight* (New York: Rutledge, 2001).
25. See Herbert Weisberg and Timothy Hill, "The Succession Presidential Election of 2000: The Battle of the Legacies" (paper delivered at 2001 American Political Science Association annual meeting). Note however that many of these independents are "leaners," who admit to favoring one party when pressed.
26. Ibid.
27. Authors' analysis of 2000 Voter News Service (VNS) state exit-poll data.
28. See John B. Judis, "The Hunted," *The New Republic,* April 17, 2000.

CHAPTER 2

1. Jeane Kirkpatrick, "The Revolution of the Masses," *Commentary,* November 27, 1972.
2. Margaret Weir and Marshall Ganz, "Reconnecting People and Politics," in *The New Majority,* ed. Stanley Greenberg and Theda Skocpol (New Haven, Conn.: Yale University Press, 1997).
3. Authors' analysis of National Election Study (NES) data.
4. Ibid.
5. Figure for 2000 from authors' analysis of Current Population Survey occupation data provided on Population Reference Bureau Web site; 1950s estimate is derived from deflating the combined figure for professional, technical, and kindred workers in *Historical Statistics of the United States.*
6. See Ruy Teixeira, *The Disappearing American Voter* (Washington, D.C.:

Brookings, 1992), chapter 3. The pattern is also observed in 1996 Current Population Survey Voter Supplement data.

7. National figure based on analysis of 2000 NES survey; it includes both those professionals who are currently working and those who are retired, as well as students, homemakers, and disabled who do professional work. Estimates for the comparison among states are based on analysis of the 1996 Current Population Survey Voter Supplement, using the 2000 NES figure as a baseline.
8. Figures for the past are from Daniel Bell's introduction to Thorstein Veblen, *Engineers and the Price System* (New York: Harcourt Brace & World, 1963), and for the present from Stephen Rose's unpublished tables on factory work and SESTAT (NSF) tables on U.S. scientists and engineers.
9. *Current Statistics on Scientists, Engineers, and Technical Workers* (DPE, 2000).
10. *Historical Statistics of the United States.*
11. This account of American economic history draws heavily upon Martin J. Sklar, *The United States as a Developing Country* (New York: Cambridge University Press, 1992), chapter 5; and Daniel Bell, *The Coming of Post-Industrial Society* (New York: Basic, 1973). See also John B. Judis, *The Paradox of American Democracy* (New York: Pantheon, 2000), chapter 4.
12. See Paul A. Baran and Paul M. Sweezy, *Monopoly Capital* (New York: Monthly Review Press, 1966), chapter 5; and David M. Potter, *People of Plenty* (Chicago: University of Chicago Press, 1954), chapter 8.
13. See Bell, *Coming of Post-Industrial Society.*
14. Figures here and before in this paragraph based on Lawrence Mishel, Jared Bernstein, and John Schmitt, *The State of Working America, 2000–01* (Ithaca, N.Y.: Cornell University Press, 2001), table 2.27, slightly adjusted to take agricultural employment into account.
15. *Historical Statistics of the United States.*
16. Authors' analysis of Current Population Survey occupation data provided on Population Reference Bureau Web site.
17. *Monthly Labor Review,* November 1999.
18. Authors' analysis of National Election Study data.
19. AnnaLee Saxenian, *Regional Advantage: Culture and Competition in Silicon Valley and Route 128* (Cambridge, Mass.: Harvard University Press, 1994).
20. David Kusnet, *Finding Their Voices* (Washington, D.C.: AFL-CIO, 2000), poll by Peter Hart Associates.
21. Harry Braverman, *Labor and Monopoly Capital* (New York: Monthly Review Press, 1998).
22. Authors' analysis of 2000 Current Population Survey Outgoing Rotation Group files.
23. See *Modern Physician,* February 26, 2001.
24. *Praxis Post,* October 4, 2000.
25. AP, June 25, 1999.
26. *Wall Street Journal,* August 8, 2001.

27. *Praxis Post,* October 4, 2000.
28. On voting by professionals, see Steven Brint, *In an Age of Experts* (Princeton: Princeton University Press, 1994); and Clem Brooks and Jeff Manza, *Social Cleavages and Political Change* (New York: Oxford University Press, 1999).
29. Based on authors' analysis of NES data for various years.
30. All data for elections prior to 1976 from authors' analysis of NES data.
31. All data in paragraph from authors' analysis of VNS national and state exit polls.
32. Kevin White, *Sexual Liberation or Sexual License* (Chicago: Ivan R. Dee, 2000).
33. Charlotte Perkins Gilman, "Economic Basis of the Woman Question," *Women's Journal,* October 1, 1898. On this subject, see Eli Zaretsky, *Capitalism, the Family and Personal Life* (New York: Perennial Library, 1975).
34. Betty Friedan, *The Feminine Mystique* (New York: Norton, 1963).
35. See Ruth Rosen, *The World Split Open* (New York: Viking, 2000).
36. Howard N. Fullerton Jr., "Labor Force Participation," *Monthly Labor Review,* December 1999.
37. Claudia Golden and Lawrence F. Katz, "On the Pill," *Milken Institute Review,* second quarter, 2001.
38. Authors' analysis of Current Population Survey occupation data provided on Population Reference Bureau Web site.
39. Authors' analysis of 1956 NES data.
40. See Jo Freeman, "Who You Know versus Who You Represent," in *Women's Movement in the United States and Europe,* ed. Mary Katzenstein and Carol Mueller (Philadelphia: Temple University Press, 1987); and Jo Freeman, *A Room at a Time* (Lanham, Md.: Roman and Littlefield, 2000).
41. White, *Sexual Liberation or Sexual License.*
42. See Tanya Melich, *The Republican War Against Women* (New York: Bantam, 1996).
43. For data and a useful discussion, see Brooks and Manza, *Social Cleavages,* chapter 5.
44. Melich, *The Republican War Against Women,* 70.
45. All data in paragraph based on authors' analysis of national exit polls for years indicated.
46. Gallup and NES data.
47. Gallup data; note that Gallup labels the category *nonwhite,* but it can safely be assumed to be almost exclusively black at that point in time. Also, the NES data, which does disaggregate blacks, shows every black respondent in the survey saying he or she voted for Johnson, so the Gallup 94 percent figure seems reasonable.
48. Data for 1968 and 1972 from the NES; 1976 to 2000 data from national exit polls.
49. Paul R. Abramson, John H. Aldrich, and David Waruhde, *Change and Continuity in the 1980 Elections* (Washington, D.C.: CQ Press, 1982), 60.

50. Teixeira, *The Disappearing American Voter;* authors' analysis of exit-poll and Current Population Survey data.
51. See Theodore White, *The Making of the President, 1972* (New York: Atheneum, 1973), 236.
52. ABC News/*Washington Post* poll.
53. Authors' analysis of 1990 and 2000 census data. We allocate bi- and multiracial individuals in the 2000 census according to the procedure suggested by James P. Allen and Eugene Turner in their paper "Estimating Primary Single-Race Identities for Reported Biracial Populations in the 2000 Census" (Department of Geography, California State University–Northridge).
54. Census data for 2000, cited on Hispanictrends.com Web site.
55. Authors' analysis of 1990 and 2000 census data.
56. This 5.4 percent figure is from the Current Population Survey (CPS) Voter Supplement. The exit poll estimate was higher, at 6.5 percent. However, we generally consider the CPS estimates to be more reliable.
57. *Los Angeles Times,* July 6, 2001.
58. Here and throughout we include Pacific Islanders with Asians as is customary in most analyses, including those done by the Census Bureau.
59. Authors' analysis of 1990 and 2000 census data.
60. Ibid.
61. VNS 2000 exit poll and 2000 Current Population Survey Voter Supplement.
62. Authors' analysis of 2000 census data.
63. See "Pilot Study" of the National Asian American Political Survey by Pei-te Lien, Margaret Conway, Taeku Lee, and Janelle Wong.
64. *Los Angeles Times,* May 23, 2001.
65. "Pilot Study."
66. The VNS exit poll had Gore with 55 percent and Bush with 41 percent, only a fourteen-point margin. Officials with the "Pilot Study" believe that the margin was wider, as indicated in their poll, and explain the difference by VNS's failure to include poll-takers who knew Chinese and other Asian languages. Note also that the *Los Angeles Times* national exit poll had Gore by twenty-five points (62–37) among Asians, close to the "Pilot Study" margin.
67. The 19 percent figure is drawn from both the 2000 VNS exit poll and from the 2000 CPS Voter Supplement; the 75 percent figure is based on the 2000 VNS exit poll but could be higher if the correct figure for the Asian-American pro-Democratic margin is close to that indicated by the "Pilot Study."
68. See Harold Meyerson, "Race Conquers All," *American Prospect,* December 3, 2001.
69. *Historical Statistics of the United States.* This 50 percent was composed of 40 percent who were blue-collar workers and 10 percent who were service workers.
70. Everett Carll Ladd Jr. with Charles D. Hadley, *Transformations of the American Party System: Party Coalitions from the New Deal to the 1970s* (New York: Norton, 1975), 231.

71. Authors' analysis of NES data; actual size of white working-class vote would be largest using an education-based (noncollege) definition, but virtually any reasonable occupation-based definition appears to still yield a figure well over 50 percent.
72. Robert J. Donovan, *Conflict and Crisis* (New York: Norton, 1977), 396.
73. Authors' analysis of the 2000 Current Population Outgoing Rotation Group files shows that Northern (that is, Northeastern and Midwestern) blue-collar workers still have a 29 percent unionization rate. Data from Derek C. Box and John T. Dunlop, *Labor and the American Community* (New York: Simon & Schuster, 1970), show that unionization rates in the early 1960s—when the overall unionization rate for nonagricultural workers was close to its level in the late 1940s—for various blue-collar occupations were generally two to three times higher than they are today. It is therefore a reasonable estimate that Northern blue-collar workers in the late 1940s had a unionization rate approaching, and probably exceeding, 60 percent.
74. Authors' analysis of NES data for years indicated; note that when we use the term *working class* without further specification we are referring to the non-college-educated—that is, those without a four-year college degree. See Ruy Teixeira and Joel Rogers, *America's Forgotten Majority: Why the White Working Class Still Matters* (New York: Basic, 2000), chapter 1, for more discussion and justification of this specification.
75. See Michael Goldfield, *The Decline of Organized Labor in the United States* (Chicago: University of Chicago Press, 1987).

CHAPTER 3

1. See Kirkpatrick Sale, *Power Shift* (New York: Random House, 1975).
2. See Robert Atkinson, "Technology and the Future of Metropolitan Economies" (Federal Reserve of Chicago, November 1995).
3. See Robert D. Atkinson and Paul D. Gottlieb, *The Metropolitan New Economy Index* (Washington, D.C.: PPI, April 2001).
4. On this point, see Richard Kaglic and William Testa, "Midwest Prospects and the New Economy," *Chicago Fed Letter*, October 2000; and Ann Markusen et al., *High-Tech and I-Tech: How Metros Rank and Specialize*, Humphrey Institute of Public Affairs, University of Minnesota (August 2001).
5. See Joe Kotkin and Ross C. DeVol, "Knowledge-Value Cities in the Digital Age" (Milken Institute, February 2001).
6. Authors' analysis of 2000 Current Population Survey Outgoing Rotation Group files; note that figures refer to metropolitan areas, not cities.
7. See Richard Florida and Gary Gates, "Technology and Tolerance" (Brookings Institution, June 2001).

8. Richard Florida, *Information Week,* November 13, 2000.
9. Authors' analysis of 2000 VNS exit poll for Colorado.
10. Authors' analysis of 2000 VNS exit poll data for states indicated.
11. Authors' analysis of 2000 VNS exit poll for Ohio.
12. All data in this paragraph from authors' analysis of county-level 2000 census data. Note that if one looks at total population growth across all ideopolis and nonideopolis counties, this considerably narrows, but does not eliminate, the growth gap discussed in the paragraph.
13. See Lou Cannon, *Ronnie and Jessie* (Garden City, N.Y.: Doubleday, 1969).
14. When we speak of the Bay Area, we generally mean the Bay Area ideopolis, which includes the San Francisco, Oakland, and San Jose PMSAs, areas tightly clustered around the city of San Francisco. This includes the counties of Alameda, Contra Costa, Marin, San Francisco, San Mateo, and Santa Clara. Sometimes the Bay Area is more broadly defined to include several counties farther north of the city: Napa, Sonoma, and Solano. And the San Francisco CMSA (Consolidated Metropolitan Statistical Area) includes all these and Santa Cruz County besides. But we will generally use the narrower definition where data permits.
15. See Markusen et al., *High-Tech and I-Tech.*
16. Democratic support was 72–23 percent among white voters with a postgraduate education, the closest approximation of professionals that the VNS affords.
17. Authors' analysis of 2000 VNS exit poll data for California; note that the VNS Bay Area designation may or may not correspond to the definition we prefer (the San Francisco, Oakland, and San Jose MSAs).
18. See Mark Baldassare, *California in the New Millennium: The Changing Social and Political Landscape* (Berkeley, Cal.: University of California Press, 2000).
19. Ideopolis-based definition, as specified earlier.
20. Central Valley defined as in Baldassare, *California in the New Millennium,* to include Butte, Colusa, Fresno, Glenn, Kern, Kings, Madera, Merced, Placer, Sacramento, San Joaquin, Shasta, Stanislaus, Sutter, Tehama, Tulare, Yolo, and Yuba counties.
21. Other races not shown in chart.
22. California is unique among states in having two credible and roughly equally sized exit polls to choose from, one conducted by VNS and the other by the *Los Angeles Times (LAT).* Here we report an average of the top-line findings from the two polls, which for Hispanics tend to be quite close.
23. The 57–40 figure is an average of the VNS and *LAT* exit polls; the 63–33 figure is the *LAT* figure.
24. Authors' analysis of 1990 and 2000 census data.
25. New Jersey Department of Labor statistics in "Projections 2008," July 2000.
26. See William Schneider, "The Battle for Saliency: The Abortion Issue in This Campaign," *The Atlantic,* October 1992.

27. *Washington Post,* November 12, 1989.
28. See John B. Judis, "A Taxing Governor," *The New Republic,* October 15, 1990; and "Bill Folds," *The New Republic,* January 28, 1991.
29. All data in paragraph except overall county results from authors' analysis of 2000 VNS New Jersey exit poll.
30. Operationalized as those with a postgraduate education (VNS collects no occupation data).
31. Jonathan Cohn, "Fade to Black," *The New Republic,* November 13, 2000.
32. Authors' analysis of 2000 VNS Pennsylvania exit poll.
33. Authors' interview with Ray Buckley, former political director of the Gore campaign in New Hampshire.
34. See Beth Gorczyca, "Peering into a Murky Future," *Herald Dispatch,* September 17, 2000. See also *Wall Street Journal,* June 13, 2001.
35. *Charleston Gazette,* November 7, 2001.
36. Stephen E. Ambrose, *Nixon: The Education of a Politician* (New York: Simon & Schuster, 1987), 606.
37. See Neal R. Pierce, *The Megastates of America* (New York: Norton, 1972).
38. Kotkin and DeVol, "Knowledge-Value Cities."
39. See Markusen et al., *High Tech and I-Tech.*
40. Bureau of Labor statistics for 1999.
41. See Paul Green and Melvin Holli, eds., *The Mayors: The Chicago Political Tradition* (Carbondale, Ill.: Southern Illinois University Press, 1995). John Kass, "The New Mayor Daley," *Chicago Tribune,* August 25, 1996.
42. Interview with authors.
43. Authors' analysis of 2000 VNS Illinois exit poll.
44. Note that this calculation does not include Lansing's Ingham County for reasons previously outlined; however, inclusion of Ingham County in this calculation would only make the result stronger.
45. MDC, Inc., *State of the South 2000* (Chapel Hill, N.C.: MDC, Inc., 2001).
46. All data in this paragraph from authors' analysis of 1996 and 2000 VNS exit polls for Missouri.
47. Interview with authors.
48. Authors' analysis of 2000 VNS Florida exit poll.
49. Authors' analysis of 1990 and 2000 census data.
50. Lance deHaven-Smith, "George W. and Jeb, a Rogue Legislature, an Activist County, Cuban Republicans, and Puerto Rican Democrats, Blue Dogs and Yellow Dogs, Dixiecrats and New Dealers, the Old South and the New South" (unpublished paper, December 2000).
51. See Michael I. Luger, "Spontaneous Technopolises and Regional Restructuring: The Case of Research Triangle, N.C.," Department of City and Regional Planning, University of North Carolina, Chapel Hill, unpublished, June 8, 1998.
52. Raleigh metro figure from analysis of North Carolina county election returns;

figure on college-educated white women from authors' analysis of 2000 VNS North Carolina exit poll.

53. "South Carolina," in *Southern Politics in the 1990s,* ed. Lamis.
54. *Decatur Daily,* April 19, 2001.

Chapter 4

1. Memo, Pat Caddell to President Carter, December 10, 1976, Press Files: Jody Powell, Jimmy Carter Library.
2. Richard Scammon and Ben Wattenberg, *The Real Majority* (New York: Coward-McCann, 1970).
3. This and following quotations from Memo, Caddell to Carter.
4. See Sidney Blumenthal, "Hart's Big Chill," *Our Long National Daydream* (New York: Harper & Row, 1988).
5. See Gary Hart, *The New Democracy* (New York: William Morrow, 1984).
6. Patrick Caddell, "The State of American Politics," October 25, 1983.
7. Exit polls have a long-term and consistent problem with overestimating the educational credentials of voters, particularly the numbers of college graduates. See appendix to this volume and appendix to Teixeira and Rogers, *America's Forgotten Majority,* for discussion of this problem.
8. Income data only available for two breaks, under and over $25,000. This translates into under and over $41,500 in 2000 dollars.
9. See Karen Paget, "The Gender Gap Mystique," *American Prospect,* Fall 1993.
10. See *New York Times,* July 22, 1984.
11. See Blumenthal, "Hart's Big Chill"; and Elizabeth Colton, *The Jackson Phenomenon* (New York: Doubleday, 1989).
12. Amiri Baraka, "What Makes Jesse Run?" *Playboy,* July 1988.
13. On the history of the Democratic Leadership Council, see Ken Baer, *Reinventing Democrats* (Lawrence, Kans.: University of Kansas Press, 2000); and interviews by authors with Will Marshall and Alvin From.
14. "Memorandum: Saving the Democratic Party," January 2, 1985.
15. See Paul Starobin, "An Affair to Remember," *National Journal,* January 16, 1993.
16. William Gallston and Elaine Ciulla Kamarck, "The Politics of Evasion: Democrats and the Presidency," Progressive Policy Institute, September 1989.
17. David Osborne and Ted Gaebler, *Reinventing Government* (New York: Plume, 1993).
18. See "The New Choice: A Progressive Agenda for the 1990s" (Washington, D.C.: Democratic Leadership Council, 1991).
19. In 1984 and 1988, male college graduates had backed the Republican presidential candidate by the same margin, 63–36 percent, but female college

graduates, who had voted for Reagan 52–47 percent in 1984, voted for Dukakis in 1988 by 51 to 49 percent. CBS/*New York Times* exit polls.

20. Clinton announcement of candidacy, July 16, 1992.
21. See Judis, *Paradox of American Democracy*, chapter 9.
22. Authors' analysis of 1994 VNS exit poll.
23. Authors' analysis of 1992 and 1996 VNS national exit polls for all figures except professionals. The latter figure is derived from authors' analysis of 1992 and 1996 National Election Studies.
24. Authors' analysis of 1992 and 1996 VNS state exit polls for Ohio and New Jersey.
25. Interview by authors.
26. Dudley Buff, Michael Hais, and Morley Winograd, "Wired Workers and the Digital Deal," *New Democrat*, November–December 1996. Later definitions of "wired workers" don't appear to include the network stipulation and may have added a specification about *preferring* to work together in a team. The slippage on the definition probably makes little difference to the usefulness (or lack thereof) of the concept.
27. Al From and Will Marshall, "Building the New Democratic Majority," *Blueprint*, fall 1998. Penn's characterization of wired workers is from "Choosing the New Economy," *Blueprint*, winter 1998.
28. See *Chattanooga Times*, January 5, 2000.
29. See Jonathan Cohn, "Play It Again, Stan," *The New Republic*, August 31, 2000.
30. Stanley Greenberg, *Middle Class Dreams* (New York: Random House, 1995, revised 1996).
31. Anna Greenberg and Stanley B. Greenberg, "Adding Values," *American Prospect*, August 2000. (Note that this essay was written before Greenberg joined the Gore campaign in late July 2000.)
32. Greenberg, *Middle Class Dreams*.
33. See "Gore's Summer Surprise," *Newsweek*, November 20, 2000; and "What It Took," *Time*, November 20, 2000.
34. A reasonable argument can also be made that Gore was hurt by distancing himself so far from the administration's very real accomplishments, especially on the economy. Note, however, that the available boost from the economy may not have been as big as commonly believed and as some political scientists asserted based on election-forecasting models. An important paper by political scientists Larry Bartels and John Zaller persuasively criticizes this viewpoint. Bartels and Zaller looked at forty-eight possible election-forecasting models using a number of standard variables, including several different economic measures. They then averaged these models' predictions, with each model's weight based on its explanatory power through the 1996 election (called Bayesian weighting). Since the historically best-performing models tended to be those based on growth in real per capita disposable income and since there had actually been a slowdown in such growth prior to the 2000 election, Bartels and Zaller found that the

weighted average prediction for Gore's percent of the two-party popular vote was only half a percentage point off the vote he actually received (as opposed to widely publicized models based on raw economic growth, which predicted anywhere from a six- to twenty-point Gore win).

35. Memo, Cadell to Carter.
36. Al From, "Building a New Progressive Majority," *Blueprint,* January 24, 2001.
37. Mark J. Penn, "Lessons of 2000," *American Prospect,* May 7, 2001; and Mark J. Penn, "Turning a Win into a Draw," *Blueprint,* January 24, 2001.
38. Press conference sponsored by Campaign for America's Future, November 10, 2000. See also Stanley Greenberg, "The Progressive Majority and the 2000 Elections," on Campaign for America's Future Web site.
39. Poll conducted November 7–8, 2000, among 2,036 respondents for the Campaign for America's Future. See also Ruy Teixeira, "Lessons for Next Time," *American Prospect,* December 18, 2000.

CHAPTER 5

1. *US News and World Report,* October 2, 2000.
2. Michael Barone with Richard Cohen and Grant Ujifusa, *The Almanac of American Politics, 2002* (Washington, D.C.: National Journal, 2001), "Introduction."
3. David Brooks, "Bush's Patriotic Challenge," *Weekly Standard,* October 8, 2001.
4. Authors' analysis of Census Bureau Historical Poverty tables, 1960–96, on their Web site.
5. John C. Green, James L. Guth, Lyman A. Kellstedt, and Corwin E. Smidt, "How the Faithful Voted: Religion and the 2000 Presidential Election," Ethics and Public Policy Center, Washington, D.C.
6. The VNS figure of 43 percent for church attendance weekly or more is much higher than the NES figure of 25 percent for every week among all adults and 30 percent among voters and the NORC figure of only 32 percent, even when combining attendance every week and almost every week. The VNS figure is probably inflated by the normative pressures of having to respond in a public place to a set of choices that are biased toward being devout (two categories that are at least weekly and another that is oddly close—"a few times a month"—among just five categories). The NES study, by contrast, actually screens people first to see if they ever attend church aside from weddings and funerals before even asking them about their level of attendance. The NORC study allows respondents to simply state their level of attendance, which is then coded into an extensive set of nine categories. The NES and NORC methods probably produce a more accurate assessment than the VNS.

7. The never-attend figure is lower in the VNS than in the other surveys—just 14 percent of voters. We believe the other surveys are more accurate for the reasons stated in the previous note.
8. Green et al., "How the Faithful Voted."
9. David Leege, "The Catholic Voter," Commonweal Foundation, June 2, 2000.
10. Peter Beinart, "The Burbs," *The New Republic,* October 19, 1998.
11. Barone et al., *Almanac.*
12. Daniel Casse, "Bush and the Republican Future," *Commentary,* March 2001.
13. NORC polling. Cited in William G. Mayer, *The Changing American Mind* (Ann Arbor, Mich.: University of Michigan Press, 1992).
14. Cited in Tom W. Smith, "Trends in National Spending Priorities, 1973–1998" (unpublished manuscript, NORC).
15. Survey conducted for Cato by Zogby polling, March 2001.
16. AARP, "Individual Accounts, Social Security, and the 2000 Election," September 2000.
17. See especially the Kaiser Family Foundation/Harvard University survey on medicare policy options, August–September 1998.
18. See John B. Judis, "Coming Attractions," *American Prospect,* December 3, 2001.
19. *Wall Street Journal,* November 14, 2001.
20. *The Bulletin's Frontrunner,* September 6, 2001.
21. David Brooks, "The Reemerging Republican Majority," *The Weekly Standard,* February 11, 2002.
22. Marshall Wittmann, Project for Conservative Reform Web site, October 23, 2001.
23. See National Resource Defense Council, "Rewriting the Rules," January 2002.

CONCLUSION

1. See John B. Judis, "Deregulation Run Riot," *American Prospect,* September–October 1999.
2. See "Negotiating Away the Environment," *Los Angeles Times,* October 30, 2001.
3. All data on health insurance coverage from Lawrence Mishel, Jared Bernstein, and John Schmitt, *The State of Working America, 2000/2001* (Ithaca, N.Y.: ILR Press, 2001).
4. Ibid.
5. See Jonathan Cohn, "Health Scare," *The New Republic,* December 24, 2001.
6. Quoted in Dionne, *They Only Look Dead.*
7. All wage data are from Mishel et al., *State of Working America.*
8. Testimony to the Senate Finance Committee, March 7, 2001.

9. *Citizens for Tax Justice,* June 18, 2001.
10. Joseph Stiglitz, "A Boost That Goes Nowhere," *Washington Post,* November 11, 2001, Sunday Outlook section.
11. See Robert McIntyre, "The $212-Billion Giveaway," *American Prospect,* November 19, 2001.
12. Quoted in Lamis, *Southern Politics.*
13. *Bergen Record,* October 1, 2001.
14. *The 700 Club,* January 8, 1992.
15. Craig Timberg, "VA GOP Attacks Democrats on Gays," *Washington Post,* August 31, 2001.
16. See Tom Willis, president of the Creation Science Association of Mid-America, quoted in the *Topeka Capital-Journal,* May 11, 1999.
17. See Ronald Bailey, "Origins of the Specious: Why Conservatives Doubt Darwin," *Reason,* July 1997.
18. See Suzanne Holland, Karen Lebacqz, and Laurie Zoloth, eds., *The Human Embryonic Stem Cell Debate* (Cambridge, Mass.: MIT Press, 2001).
19. Michael Kinsley, *Time,* June 25, 2001.

AFTERWORD

1. Gallup poll, September 7–10, 2001.
2. *Weekly Standard,* November 18, 2002.
3. Gallup poll, September 7–10 and October 11–14, 2001.
4. Gallup poll data.
5. Spencer Ackerman and John B. Judis, "The First Casualty," *The New Republic,* June 30, 2003.
6. Gallup poll data.
7. Gallup poll, October 31–November 1.
8. Gallup poll, October 3–6.
9. John B. Judis, "Soft Sell," *The New Republic,* November 11, 2002.
10. Authors' analysis of 2002 VNS data.
11. *Los Angeles Times,* November 4, 2002. See also Ruy Teixeira, "Where Democrats Lost,"*American Prospect,* November 12, 2002.
12. David W. Moore and Jeffrey M. Jones, "Late Shift Toward Republicans in Congressional Vote," Gallup poll analysis, November 4, 2002.
13. Fabrizio, McLaughlin and Associates poll.
14. See David Gopoian, "Restoring the Gore Coalition." Private study circulated among Democratic strategists.
15. Authors' analysis of 2002 VNS exit poll data.
16. Ibid.
17. For a detailed critique of this thesis, especially the limited potential of exurban growth to change political trends in large metropolitan areas, see Ruy

Teixeira, "Deciphering the Democrats' Debacle," *The Washington Monthly*, May 2003.

18. Political Money Line (www.tray.com). See also the seminal articles on campaign finance by Thomas B. Edsall: "Republicans, Big Cash Edge," November 7, 2002 and "Soft Money Bank," November 22, 2002 in *The Washington Post* and "Campaign Reform Boomerang," *American Prospect*, September 2003.

APPENDIX

1. Samuel Popkin and Michael McDonald, "Who Votes?" *Blueprint: Ideas for a New Century* (Washington, D.C.: Democratic Leadership Council, fall 1998).
2. For more discussion, see the appendix to Teixeira and Rogers, *America's Forgotten Majority*.

ACKNOWLEDGMENTS

The genesis of this book goes back to the New Synthesis lunch group that we started in Washington in early 1995 and ran more or less continuously until 2000. At the time, Democrats were fighting with each other over whether it was more important to emphasize "economics" or "values," "populist" or "quality of life" issues. We believed, then and now, that what was needed was a synthesis of the two approaches. Thanks to all who participated in these monthly luncheons.

The book would not have been possible without our editor, Lisa Drew at Scribner, who believed in the book and strongly supported it every step of the way. It would also not have been possible without a timely and generous grant that John Judis received from Bill Moyers and the Florence and John Schumann Foundation.

We received a lot of help from people who read all or part of the manuscript and provided valuable advice. Jonathan Cohn did a heroic job of making substantive comments and improving our prose. Guy Molyneux's criticisms inspired an important addition to our argument. Jo Freeman made helpful comments throughout. E. J. Dionne, Ryan Lizza, Harold Meyerson, and Mac McCorkle provided useful comments and corrections.

We also received a lot of assistance in doing our research. Dave Leip's Web site on U.S. elections provided the primary source for our county-level analysis of the presidential vote. Steve Rose shared his data on occupational change with us. Manish Patel and Melissa Corbin helped us build our database. Corbin and Natasha Udugama helped with charts and other research-related tasks. Tim Parker was invaluable in helping us with analysis of Census Bureau data. Alex Tait assisted with maps. And John Lampe helped with access to the University of Maryland library.

Others provided materials, advice, and research tips that were immensely helpful. They include Robert Atkinson, Sid Blumenthal, Ray Buckley, Jim Chapin, Frank Foer, Jim Gilbert, Stan Greenberg, David Lee, Will Marshall, Harris Meyer, Don Rose, Fred Siegel, Ken Warren, and Jason Zengerle. Glen Hartley and Lynn Chu negotiated our contract with Scribner.

We thank our families (Robin Allen, Lauren and Ian Teixeira; Susan Pearson, Hilary and Eleanor Judis) for putting up with us during the writing.

INDEX